ANSELM OF CANTERBURY
VOLUME THREE

ANSELM
OF CANTERBURY

VOLUME THREE

TWO LETTERS CONCERNING ROSCELIN
THE INCARNATION OF THE WORD
WHY GOD BECAME A MAN
THE VIRGIN CONCEPTION AND ORIGINAL SIN
THE PROCESSION OF THE HOLY SPIRIT
THREE LETTERS ON THE SACRAMENTS

Edited and Translated by
Jasper Hopkins and Herbert Richardson

THE EDWIN MELLEN PRESS
Toronto and New York

Library of Congress Catalog Card Number 74-19840
ISBN 0-88946-350-6 (Vol. III)
0-88946-977-6 (Set of 4 vols.)

First Edition by The Edwin Mellen Press 1976
© 1976 The Edwin Mellen Press
Toronto and New York

CONTENTS

Translators' Preface	vii
Two Letters Concerning Roscelin	1
The Incarnation of the Word	7
Why God Became a Man	39
The Virgin Conception and Original Sin	139
The Procession of the Holy Spirit	181
Three Letters on the Sacraments	231
Abbreviations	250
Notes	251

TRANSLATORS' PREFACE

This is the third volume in the series of St. Anselm's complete treatises. It contains, among other texts, his paramount contribution to the history of theology: viz., the *Cur Deus Homo*. Through the years, the complex argument therein set forth has been subjected to intense examination. In particular, the moral principles undergirding the Anselmian theory of atonement have been scrutinized thoroughly. Yet, no final agreement unites interpreters of this theory. Some still stress the feudal conceptions of honor and of service as indispensable focal points for Anselm's picture of man's relation to God. Others, by contrast, emphasize the code of Roman Law and suggest that its construal of human justice was transferred by Anselm to apply to the divine agency. Still others believe that Anselm's moral conceptions were primarily influenced by the ecclesiastical penitential system with its scale of merits and its insistence that penance be proportional to the gravity of the sin. Amid the on-going historical debate, what remains incontrovertible is that Anselm's theory of atonement stands or falls just as surely with its conception of morality as with its doctrine of Christology.

In fact, Anselm's moral reasoning may be sketched as follows. Obviously, an individual who steals from another ought to give back what he has stolen. But he ought, in addition, to make compensation for the injury he inflicted upon the other in removing what is rightfully his. Similarly, when Adam sinned he stole from God what is rightfully His, viz., His honor. For by virtue of being God's creature a man owes to God the honor of voluntary submission to His will. In sinning, Adam willed something contrary to God's will for him. Thereby, he rebelled against God and, in intent, stole himself from God's dominion, bringing to God dishonor, as it were. For by marring his own nature through spurning righteousness, Adam reflected discredit upon the workmanship of God in the creation of human nature. Indeed, since every craftsman is lauded in proportion to the perfection of his creation, the marring of man's perfection through man's own fault detracted from the manifestation of God's wisdom and goodness. Accordingly, Adam was required (1) to resume paying the debt of voluntary submission to God's will and (2) to make compensation, or satisfaction, for the injury inflicted upon God as a result of the marring of human nature. Only by meeting these two requirements would Adam *fully* restore God's honor. But Adam was unable to resume being fully submissive to God, because, having forsaken uprightness, his will had no power to recover it. Moreover, even if *per impossibile* he had been able to meet the first requirement, he still would not have been able to fulfill the second. For in order to make satisfaction for his sin, he would need to perform a service meritorious enough to counterbalance the injury done by the sin. Now, reasons Anselm, any violation of God's command is so grave that it ought not to be committed even in the following circumstance: viz., where to refuse to obey God would keep our entire world — and an infinite number of other such worlds — from perishing. Clearly, Anselm is so appreciative of God's majesty that he regards any infringement upon it as intolerably horrible. Just as a slight done to a king is more serious than a similar slight done to one's neighbor, so an offense against the Supreme Being is vastly more dreadful than a corresponding offense against one's fellow-man.

At this juncture Anselm draws an inference from his moral rule that satisfaction ought to be proportional to the transgression: Adam ought to offer as satisfaction for his sin *something greater than is that for whose sake he was obligated not to dishonor God.* Since he was obligated not to dishonor God even at the expense of the universe's perishing, he was required to render something whose value surpasses the totality of things which are other than God. But only God can make such a payment, though only a man ought to. Therefore, if payment is to be made, it must be made by a God-man. Hence, God, in the person of the Son, assumed a human nature into a unity of person with His divine nature in order, by becoming a man, to pay with His human life the debt of all other men's sins. For since Jesus was sinless He was not required to die. He could thus meritoriously yield up His life to the honor of God by letting Himself be put to death for "blasphemy" rather than disobediently denying that He was the Son of God.

Here Anselm introduces a further moral consideration: Since the evil of sinning against the person of God is the greatest conceivable evil, the goodness of the God-man's life must be the greatest conceivable goodness. Thus, in rendering up His life Jesus gave for the honor of God something which surpasses in value the totality of all things other than God. Such a meritorious service ought not to go unrewarded. But since this man is Himself God He is in need of nothing. Therefore, He may acceptably request that the reward be credited to cancel the debt of Adam's sin.

Anselm goes on to explain why the debt for Adam's sin passes down to all those who are naturally descended from him, and how through humbly petitioning for forgiveness they too may draw upon the reserve of Christ's merit. In fact, Anselm's theory of atonement really only makes sense in the light of his doctrines of original sin and sacramental grace. His treatment of these topics evidences that he is sensitive to the charge that God is unjust in punishing Adam's descendants for *Adam's* sin. Accordingly, in *De Conceptu Virginali* he attempts to vindicate the justice of God by denying that any of Adam's progeny are condemned for Adam's sin, even though because of Adam's sin they have sin of their own from which their condemnation follows.

Anselm's intricate distinctions, together with his ingenious strategy for elucidating the moral basis which legitimates the divine program of redemption, deserve our admiration. Admittedly this moral basis can be challenged; and in the twentieth century it may even appear to some to be simply a relic of medieval Christendom. Yet, given Anselm's framework of Christian orthodoxy, let no one underestimate the skill required to construct a theory that reconciles divine mercy with divine justice. And whatever might be the failings of Anselm's theory, let no one fail to recognize its vast superiority, both morally and theologically, over the devil-ransom theory it replaced.

As a spokesman for Christian orthodoxy Anselm does not always make unprecedented points in medieval debate. On the contrary! Because he is working within a *tradition*, his self-envisioned task is to perfect this tradition rather than to reconstruct it. His originality comes in setting the tradition in array by consistently extending its lines of reasoning, analyzing its liturgical terminology, systematizing its separate dogmas, and faulting its opponents' misconceptions. In attacking the heresies of Sabellianism, tritheism, Eutycheanism, Apollinarianism, and Pelagianism, Anselm is really only promoting the position taken by the Nicene Fathers and by Augustine. To this hydra of heresies — already grievously wounded, but risking to raise its many heads once more in the eleventh century — Anselm delivers a *coup de grâce*.

The eleventh century was a period of conquest and reform. The Norman Invasion of 1066 paved the way for the influence of Lanfranc and his pupil Anselm to be extended across the English Channel. The proclamation of Pope Urban II in 1095 set in movement the First Crusade. And the moral idealism of the Gregorian Reform engendered the long, rancorous controversy over investiture. Anselm did not escape the stress and distress of this power-struggle. We recognize from his self-imposed exile how frustrating he found his role as ecclesiastical prelate vis-à-vis King William Rufus. And we can sympathize with his preference for the solace of Capua, where he finished the *Cur Deus Homo*, already started in England. Indeed, his monumental legacy to the history of the Church is constituted more by his intellectual writings than by his devotional outpourings, his official directives, or his personal correspondence. And yet, from his prayers, meditations, and letters, as well as from Eadmer's biography, we acquire the humanizing perspective necessary to correct the one-sided picture of him as only the Father of Scholasticism.

. . . .

The translations which appear in this third volume are more literal than those published earlier in *Trinity, Incarnation, and Redemption: Theological Treatises* (Harper & Row, 1970). However, since these earlier versions (now out of print) were the basis for the present ones, acknowledgement is due to the following people who formerly collaborated with us: George Peck (*Epistolae 129 et 136. Epistola de Incarnatione Verbi*); Douglas Johnson and Ray Phyles (*De Conceptu Virginali et de Originali Peccato*); Lee Gibbs and Warren Lewis (*De Processione Spiritus Sancti*); Lucien Richard (*Epistolae de Sacramentis*).

Special appreciation is due to the University of Minnesota for

Translators' Preface

its support of this entire project through a modest research grant and a single-quarter leave. We are also grateful to Carl Brandt and Sandra Menssen, who typed the manuscripts of Vols. I–IV, and to Thomas Baker, Vicki Field, Ann Forestell, Ruth Anne Ruud, and Peter Shea, who assisted with the proofreading.

Jasper Hopkins
Philosophy Department, University of Minnesota

Herbert Richardson
St. Michael's College, University of Toronto

NOTE: Where, for clarification, words from the Latin text have been inserted into the translations, the following rule has been employed: When the Latin term is noted exactly as it appears in the Latin text, parentheses are used; when the case-endings of nouns have been transformed to the nominative, brackets are used.

The numbering of the Psalms accords with the Douay Version and, in parentheses, with the King James (Authorized) Version.

The symbol ~ indicates negation.

TWO LETTERS CONCERNING ROSCELIN
(Epistolae 129 et 136)

TWO LETTERS CONCERNING ROSCELIN

TO JOHN THE MONK[1]

Brother Anselm to my lord and beloved brother John: may you always make progress toward the better things.

Because I have been wanting to speak about the matter more fully, I have delayed so long in replying to the letter which Your Love sent me regarding that man[2] who makes the following claim: "In God, either the three persons are three things or else the Father and the Holy Spirit were incarnate with the Son." But being hindered by many demands upon my time since receiving your letter, I have not been at liberty [to write at length]. Thus, for the moment, I send a brief reply about this matter. However, I intend to deal with the topic more fully in the future, if God will deign to grant me the opportunity.

As for his claim, then, that the three persons are three things: he wants it to be interpreted either in accordance with three *relations* (i.e., in accordance with the fact that God is spoken of as the Father and the Son and the spirit who proceeds from the Father and from the Son) or else in accordance with that which is called God [i.e., in accordance with God's *deity*]. Now, if he is saying that the three relations are three things, he is saying it superfluously. For no one denies that in this respect the three persons are three things — provided we carefully discern in what sense these relations are called things, and what kind of things they are, and whether or not they affect the substance, as do many accidents. Yet, because of his adding that the will or power of the three persons is one, he seems not to understand in the foregoing respect the three things of which he is speaking. For these three persons have their will or power not in accordance with their relations but in accordance with the fact that each of the persons is God. Now, if he says that the three persons are three things with respect to the fact that each of them is God, then either he wants to establish three gods or else he does not understand what he is saying. May these remarks temporarily satisfy Your Love as an indication of what I believe regarding the aforementioned claim. And may you continue always to fare well.

Concerning your request to dwell with me before you set out for Rome: as far as regards my love for Your Honor, be assured that I would gladly consent. But, as I see it, [your sojourn] would be of little use to you, on account of my busy schedule; and, in fact, it would be a hindrance to you. For I am absolutely certain that unless you remain with the bishop[3] until you set out, he will be of little or no assistance to you with respect to what you are obliged to do. Nor am I able to do anything which would be of benefit for the journey you are to undertake.

TO FULCO, BISHOP OF BEAUVAIS[1]

To my lord and very dear friend Fulco, venerable bishop of Beauvais: brother Anselm, by title abbot of Bec, [sends] greeting.

I hear — but nevertheless cannot entirely believe — that the cleric Roscelin makes the following claim: "In God, either the three persons are three things — [existing] in separation from one another (as do three angels) and yet [existing] in such way that there is one will and power — or else the Father and the Holy Spirit were incarnate. Moreover, [the three persons] could truly be called three gods if custom allowed it." He maintains that Archbishop Lanfranc (of venerable memory)[2] was of this opinion and that I am presently of it. I have been told that on account of all this a council[3] is to be called in the near future by Rainaldus, venerable archbishop of Rheims. Accordingly, since I anticipate that Your Reverence will be present there, I want to instruct you on how you ought to answer on my behalf if the matter needs [my response].

Archbishop Lanfranc's life, known to many religious and wise men, sufficiently excuses him from the above charge (for no such thing was ever before said about him); and his absence and death prohibit any new accusation concerning him. Concerning me, however, I wish all men to have the following true opinion. I hold those doctrines which we confess in the creeds[4] when we say: "I believe in God the Father Almighty, Creator [of heaven and earth]"; and "I believe in one God, Father Almighty, Maker [of heaven and earth]"; and "Whoever wishes to be saved: before all things it is necessary that he hold the Catholic faith." [And I hold] the doctrines which follow [from these creeds]. I believe with my mind and confess with my mouth these three bases of the Christian confession which I have just mentioned. [And I so believe and confess them] that I am certain that whoever wishes to deny any part of them, and whoever expressly asserts as true the blasphemy which I mentioned having heard that Roscelin is stating, is anathema — whether he be a human being or an angel. And I will say by way of confirmation: as long as he persists in this obstinacy let him remain anathema, for he is not at all a Christian. But if he was baptized and was brought up among Christians, then he ought not at all to be given a hearing. No explanation for his error should be demanded of him, and no explication of our truth should be presented to him. Rather, as soon as the detection of his falsehood is beyond doubt, either let him anathematize the poison which he produces and spews forth or let him be anathematized by all Catholics unless he recants. For it is pointless and most foolish to call back into the uncertainty of unsettled questions that which is most firmly established upon a solid rock — [to do so] on account of every single man who lacks understanding. For our faith ought to be rationally defended against the impious, but not against those who admit that they delight in the honor of the name "Christian." From these latter it must be rightly demanded that they hold firmly to the pledge made at baptism, but to the former it must be demonstrated rationally how irrationally they despise us. For a Christian ought to advance through faith to understanding, instead of proceeding through understanding to faith or withdrawing from faith if he cannot understand. But when he is able to attain to understanding, he is delighted; but when he is unable, he reveres what he cannot apprehend.

I request that this letter of mine be taken by Your Holiness to the council already mentioned; or, if perhaps you are not going, I ask that it be sent through one of your men of learning. If the matter has need of my name, then let my letter be read aloud in the hearing of the entire assembly. But if [the matter does] not [have need of my name], there will be no necessity for making my letter public. Farewell.

THE INCARNATION OF THE WORD
(*Epistola de Incarnatione Verbi*)

THE INCARNATION OF THE WORD[1]
(*Epistola de Incarnatione Verbi*)

To the supreme Pontiff Urban,[2] Lord and Father of the universal Church as it sojourns on earth, Brother Anselm, sinner in life, monk in habit, called to be bishop of the chief city Canterbury (by either the command or the permission of God), [offers] due subjection, with humble service and devout prayers.

I

Divine providence has chosen Your Holiness, and has appointed you custodian of the Christian faith and life, and ruler of the Church. Therefore, if anything which is contrary to the Catholic faith arises in the Church, there is no one else to whom it is more rightly referred for authoritative correction. And if anyone responds to error, there is no one else to whom this response is more safely referred for prudent scrutiny. Therefore, just as I am not able [to send] the present letter more appropriately to anyone else, so I send it to no one more willingly than to Your Wisdom — so that if anything in it needs to be corrected, it may be set right by your judgment, and so that what holds to the rule of truth may be confirmed by your authority.

When I was still abbot[3] at the monastery in Bec, the following assertion was advanced by a certain cleric[4] in France: "If the three persons in God are only one thing (*res*) — and are not three things, each one [existing] separately in itself (as do three angels or three souls) and yet [existing] in such way that they are wholly the same in will and in power — then the Father and the Holy Spirit were incarnate with the Son." When this error was brought to my attention, I began a letter against it. However, I thought it not worth completing, even though a part of it had been written. For since he against whom it was being written had abjured his error in the council[5] called by Rainaldus, venerable archbishop of Rheims,[6] and since there did not seem to be anyone who was unaware that this man had been mistaken, I thought there to be no need for it. (That part of the letter which I had written was, however, transcribed by certain brothers, without my knowledge, and passed on to others to read. I mention this (1) so that if this part should come into anyone's hands, then although it contains nothing false, it should nevertheless be discarded as incomplete and unpolished, and (2) so that what I there began should here be required to be more carefully undertaken and to be completed.)

Now, after I was seized in England and bound to the episcopate[7] by some unfathomable ordinance of God, I heard that the author of the above-mentioned novelty was persisting in his opinion and was saying that he had abjured his earlier statements only because he was afraid of being killed by the people. For this reason, then, certain brothers petitioned me, urging that I solve the problem in which he was so entangled that he believed he could extricate himself only by committing himself either to the incarnation of God the Father and God the Holy Spirit or else to a plurality of gods. And I, in turn, petition that no one think me to have been so presumptuous as to suppose that the strength of the Christian faith needs the assistance of my defense. Indeed, if, when there are so many holy and wise men everywhere, a contemptibly insignificant man like me were to try to write something to strengthen the foundation of the Christian faith, as if it stood in need of my defense, then assuredly I could be justly called presumptuous and could be viewed as a laughing stock. For if other men saw me — loaded with stakes and ropes and the customary items used to tie down and to render steadfast what is likely to collapse — working around Mount Olympus in order to strengthen it lest as the result of some shock it collapse or be destroyed, it would be amazing if they could restrain themselves from laughter and derision. How much more [this would happen] if with my arguments I should try to strengthen and to render steadfast, as if it were tottering, that stone which, "cut out without hands from a mountain, struck and smashed the statue" which Nebuchadnezzar saw in a dream — that stone which has now become "a great mountain and has filled the whole earth"![8] Would not those many holy and wise men, who rejoice in having their lives founded upon this mountain's eternal stability, be entitled to be indignant with me and to consider my effort to be the

De Incarnatione Verbi

result not of serious learning but of frivolous boasting? Therefore, if in this letter I deal with anything that has to do with the stability of our faith, it is not in order to confirm that stability but to satisfy the requests of my brethren who asked for the discussion.

But if the one who expressed the above-mentioned opinion has already been corrected by God and has returned to the truth, then let him not at all suppose that I am speaking against him in this letter, since he is no longer what he was. For if he was "once darkness, but is now light in the Lord,"[9] we ought not to accuse the darkness which no longer exists but to approve the light which shines. But whether he has as yet returned to the light or not, I perceive that there are many who are struggling with the same problem. Accordingly, even though their faith surmounts the reasoning which to them seems inconsistent with faith, I do not think it superfluous to resolve this inconsistency.

But before I examine this question I will say something to curb the presumption of those who, with blasphemous rashness and on the ground that they cannot understand it, dare to argue against something which the Christian faith confesses — those who judge with foolish pride that what they are not able to understand is not at all possible, rather than acknowledging with humble wisdom that many things are possible which they are not able to comprehend. Indeed, no Christian ought to question the truth of what the Catholic Church believes in its heart and confesses with its mouth. Rather, by holding constantly and unhesitatingly to this faith, by loving it and living according to it he ought humbly, and as best he is able,[10] to seek to discover the reason why it is true. If he is able to understand, then let him give thanks to God. But if he cannot understand, let him not toss his horns in strife but let him bow his head in reverence. For self-confident human wisdom can, by thrusting, uproot its horns more quickly than it can, by pushing, roll this stone. For when certain men begin to grow "horns" of self-confident knowledge, then (being ignorant of the fact that if someone thinks he knows something, he does not yet know it as he ought to know it) they are accustomed to mount up presumptuously unto the loftiest questions of faith before they possess spiritual wings through firmness of faith. Consequently, when they try to ascend to those questions which first require the ladder of faith (as it is written, "Unless you believe you will not understand"),[11] but try to ascend in reverse order by means of first understanding, they are constrained to fall into many kinds of errors on account of their defective understanding. For it is apparent that they have no foundation of faith who, because they cannot understand what they believe, argue against the truth of this same faith — a truth confirmed by the holy Fathers. It is as if bats and owls, which see the sky only at night, were to dispute about the midday rays of the sun with eagles, which with unblinded vision gaze directly at the sun.

So *before* we examine and judge the deep things of faith, the heart must be cleansed by faith — just as God is spoken of as "cleansing their hearts by faith."[12] And the eyes must be enlightened through keeping the precepts of the Lord, because "the precept of the Lord is light, enlightening the eyes."[13] And through humble obedience to the testimonies of God we ought to become as little children in order to learn the wisdom which the testimony of the Lord gives, testimony "faithful, giving wisdom to little ones."[14] Thus, the Lord says: "I thank You, Father, Lord of heaven and earth, because You have hidden these things from the wise and the prudent and have revealed them to little ones."[15] Putting aside the things of the flesh, let us live according to the Spirit *before*, I say, we examine and judge the deep things of faith. For he who lives according to the flesh is carnal or natural (*animalis*); and of him it is said that "the natural (*animalis*) man does not perceive the things which are of the Spirit of God."[16] But he who "by the Spirit puts to death the deeds of the flesh"[17] is made spiritual; and it is read of him that "the spiritual man judges all things, but is himself judged by no one."[18] For it is true that the more richly we are fed on those things in Sacred Scripture which nourish us through obedience, the more precisely we are carried on to those things which satisfy through understanding. Indeed, it is vain for someone to try to say "I have understood more than all my teachers" if he does not dare to add "because Your testimonies are my meditation."[19] And he utters falsely "I have understood more than the ancients" if he is unaware of the continuation: "for I have sought Your commandments."[20] Assuredly, what I am saying is this: He who does not believe will not understand. For he who does not believe will not experience; and he who has not experienced will not know. For the more experiencing-a-thing is superior to merely

De Incarnatione Verbi

hearing about it, the more knowledge from experience surpasses knowledge at second hand.[21]

And not only is the mind prevented from rising to the understanding of higher things when it lacks faith and obedience to the commandments of God, but by the neglect of good conscience even the understanding which has already been given is sometimes removed and faith itself overturned. For the apostle says of certain ones: "When they knew God, they did not glorify Him as God or give Him thanks; but they became futile in their thinking, and their foolish hearts were darkened."[22] And when the apostle instructed Timothy to "fight the good fight," he stated: "having faith and a good conscience, for rejecting conscience some men have made shipwreck of their faith."[23] Therefore, let no one plunge rashly into complex questions concerning divine things without first striving in firmness of faith for earnestness of life and of wisdom — lest running through a misleading mass of sophistries with frivolous lack of care, he be ensnared by some persistent falsehood.

All men are to be warned to approach questions concerning the Sacred Page with utmost care. Nevertheless, in particular, those dialecticians of our day (or rather, heretics of dialectic) who think that universal substances are only vocal sounds [*flatus vocis*],[24] and who cannot comprehend that a color is something distinct from the material object or that a man's wisdom is something distinct from his soul, ought to be blown right out of the discussion of spiritual questions. Indeed, in the souls of these dialecticians, reason — which ought to be the ruler and judge of all that is in man — is so covered over by corporeal images that it cannot extricate itself from them and cannot distinguish from them those things which it ought to contemplate purely and in isolation. For example, how will someone who does not yet understand how several men are one man in species be able to comprehend how in that highest and most mysterious Nature several persons — each one of whom, distinctly, is perfect God — are one God? And how will someone whose mind is too darkened to distinguish between his horse and its color be able to distinguish between the one God and His several relations? Finally, someone who cannot understand a human being [*homo*] to be anything except an individual shall not at all understand a human being to be anything except a human person, for every individual man is a person.

How, then, shall he be able to understand that a humanity [*homo*], though not a person, was assumed by the Word? That is, another nature but not another person was assumed.

I have said these things so that no one will presume to examine the highest questions of faith before he is ready, or so that if he does so presume no difficulty or impossibility of comprehending will be able to shake him from the truth to which he has been holding by faith.

Now we must come to the matter on account of which we began [this letter].

2

This man who is said to maintain that the three persons [of the Trinity] are like three angels or three souls also says, so I hear: "The pagans defend their law; the Jews defend theirs. Therefore, even we Christians ought to defend our faith." Let us hear how this Christian defends his faith: "If," says he, "the three persons are only one thing — and are not three things, each one [existing] separately in itself (as do three angels or three souls) and yet [existing] in such way that they are wholly the same in will and in power — then the Father and the Holy Spirit were incarnate with the Son." Look at what this man says! Look at how this Christian defends his faith! Assuredly, either he wants to confess that there are three gods, or else he does not understand what he is saying. Now, if he confesses that there are three gods, he is not a Christian. On the other hand, if he affirms what he does not understand, he ought not to be given credence.

We should not reply to this man by reference to the authority of Sacred Scripture, because either he does not believe Scripture or else he interprets it in a perverse sense. For what does Sacred Scripture say more plainly than that there is only one God? Therefore, his error must be demonstrated by reference to the reasoning by which he tries to defend himself. In order to accomplish this demonstration more easily and briefly, I shall discuss only the Father and the Son, because by their own proper names these two persons are clearly indicated to be distinct from each other. (For the name "Holy Spirit" is not alien to the Father and to the Son, since each of them is both spirit and holy.) However, what we shall discover in the case of the Father and the Son

De Incarnatione Verbi

concerning the unity of substance or the plurality of persons will be known without doubt to hold true for each of the three.

Suppose [my opponent][25] to be saying, then: "If the two persons, Father and Son, are not two things . . . ." Let us ask first what he means here by "two things." For we believe that each of the persons is that which is common to both and that which is proper to Himself. For the person of the Father is both God (To be God is common to Him with the Son) and Father (To be Father is His distinguishing property). Similarly, the person of the Son is both God (To be God is common to Him with the Father) and Son (This person alone is called Son). In the case of these two persons, therefore, one thing is common, viz., to be God, and two things are proper, viz., to be Father and to be Son. Now, whatever is common to them — such as to be omnipotent and to be eternal — is understood only in this joint way. And those things which are proper to each — such as to be the begetter or the one who begets (for the Father), to be the Word or the one who is begotten (for the Son) — are signified by the two names "father" and "son."

Therefore, when [my opponent] says that these two persons are two things, I ask what in this instance he is calling two things. Is it that which is common to them or is it those things each of which is proper to one person alone? Now, if he says that "two things" indicates two distinguishing properties, viz., to be Father and to be Son — yet so that what is common to the Father and the Son is only one thing and not more than one — then he is speaking superfluously, because no Christian confesses that with respect to these two distinguishing properties the Father and the Son are one thing; rather [every Christian confesses that they are] two [things]. For we customarily apply the word "thing" ("*res*") to whatever we in any way say to be something (*aliquid*). Now, whoever says of God that He is Father or is Son says something about Him. Moreover, everyone knows that in the case of God, the Father is not the Son and the Son not the Father, even though in the case of a given human being the father is a son and the son a father if the same man is both a father and a son. This difference [between the two cases] occurs because in the case of God, "father" and "son" are predicated in opposition to each other. However, in the case of the given human being the terms are not predicated in relation to each other; rather, the man is called father in relation to a second man, who is his son, and he is called son in relation to a third man, who is his father.

In this way, then, nothing prevents our saying that the two persons, Father and Son, are two things — provided we understand what kind of things they are. For the Father and the Son are two things not in the sense that their substance is two things but in the sense that their relations are two things. Nonetheless, [my opponent] clearly shows, by what he adds, that this is not the manner in which he understands the two persons to be two things. For when he says "If the three persons are only one thing and are not three things," he then specifies: "[each one existing] separately in itself." Indeed, he is seen to be setting forth a separation such as would prevent the Father and the Son from being present together in the same man. For only through this separation does he think that he can free the Father from sharing in the incarnation with the Son. For if he believes that God, who is Father and Son, is only one, he does not see that the Father and the Son can be separated (so as not to be together in the same man) according to the separation in terms of which it is one thing to be the Father and another to be the Son, since paternity and filiation are different from each other. Therefore, he is speaking of a separation of the persons of the Father and the Son other than that separation by which the Father and the Son are different from each other in accordance with their respective distinguishing properties. (For in accordance with this latter separation he does not understand the incarnation to be alien to the Father; indeed, if the Father and the Son exist simultaneously, he believes it to follow that the Father shares incarnation with the Son.) Or else if he is speaking about this latter separation, he labors in vain, as I have already said, for this is the manner in which the Christian faith understands the Father and the Son to be two things.

Now, when he says "as do three angels or three souls," he shows plainly that he is not talking about that plurality or that separation which is in these persons according to their distinguishing properties. Certainly "two angels" or "two souls" is not predicated of anything that is numerically one and the same. Nor is anything numerically one predicated of two angels or of two souls — as, for example, we predicate "father" or "son" of God, who is numerically one, and predicate "numerically one God" of the Father and the Son. For we believe and say that God is Father and that God is Son — and conversely, that the Father is God and that the Son is God. And yet we believe and say not that there is more than one God but rather that God is one in number as in nature, even though the Father and the Son are not one but two.

Now, we predicate "angel" and "soul" substantially, not relationally. (For although the name "angel" is taken from a function — since "angel" means "messenger" — nevertheless it is understood to indicate a kind of substance, just as does "soul.") That this is [my opponent's] understanding of the matter is evidenced by his saying, on equal footing, "as do three *angels* or three *souls*." Therefore, he means the kind of plurality and separation which a plurality of angels or of souls has, i.e., which a plurality of substances has. Furthermore, he is seen to display this viewpoint clearly when he adds "in such way that they are wholly the same in will and in power." For he understands will and power in these several things analogously to [will and power] in several angels or souls. Now, this viewpoint would be unintelligible if these were being regarded as several things with respect to properties-of-persons rather than with respect to what is predicated of them jointly. For the Father and the Son do not at all have any will or power with respect to their distinguishing properties, i.e., with respect to paternity and filiation; rather, they have will and power with respect to their divine substance, which is common to them.

Therefore, if he means that the three persons are three things with respect to their *distinguishing properties*, it is plain how superfluously he makes this statement. And when he adds "as do three angels or three souls" it is also plain how inconsistently [he does so].

3

On the other hand, if [my opponent] is saying that these persons are two things with respect to what is *common* to them (i.e., with respect to the fact that by Himself each is, and together all are, one perfect God), then first of all I pose the question of whether he is a Christian. He will reply, I suppose, that he is. Accordingly, he believes that God is one, that He is three persons (viz., Father, Son, and Holy Spirit), and that only the person of the Son was incarnate, although with the cooperation of the other two. Now, whoever believes these doctrines maintains that anyone who wants to contradict any one of them is not a Christian. Thus, if he believes these doctrines, he denies that anyone arguing against them is a Christian.

Let us now consider, however, whether he himself is trying to undermine this faith. Accordingly, when he asserts — to continue (as I have been doing) to state about two persons what is understood of all three — when, I say, he asserts that "If the two persons are one thing and are not two things (as are two angels or two souls), it follows that if the Son was incarnate then so also was the Father," I think that he is reasoning with himself accordingly:

> If God is numerically one and the same thing, and if this very thing is Father and Son, then when the Son was incarnate how is it that the Father also was not incarnate? Indeed, an affirmation and its denial are not both true of one and the same thing at the same time; but nothing prevents us from affirming something of one thing while at the same time denying it of another. For instance, it is not the case that the same man Peter both is and is not an apostle. And even if under one name he is affirmed to be an apostle and under another name is denied to be an apostle (as, for example, "Peter is an apostle" and "Simon is not an apostle"), not both of the statements are true, but rather one of them is false. But "Peter is an apostle" and "Stephen is not an apostle" can both be true, because Peter and Stephen are different men. Hence, if the Father is numerically one and the same thing as the Son, and is not a thing other than the Son, then it is not true that something ought to be affirmed of the Son and denied of the Father, or affirmed of the Father and denied of the Son. Therefore, whatever the Father is, the Son is as well; and what is said of the Son ought not to be denied of the Father. Now, the Son was incarnate. Therefore, the Father also was incarnate.

Now, if this reasoning were sound, then the heresy of Sabellius would be true. For if what is said of the one person were said also of the other simply because the two persons are one thing, then just as the Son is called *Son* and *Word* and *Begotten*, so these terms would be predicated of the Father as well. And just as the Father is *Father* and *Begetter* and *Unbegotten*, so these terms would have to be predicated of the Son as well. But if so, then the Father would not be different from the Son, nor would the Son be different from the Father. Hence, they would not be two persons but would be one person. For if we grant that God is Father and Son, then the Father and the Son are called two persons because they are believed to be different from each other. For a father is

De Incarnatione Verbi

always the father of someone, and a son is always someone's son; a father is never his own father, nor is a son ever his own son. Rather, the father is other than the one of whom he is the father; and, similarly, the son is other than the one whose son he is. Therefore, if there were not in God one who is the Father and another whose father he is, nor one who is the Son and another whose son he is, then God would falsely be called Father or Son. For if in God there were not someone different from the Father — someone of whom the Father is father — then there could not be a father. And, similarly, if in God there were not someone different from the Son — someone of whom the Son is a son — then there could not be a son. Thus, there would be no basis for affirming these two persons in God, for they are called two because God is Father and God is Son, and because the Father is always one and the Son always another.

Do you see, then, how our faith would be destroyed in conformity with the opinion of someone who thinks that if the several persons in God are one thing and not more than one thing, then, as a consequence, the Father was incarnate with the Son? For if this inference of his were true, then the result would be not only what I mentioned about the Father and the Son but also such great confusion with respect to all three persons that whatever is said with respect to the individual properties of any one of them would have to be said commonly of all three. Hence, (just as I have shown[26] in the case of the Father and the Son) there would be no basis for differentiating from each other the Father, the Son, and the Holy Spirit, who proceeds from the Father and the Son. Consequently, there would not be any relation in God, since a relation exists in no way in God except according to that whereby the persons are different from one another. And so there would be no plurality of persons.

Indeed, if we posit that the three persons are one thing, then either his inference[27] does not follow or else all the things that I have just been saying[28] follow together. For the logic of my inference is similar [to that of his] in all respects. So why does he proceed with the incarnation as if it alone posed a problem? Why does he not rather say: "If the three persons are one thing, then there are not three persons"? For he can raise this problem about the time before the incarnation just as well as about the time after the incarnation.

4

On the other hand, if he at all means to claim that the three persons, insofar as each is God, are not one thing but are three things, each one independent, as are three angels, then it is quite clear that he is setting up three gods. Yet, perhaps he himself does not say "as are three angels or three souls" but only affirms that the three persons are three things, without the addition of any comparison. (Perhaps the one who commended this man's question to me introduced this comparison on his own.) Why, then, is he misled or does he mislead others by the word "thing"? For the word "God" signifies this very thing. Undoubtedly, either he will deny that this thing in which there are three persons (or, rather, this thing which we confess to be three persons) is God, or else (if he does not make this denial) it follows that just as he asserts that the three persons are three things and not one thing, so he also affirms that these three persons are three gods and not one God. And let Christians judge how impious these statements are.

But he will reply: "The fact that I say 'three things' does not compel me to admit three gods, because these three things are together one God." And I say that, as a consequence, no one of these three things considered by itself (i.e., no one of these persons considered by Himself) would be God; rather, God would consist of the three things. Hence, the Father would not be God, the Son would not be God, the Holy Spirit would not be God — because God would have to be spoken of by naming the three together and not by mentioning any one or two of them. And this is as impious as the preceding statements. For if this view were correct, God would not be a simple nature but would be a nature composed of parts. Now, if [my opponent] has an uncluttered intellect, undarkened by a multiplicity of images, he understands that things-simple excel things-composite (insofar as simplicity and composition are concerned). For everything composite must be able to be divided either actually or conceivably; but this divisibility cannot be understood to hold true of things simple. For no intellect can dissolve into parts something whose parts cannot be conceived. Therefore, if God is composed of three things, then either no nature is simple or else there is some other nature which in some respect is more excellent than the nature of God. But it is clear how false both of these alternatives are. Now,

De Incarnatione Verbi

if [my opponent] is one of those modern dialecticians who believe that nothing exists except what they can imagine, and if he does not think there to be anything in which there are no parts, at least he will not deny understanding that if there were something which could neither actually nor conceivably be divided, it would be greater than something which can be divided at least conceivably. Thus, if everything composite can be divided at least in thought, then when [my opponent] says that God is something composite, he is saying that he is able to understand that something is greater than God. Hence, his intellect passes beyond God — a feat which no intellect can perform.

5

But now let us look at what he adds as if to ward off the inconsistency which is seen to arise if the three persons are three things: "and yet [existing] in such way that the will and power of these three things is one." Here we must ask: Are these three things divine natures (1) with respect to that which they are understood to be in separation from one another, (2) with respect to their common will and power, or (3) neither with respect solely to what they have separately nor with respect to what is common to them but with respect to both of these together? (~1) To be sure, if they possessed deity with respect to what they are separately, then there would be three gods. And they could be understood to be divine apart from reference to their will and power. For what is proper is always understood separately from what is common, and what is common is always understood separately from what is proper. The divine nature, though, cannot at all be conceived without reference to will and power. (~2) But if with respect to one common will and power they were God, whether they are considered singly or two at a time or all three together — what would these three discordant things be doing in the Godhead? For only through some other thing (*per aliud*) could these three things harmonize into a unity of deity; moreover, they could be of no avail either toward perfecting or toward at all assisting the divine existence. For if one will and power suffice for God's perfection, what are these three things which God needs, or to what end does He need them? Indeed, we believe that God is not in need of anything. So it would be pointless to think that these things are in

God. (~3) But if God were constituted not by these three things exclusively nor by will and power exclusively but by all of them together, then, I repeat, He would be composed of parts and would be comprised by things which, by themselves, are neither God nor gods.

But if [my opponent] says that these three things are called God by virtue of their power and will, just as a man is called king by virtue of his kingly power, then "God" would not be the name of a substance; but, rather, the three things (whatever they are) would be called three gods accidentally, just as three men who have the same kingly power are called three kings; for three men cannot be one king. How abominable this view is I need not say.

I would have to fill a large book should I wish to write out the absurdities and impieties which would follow (1) if it were true that because these three persons are one thing with respect to what we predicate commonly of all three, the incarnation of one person of God requires the incarnation of the remaining two persons, or (2) if [it were true that] because the Son alone was incarnate, [the three persons] are three separate things, as he against whom I have made these replies supposes. Hence, it is clear how little he ought to be eager to argue about profound matters — especially about issues concerning which one does not err without danger.

6

But perhaps [my opponent] will say to me:[29]

> Just as to you it seems that if the conclusion I reach follows logically, then the conclusions you reach follow with equal necessity, so to me it seems that my inference does follow logically. Therefore, show that my inference does not follow logically, and I will admit with you that no inconsistency is entailed if the Son alone was incarnate or if the three persons are one thing. But if you fail to show this [inconsequence], then instead of solving the disputed point you render it more difficult to solve, since you join with me in proving that numerous inconsistencies arise from it. Now, if these inconsistencies must be rejected, then we both ought, alike, to conclude that "if the Son alone was incarnate, then the three persons are not one thing, or else if they are one thing, then all three persons, alike, were incarnate."

Accordingly, I must show (1) in what respect [my opponent] is mistaken, (2) how from the incarnation of the Son alone it does not follow that the three persons are three separate things and

De Incarnatione Verbi

(3) how it does not follow that if the three persons are one thing they were all incarnate. But assuredly the holy Fathers (and especially blessed Augustine), following the apostles and evangelists, have argued with irrefutable reasoning with God is three persons and yet one unique, individual, and simple nature. Still, if anyone will deign to read my two short works, viz., the *Monologion* and the *Proslogion* (which I wrote especially in order [to show] that what we hold by faith regarding the divine nature and its persons — excluding the topic of incarnation — can be proven by compelling reasons apart from [appeal to] the authority of Scripture) — if, I say, anyone is willing to read these works, then I think that he will there discover, with regard to the matter before us, arguments which he will neither be able to disprove nor will want to treat lightly. If in those writings I have asserted any points which I have not read elsewhere or do not remember having read elsewhere, I ought not at all, I think, to be reproached for having done so. For I asserted these points not as one teaching what our instructors were ignorant of, and not as one correcting what they did not put well, but as one saying something which, it seems, they were silent about, something which nonetheless was consistent with, not in discrepancy with, their teachings. And I advanced these points (1) in order to defend our faith against those who, while unwilling to believe what they do not understand, deride those who do believe, and (2) in order to assist the devout striving of those who humbly seek to understand what they most steadfastly believe. However, I do not want to inflict upon readers of this letter the task of searching out some other writing in order to know by clear reasoning as well as by faith that the three persons are not three gods but only one, or that the incarnation of God with respect to one of His persons does not necessitate that the same God be incarnate with respect to His other persons. Accordingly, I shall now append an argument which I believe is sufficient to refute the view of this self-styled defender of our faith.

He asserts plainly that either the Father and the Holy Spirit were incarnate with the Son or else these three persons are three separate things. Now, surely he understands this separation to be such that neither the Father nor the Holy Spirit is in the Son. For if the other two persons are in the Son and the Son is in a man, then they also are in that man. Therefore, since the three persons are together in the same man: [my opponent] thinks it to follow that if the three are one thing, the person of the Son cannot at all be incarnate in this man in separation from the other two persons. Nevertheless, he does not deny that there are three persons or that the Son was incarnate.

I have already demonstrated that if the three persons are three separate things, either there must be three gods or else the other absurdities mentioned earlier must be true. Accordingly, with the help of the one and only God I shall now show briefly,[30] first of all, that even if there were three gods, this fact would not help him to keep the Father and the Holy Spirit from being incarnate — even though he thinks they can be kept from incarnation only if they are more than one god.[31] Next, I shall show that there is only one God and not more than one. Finally, I shall make it clear that although the three persons are one God, the incarnation of any one of them does not necessitate the incarnation of the others as well but, instead, renders it impossible.

7

Assuredly, it is a characteristic of the Divine Nature so to exist always and everywhere that never and nowhere does anything exist without its presence.[32] Otherwise, it would not at all be powerful everywhere and always; and that which is not powerful everywhere and always is not at all God. Now, if [my opponent] claims that it is not this Divine Substance but is its power which is present always and everywhere, he will not, however, deny that God possesses His power either accidentally or substantially. But God does not have power accidentally, because although every subject can exist or be conceived apart from its accidents, God can neither be nor be conceived apart from His power. So if God has His power substantially, either it is a part of His being, or else it is that very thing which His entire being is. But it is not a part, because (as has already been mentioned) that which has parts can be divided either actually or conceivably, and division in either way is totally foreign to God. Therefore, the being of God and the being of His power are the same. Thus, just as the power of God is present always and everywhere, so whatever God is is present always and everywhere. Therefore, when the aforementioned self-styled defender of our faith says that there are three gods, he

De Incarnatione Verbi

cannot show how they exist separately — with respect to that separation in terms of which he supposes himself to free the Father and the Holy Spirit from incarnation. Hence, [positing] a plurality of gods cannot help him to keep the Father and the Holy Spirit from being incarnate, for in this plurality of gods cannot be found that separation without which, as he believes, the freedom from incarnation is not at all possible.

8

However, that there is only one God and no more than one is easily proved from the consideration that either (1) God is not the Supreme Good or else (2) there is more than one Supreme Good or else (3) instead of there being several gods there is only one God. (~1) But no one denies that God is the Supreme Good, because whatever is less than something else is not at all God, and whatever is not the Supreme Good is less than some other because it is less than the Supreme Good. (~2) And, assuredly, it is not the case that the Supreme Good admits of plurality and thus that there are several Supreme Goods. For if there were several Supreme Goods, they would be equal. But, indeed, the Supreme Good is that which so excels other goods that it has neither an equal nor a superior. Therefore, there is only one Supreme Good. (3) Hence, instead of there being several gods, there is only one God — just as there is only one Supreme Good and [only one] Supreme Substance, Supreme Being, or Supreme Nature, which, by a process of reasoning exactly similar to that in the case of the Supreme Good, is proved to be unable in any respect to be spoken of plurally.

9

Although this one and only God is three persons — Father, Son, and Holy Spirit — it is not necessary (as my opponent thinks) for the other persons to be incarnate when the Son is incarnate; on the contrary, it is impossible. For [my opponent] concedes that since they are different from one another they are several persons. Indeed, if they were not different from one another, they would not be more than one. (In order to explain more briefly and easily what I want to, I will continue to speak, as

I have done above, only of the Father and the Son; for by considering them it will be clear what must be understood about the Holy Spirit.) Accordingly, because the Father and the Son are not two substances it is not with respect to substance that they are different from each other and are more than one. The Father is not one substance and the Son another; rather, the Father and the Son are one and the same substance. But because the Father and the Son are two persons and are different from each other (rather than being one and the same person) it is with respect to person that they are more than one and are different from each other.

So [my opponent] says: "If the Son was incarnate, and if the Son is not a different thing from the Father but is numerically one and the same thing as the Father, then it must be the case that the Father also was incarnate. For it is impossible that a thing which is numerically one and the same both be and not be, at the same time, incarnate in the same man." I reply that if the Son was incarnate and if the Son is not numerically one and the same person as the Father, but is another person, then it does not follow that, necessarily, the Father also was incarnate. For it is possible that one person be incarnate in a given man and that at the same time another person not be incarnate in this man.

But [my opponent will perhaps say]: "If God the Son was incarnate and if God who is the Son is not other than, but is numerically one and the same as, God who is the Father, then even though the Father and the Son are different persons, the necessity that the Father also be incarnate with the Son because of the unity of deity seems to outweigh the possibility that because of the diversity of persons the Father was not incarnate at the same time." Notice how he who says this is lame in both feet regarding the incarnation of the Son of God.[33] For whoever rightly understands His incarnation believes that He assumed a human nature [*homo*] into a unity with His person, rather than into a unity with His nature. But [my opponent] dreams that a human nature was assumed by the Son of God into a unity of nature rather than into a unity of person. For if this were not his view, he would not have said that the necessity that the Father be incarnate with the Son because the Father and the Son are one God outweighs the possibility that because they are more than one person the Father was not incarnate at the same time. Therefore, regarding the incarnation of the Son of God, who is one nature with the Father and a different person from the Father: whoever thinks that this incarnation so accords with the unity of nature that the Son cannot be incarnate apart from the Father, and whoever does not understand that the incarnation so accords with the unity of person that the Father cannot be incarnate with the Son, is lame in both feet, i.e., in both respects.

Indeed, God assumed a human nature not in such way that the divine nature and the human nature were one and the same[34] but in such way that the person of God and the person of the man were one and the same. But this [assumption of a human nature] can only occur in the case of one person of God. For it is incomprehensible that different persons be one and the same person with one and the same man. For if one man were one person with several other distinct persons, then [here would be an instance in which] a plurality of persons who are different from one another would have to be one and the same person — something impossible. Therefore, when God is incarnate with respect to any one of His persons, it is impossible that He be incarnate with respect to another of His persons as well.

10

Although it was not my purpose [to explain] in this letter why God assumed a human nature into a unity of person with the Son rather than into a unity with either of the other persons, nevertheless since mention of the matter has been made, I think that an explanation must be given.[35]

Assuredly, if the Holy Spirit had been incarnate — just as the Son was incarnate — the Holy Spirit would have been the son of a human being. Hence, there would be two sons in the Divine Trinity, viz., the Son of God and the son of a human being. Thus, a certain confusing ambiguity would arise when we would speak of God the Son. For both [of the persons] would be God and a son, though one would be the Son of God, the other the son of a human being. Moreover, since the one son would excel by virtue of the dignity of His greater parent, and since the other son would be subordinate because of the lowliness of His lesser parent, there would occur — with respect to their being sons — a seeming inequality in two persons who ought in every respect to be equal. For the greater the nature of God is than the nature of a man, the more becoming it is to be the Son of God than to be the son of a human being. Therefore, if the Holy Spirit had been begotten of a virgin, then since the Son of God would have had a uniquely more excellent birth (viz., from God), and since the Holy Spirit would have had only a lesser birth (viz., from a human being), the one person would be greater and the other lesser with respect to the dignity of birth — an inadmissible consequence.

On the other hand, if the *Father* had assumed a human nature into a unity with His own person, the plurality of sons would have produced not only the same[36] unbefittingness in God but also an additional one. For if the Father were the son of a virgin, then two persons in the Trinity would have the name "grandson"; for the Father would be the grandson of the parents of the virgin, and His son would be the grandson of the virgin (even though His son would have received nothing from the virgin).

Therefore, since it is impossible for there to be even any small unbefittingness in God, no person of God other than the Son ought to have been incarnate. For if *He* is incarnate nothing inadmissible follows. As for the fact that the Son is said to be less than the Father and the Holy Spirit from the point of view of His humanity: these two persons do not excel the Son, because even the Son has that very majesty by which these two persons are greater than His humanity and by which He Himself, with them, excels His own humanity.

There is another reason why incarnation befits the Son more than another [of the persons]. He who was to be incarnate was going to pray on behalf of the human race. And the human mind understands it to be much more suitable for the Son to supplicate the Father than for either of the persons other than the Son to make supplication to either of the persons other than the Father — even though this supplication is made not by the Son's divinity but by His humanity to His divinity. The Son of God makes this supplication [on behalf of the human race] because by virtue of a unity of person the Son of God is a man.

Furthermore, the one who was going to assume a human nature was going to come in order to war against the Devil and to intercede, as I have said, on behalf of man. Now, by an act of robbery[37] both the Devil and man willed to make themselves like unto God when they exercised an autonomous will [*propria voluntas*].[38] And because by an act of robbery they [thus] willed,

De Incarnatione Verbi

they willed only by falsehood, inasmuch as they could only [thus] have willed unjustly. Now, the will of an angel or of a man is autonomous when it wills contrary to the will of God. For when someone wills that which God forbids him to will, he has no author of his will except himself; so his will is autonomous. Now, even though a man might at some time submit his will to the will of another man, still this willing is autonomous if it is in opposition to God. For he only submits his will in order to obtain something that he wants, and thus he himself is the author of the reason why he submits his will to another will. Hence, his will is an autonomous will and is not [in one sense] submitted to another will. Yet, it is the prerogative of God alone to have an autonomous will — i.e., a will which is subject to no other will. Therefore, whoever else exercises an autonomous will tries to attain unto the likeness of God by an act of robbery, and is convicted of depriving (as far as it lies in his power to do so) God of His proper dignity and unique excellence. For if there were another will which were subject to no other will, then the will of God would not be superior to all other wills, nor would it be that will which no other will excels. Therefore, none of the three persons of God more fittingly "emptied Himself and took on the form of a servant"[39] (in order to vanquish the Devil and to intercede on behalf of man, who by an act of robbery had presumed unto a false likeness of God) than did the Son, who, being the brilliance of the eternal light and the true image of the Father, "thought it not robbery to be equal to God"[40] but by virtue of a true equality and likeness said, "I and the Father are one" and "He who sees me sees the Father also."[41]

Indeed, no one can more justly vanquish or punish a criminal, or more mercifully spare him or intercede on his behalf, than someone against whom the wrong is shown to be the more specifically committed. Nor can anything be more fittingly opposed to falsehood in order to vanquish it, or more fittingly applied to it in order to cure it, than is truth. Now, those who have presumed unto a false likeness to God are seen to have sinned the more specifically against Him who is believed to be the true likeness[42] of God the Father. But the Son assumed a human nature into a unity with His person, as I have said, in order that two natures — one divine and one human — would be one person.

11

Nevertheless, because an argument can be given on the basis of which Christ can seem (to those viewing the matter too carelessly) to exist of and in two persons, I think it valuable to say something about this unity of person, which we most steadfastly believe *not* to be a unity of two persons in Christ. For there are those who argue:

> How is it that we do not say that in Christ there are two persons even as there are two natures? For even before the assumption of human being [*homo*][43] God was a person; and after the assumption of human being He did not cease to be a person. Moreover, the human being that was assumed (*homo assumptus*) is a person because every individual human being is known to be a person. Therefore, the person of God who existed before the incarnation is one person, and the person of the assumed human being is another. Hence, just as Christ is both God and a man, so there are seen to be two persons in Him.

This argument seems to prove — because of the fact that God is a person and the assumed man (*homo assumptus*) is a person — that there are two persons in Christ. But the argument is not sound. For just as in God one nature is several persons, and the several persons are one nature, so in Christ one person is several natures and the several natures are one person. For just as the Father is God and the Son is God and the Holy Spirit is God, and yet there is one God and are not three gods, so in Christ the divine being (*deus*) is a person and the human being (*homo*) is a person, and yet there is one person and are not two persons. For in Christ the divine being is not one [individual] and the human being another (even though in Christ the divine being is one thing and the human being another). On the contrary, the same [individual] who is human is also divine. For the "Word made flesh"[44] assumed another nature, not another person. Now, when the word "man" ("*homo*")[45] is used, only the nature which is common to all men is signified. But when we say, demonstratively, "this man" or "that man," or use the proper name "Jesus," we designate a person — who has not only a nature but also a collection of distinguishing properties[46] by which the common[47] human nature is individuated and marked off from other individuated human natures. When this designation occurs, not just any man at all is understood [to be referred to] but only [the individual] who was announced by the angel — [the indi-

De Incarnatione Verbi

vidual] who is both divine and human, Son of God and Son of the Virgin (and whatever else it is true to say about Him in accordance with His deity and His humanity). For it is not possible to designate personally or to name personally the Son of God without designating or naming the Son of man; nor is it possible to designate or name the Son of man without designating or naming the Son of God. The reason for this impossibility is (1) that the same [individual] who is the Son of man is also the Son of God and (2) that the Word and the assumed man have the same collection of distinguishing properties. Now, it is impossible for two different persons to have the same collection of distinguishing properties or for these persons to be called by each other's name. For Peter and Paul do not have the same collection of distinguishing properties; and Peter is not called Paul, nor is Paul called Peter.

Therefore, when the "Word was made flesh,"[48] He assumed a nature. And only this nature is signified by the word "man"; moreover, it is always a different nature from the divine nature. The Word did not assume another person, because the Word has the same collection of distinguishing properties as does the assumed man. For man and the man-as-assumed-by-the-Word (viz., Jesus) are not the same thing. For the word "man"[49] (as I have said) signifies only [human] nature; but the phrase "the assumed man" or the name "Jesus" signifies not only [human] nature (i.e., humanity) but also a collection of distinguishing properties which is the same for the Word and the assumed man. Therefore, lest we be saying that that man is no more personally identical with the Word than is any other man, we do not say that the Word and man,[50] in an unrestricted sense, are the same person. Rather, we say that the Word and the assumed man, viz., Jesus, [are the same person]. Similarly, lest we seem to be confessing that the assumed man is the same person as the Father and the Holy Spirit, we do not believe that the assumed man is the same person as God, in an unrestricted sense. Rather, [we believe that the assumed man is the same person] as the person who is Word and Son. But since the Word is God and since the assumed man is human, it is true to say that God and man are the same person. Yet, by "God" must here be understood the Word; and by "man" must here be understood the Son of the Virgin.

Except for the statement I quoted above,[51] I have had access to nothing from the writings of the opponent to whom I am responding in this letter. Nonetheless, I think that the truth of the matter has been made so evident by what I have said that anyone who is intelligent will plainly recognize that nothing said against this truth contains the force of truth.

12

But if when recalled from [subscribing to] a multiplicity of gods [my opponent] rejects the plurality of persons in God, he does so because he does not know what he is talking about. He has in mind not God or His persons but something like a plurality of human persons; and because he sees that it is not possible for one man to be several persons, he denies that God is several persons. But we speak of three persons in God not because they are three separate things as are three men but because they have a certain likeness [*similitudo*] to three separate persons. Let us consider this point in regard to the Father and the Son, and let the same consideration be understood [to apply to] the Holy Spirit.

Accordingly, let us take the case of a man who is only a father without being a son, and of his son, who is only a son without being a father (viz., the case of Adam and Abel). We say, then, of Adam the father and of Abel the son that the father is not the son and the son it not the father. For Adam and Abel are two men and are separate persons; and there is not anyone of whom Adam is the son or anyone of whom Abel is the father. Similarly, then, even though there are not two gods, we confess that, in God, the Father is not the Son and the Son is not the Father, because the Father does not have a father and the Son does not have a son. Similarly, the Holy Spirit is not the Father or the Son, because there is no one whose father He is or whose son He is. Therefore, the Father and the Son and the Holy Spirit are called three persons not because they are three separate things but simply because they are three, and are different from one another, and cannot be called by one another's names (just as I have shown about the father and the son in the case of different human persons).

13

But suppose that — on the ground that he cannot understand it in God and does not see any instance of it in other things — [my

De Incarnatione Verbi

opponent] denies that something *one* can be called something *three* and that something *three* can be called something *one* (in such way that the three are not called by one another's respective name) as we do in the case of the one God and His three persons.[52] In that event, let him tolerate something which his intellect cannot comprehend to be in God. And with things that are enclosed by place or time or are composed of parts let him not compare that Nature which is above all other things and is free from every law of place, time, and composition of parts. Instead, let him believe that something holds true of this Nature which cannot hold true of those things; and let him submit to Christian authority without contending against it.

However, let us see whether among created things, which are subject to the law of place, time, and composition of parts, we can to some extent find that which [my opponent] denies to hold true of God. Suppose[53] that there is a spring from which originates and flows a river that later accumulates into a lake; and let its name be the "Nile." Accordingly, we speak so separately of the spring, the river, and the lake that we do not call the spring "river" or "lake," nor call the river "spring" or "lake," nor call the lake "spring" or "river." And yet, the spring is called the Nile, the river is called the Nile, and the lake is called the Nile. Moreover, the spring and the river taken together are called the Nile, the spring and the lake taken together are called the Nile, and the river and the lake taken together are called the Nile. Furthermore, the spring, the river, and the lake — all three taken together — are called the Nile. Nevertheless, whether the name "Nile" is applied to each separately or to two in combination or to all three together, there are not different Niles; there is one and the same Nile. Hence, the spring, the river, and the lake are three; and they are one Nile, one stream, one nature, one body of water — none of which can be said to be something three, for there are not three Niles or three streams or three bodies of water or three natures. Nor are there three springs or three rivers or three lakes. Here, then, is an example in which something three is called something one and something one is called something three, without the three being called by one another's respective name.

But if [my opponent] objects that the spring, the river, or the lake neither singularly nor in combinations of two are the complete Nile but are only parts of the Nile, then let him think of this whole Nile, from when it began until when it shall end, as its whole lifespan, so to speak. For it does not exist as a spatial or a temporal whole at once but exists through parts and will not be complete until it ceases to exist. In this respect it is like a statement, which is not complete as long as it issues from the fountain of the mouth, so to speak; and when it *is* complete it no longer exists. Now, if anyone considers the matter in this way and understands it carefully, he will realize that the whole Nile is the spring, the whole Nile is the river, and the whole Nile is the lake, and that the spring is not the river or the lake, the river is not the lake or the spring, and the lake is not the spring or the river. For the spring is not the same as the river or the lake, even though the river and the lake are the same thing that the spring is, viz., the same Nile, the same stream, the same body of water, the same nature. Therefore, here is a case in which one complete whole is called something three and something three is called one complete whole, without these three being called by one another's respective name. However, in the case of that Nature which is perfectly simple and perfectly free from the law of all space and time, the foregoing kind of predication occurs in quite a different manner and much more perfectly. Nevertheless, if this kind of predication is seen [to occur] to some extent with respect to something which is composed of parts and is spatial and temporal, then it is not beyond belief for it to occur perfectly in the case of that Nature which is supremely free [of spatial and temporal parts].

Here we ought also to take into consideration — even as we speak [in a similar fashion] of the Father and the Son and the Holy Spirit — that the spring does not exist from the river or from the lake; but the river so exists only from the spring (and not from the lake), and the lake so exists from both the spring and the river, that the whole river exists from the whole spring, and the whole lake exists both from the whole spring and the whole river. Furthermore, we ought to take into consideration that the river exists from the spring in one way, whereas the lake exists from the spring and the river in another way, so that the lake is said not to be the river — just as in His own way the Word exists from the Father, whereas the Holy Spirit exists from the Father and the Word in another way, so that the Holy Spirit is not the Word, or the Son, but is the one who proceeds.

14

In addition, I want to mention a comparison which is not without some resemblance to the incarnation of the Word, even though the dissimilarity is great. Perhaps one who reads this comparison will treat it with disdain; nonetheless, let me say that I would not altogether disdain the comparison should someone else make it: If the river ran from the spring to the lake through a pipe, then even though the river is not a different Nile from the spring and the lake, is it not the river alone that is "en-piped,"[54] so to speak — just as the Son alone is incarnate, even though He is not a different God from the Father and the Holy Spirit?

15

But since these earthly things are very far removed from the Supreme Nature, let us with the help of that Nature lift up our minds to it, and with regard to it let us consider briefly some aspects of what we mean.

God is nothing other than simple eternity itself. But a plurality of eternities is unintelligible.[55] For if there were a plurality of eternities, they would be either outside or inside one another. Now, nothing is external to eternity. Therefore, it is not the case that eternity is external to eternity. Likewise, if they were outside one another, they would exist in different places or times — something incompatible with eternity. Therefore, there is not a plurality of eternities outside one another. On the other hand, if we say that there is a plurality of eternities within one another, we ought to know that however often eternity is repeated within eternity, it is only one and the same eternity. For a nature which, when repeated within itself, always integrates into a perfect unity with itself is of greater worth than a nature which admits of plurality. For where there is plurality there is diversity; and where there is diversity there is not perfect harmony. Indeed, perfect harmony is that which integrates into a unified identity and identical unity. Therefore, if perfect harmony is better than imperfect harmony, and if it is impossible for anything imperfect to exist in the Supreme Good (which is eternity itself), then it is not possible for the nature of eternity to admit of plurality. Hence, however often eternity is repeated within eternity, it is always only one and the same eternity.

In a similar way, the foregoing remarks also apply to many other things. For example, omnipotence within omnipotence is only one omnipotence. Or to cite one of those things which do not have a divine nature but in which the case is similar: a point within a point is only one point. For a point (such as the middle point of the world or a point of time, e.g., the present moment) has some similarity to eternity and is of no small use for the investigation of eternity. This issue must be discussed more fully elsewhere. Here let it suffice [to note] only that, like eternity, a point is simple (i.e., without parts) and indivisible; and so a point together with a point, without an interval, is only one point — just as eternity together with eternity is only one eternity.

Therefore, since God is eternity, there is no plurality of gods; for God is not external to God, nor does God within God add numerically to God. Thus, there is always and only one and the same God. Hence, when God is begotten of God, then since what is begotten is not outside of that from which it is begotten, the offspring is in the parent and the parent in the offspring,[56] i.e., there is one God, who is Father and Son. And when God proceeds from God, who is Father and Son, and does not go outside of God, God (i.e., God the Holy Spirit) remains in God from whom He proceeds; and there is one God, who is Father, Son, and Holy Spirit. And since this begottenness and this procession do not have a beginning — Were it otherwise, then an eternity which is begotten and an eternity which proceeds would have a beginning (a consequence which is false) — we absolutely ought not, and absolutely cannot, think that God ever began to be the Father, the Son, or the Holy Spirit.

16

However, just as the divine substance preserves its eternal and singular unity, so the nature of these relations (viz., of the Father and of the Son; of the one proceeding and of Him from whom He proceeds) retains its inseparable plurality. For just as it is necessary that God always be one and the same rather than many, so with respect to these relations the Father is never identical with His Son, and He who proceeds is never identical with Him from whom He proceeds. Rather, the Father is always different from the Son, and He who proceeds is always different from Him from whom He proceeds; and no one of the three can ever be called by either of the others' names. Therefore, when God is begotten of God or when God proceeds from God, the substance cannot lose its singularity nor the relations their plurality. For this reason, in God the one thing is three things and the three things are one thing, and yet the three are not called by one another's respective name. Now, in a Nature which is above all other things and is unlike all other things, it ought not to be preposterous that there is something of which an example cannot perfectly be found in other things. Now, the Latins call these three things *persons*, whereas the Greeks call them *substances*.[57] For just as we say that in God one substance is three persons, so they say that one person is three substances. By the word "substance" they signify in God exactly what we signify by the word "person"; and they are not at all at variance with us in faith.

As for how the Son is begotten of the Father, and how the Holy Spirit proceeds from the Father and the Son without being a son: since in this life we cannot behold [this truth] "as it is,"[58] Blessed Augustine, "as through a glass, darkly,"[59] has studied [the matter] carefully in his book *On the Trinity*; and to the best of my ability I also have discussed [it] in my *Monologion*, which I alluded to earlier.[60] Now, if anyone wants to know why, although there is no sexual distinction in the Supreme Being, the parent in the Supreme Being is called father rather than mother, or the offspring called son rather than daughter, or why only the Father is called unbegotten, only the Son called begotten, and only the Holy Spirit called neither begotten nor unbegotten, then he will find [the answers] clearly [stated] in this same small book of mine.[61]

ND A MAN
(Cur Deus Homo)

COMMENDATION[1] OF THIS WORK TO POPE URBAN II

Succeeding the Apostles, many of our holy Fathers and holy teachers make very many significant points regarding the rational basis of our faith. They do so not only in order to confound the foolishness of unbelievers and to break through their hardheartedness, but also in order to nourish those who, having hearts already cleansed by faith, delight in the rational basis of our faith — a rational basis for which we ought to hunger once [we have] the certainty of faith. Although our holy Fathers make so many significant points that we do not expect either in our own day or in future times anyone to be equal to them in contemplating the truth, nevertheless if anyone who is steadfast in faith wants to engage in investigating the rational basis for his faith, I think he ought not to be reproached. For because "the days of man are short,"[2] the holy Fathers were not able to say all of the things which they could have said if they had lived longer. Moreover, the rational basis of truth is so extensive and so deep that it cannot be exhausted by mortals. Furthermore, within His Church, with which He promises to remain unto the end of the world, the Lord does not cease to impart the gifts of His grace. And — to mention only one passage in which the Sacred Page summons us to rational investigation — the passage "Unless you believe you will not understand"[3] clearly advises us to direct our attention toward understanding, for it teaches us the way in which we ought to advance to understanding. Finally, since I discern that the understanding which we acquire in this life is a middle-way between faith and sight, I think that the more anyone advances to understanding, the closer he comes to the actual seeing for which we all long.

Strengthened, then, by these considerations, I endeavor (although I am a man of meager learning) to rise up a bit higher in order to behold (to the extent that heavenly grace deigns to grant me) the rationale for those doctrines which we believe. And when I find some point which I did not previously notice, I shall willingly disclose it to others, so that I may learn from another's judgment what I ought to believe confidently.

Therefore, Pope Urban, my father and lord, you who are worthy of all Christians' loving reverence and reverential love, and whom God's providence has established as supreme pontif within His Church: since I can present the enclosed treatise to no one else more rightly, I present it to the scrutiny of Your Holiness, so that by the authority of Your Holiness what is therein deserving of acceptance may be approved and what must be corrected may be amended.

PREFACE

There are certain men who without my knowledge copied for themselves the first parts of the enclosed work before it was completed and perfected. Because of these individuals I have been forced to finish this treatise as best I could and more hastily than suited me, and hence in a more abbreviated form than I had intended. For if I had been permitted to publish it unhurriedly and at a convenient time, I would have added many things which I have left unsaid. With great tribulation of heart — God knows the source and the cause[1] of my having suffered this — I began it in England upon request and finished it in the province of Capua as an exile. In accordance with the subject-matter with which it deals I entitled it *Why God Became a Man*; and I divided it into two short books. The first of these contains the answers of believers to the objections of unbelievers who repudiate the Christian faith because they regard it as incompatible with reason. And this book goes on to prove by rational necessity — Christ being removed from sight, as if there had never been anything known about Him — that no man can possibly be saved without Him. However, in the second book — likewise proceeding as if nothing were known of Christ — I show with equally clear reasoning and truth that human nature was created in order that the whole man (i.e., with a body and a soul) would some day enjoy a happy immortality. And I show the necessity of man's attaining this end for which he was created, and [that it can be attained] only by means of a God-man.[2] And I show that all the things which we believe about Christ ought, necessarily, to occur.

I ask all those who wish to copy this volume to affix this preface, together with all the chapter titles, before the beginning of the text.[3] This way anyone into whose hands the volume comes will see on its countenance, so to speak, whether the whole body of the text contains anything which he may deem important.

CHAPTER TITLES OF BOOK I

1. The central problem governing the entire work.
2. How the things to be said are to be construed.
3. The objections of unbelievers and the replies of believers.
4. These answers seem to unbelievers to lack cogency and to be pictures, as it were.
5. The redemption of man could not have been accomplished through any other person than a divine person.
6. How unbelievers find fault with our saying that God has redeemed us by His death, that in this way He has shown His love for us, and that He has come to vanquish the Devil on our behalf.
7. The Devil had no just claim against man. Why the reason for God's liberating man in this manner seems to have been based in the Devil.
8. How although the lowly things which we affirm of Christ do not apply to His divinity, nonetheless to unbelievers it seems unfitting that these things are affirmed of Him with respect to His humanity. Why it seems to them that this man did not undergo death willingly.
9. He died willingly. The meaning of the following texts: "He became obedient unto death"; "For this reason God has also exalted Him"; "I have not come to do my will"; "God spared not His own son"; "Not as I will but as You will."
10. How these same texts can rightly be interpreted in another way.
11. What sinning and making satisfaction for sin are.
12. Whether it is fitting for God to forgive sin out of mercy alone, apart from any repayment of debt.
13. Nothing ought less to be tolerated in the order of things than that the creature remove the honor owed to the Creator and not repay what he removes.
14. How the punishment of a sinner honors God.

15. Whether God lets His honor be violated even slightly.
16. The reason that the number of angels who fell is to be made up from among human beings.
17. Other angels cannot be substituted for fallen ones.
18. Whether there will be more holy men than there are evil angels.
19. Man cannot be saved without satisfaction for sin.
20. Satisfaction ought to be proportional to the measure of the sin. Man cannot make satisfaction by himself.
21. How grave sin is.
22. How when man permitted himself to be conquered by the Devil he did an injury to God for which he is unable to make satisfaction.
23. What it was that man, when he sinned, removed from God and cannot repay.
24. As long as man does not repay to God what he owes, he cannot be happy and is not excused because of his inability.
25. Necessarily, man is saved through Christ.

CHAPTER TITLES OF BOOK II

1. Man was created *just* in order to be happy.
2. Man would not have died if he had not sinned.
3. Man will be resurrected with the body in which he lives during this present life.
4. God will accomplish with human nature that which He began.
5. Although [what God began] must be accomplished, nevertheless He will not accomplish it under the constraint of necessity. There is a necessity which diminishes or eliminates gratitude, and there is a necessity which increases it.
6. Only a God-man can make the satisfaction by means of which man is saved.
7. It is necessary that one and the same being be fully divine and fully human.
8. God ought to assume a human nature from the race of Adam and from a virgin woman.
9. It is necessary that the Word alone and a human nature conjoin in one person.
10. This man is not required to die. How He is able to sin and not able to sin. Why He and an angel ought to be praised for their justice even though they cannot sin.
11. He dies of His own power. Mortality does not pertain to sinless human nature.
12. Although He shares our misfortunes, He is not unhappy.
13. It is not the case that along with our other infirmities He has ignorance.
14. How His death outweighs the number and the magnitude of all sins.
15. How His death blots out even the sins of those who put Him to death.
16. How God assumed from the sinful mass a sinless human nature. The salvation of Adam and of Eve.

17. In God there is neither necessity nor impossibility. There is a necessity which compels and a necessity which does not compel.
18. How the life of Christ is paid to God for the sins of men. The sense in which Christ ought, and the sense in which He ought not, to have suffered.
19. How very reasonable it is that human salvation results from His death.
20. How great and how just the mercy of God is.
21. It is impossible for the Devil to be reconciled.
22. The truth of the Old and of the New Testament has been proved within the statements that have been made.

WHY GOD BECAME A MAN[1]
(*Cur Deus Homo*)
BOOK I

Chapter One: The central problem governing the entire work.

In reply to those who make inquiry, I am accustomed to give the rational bases of a particular problem of our faith. On numerous occasions and with very great fervor many individuals have urged me, both by word of mouth and in letters, to write down these considerations for posterity. For they say that these considerations please them; and they regard them as satisfactory. They make their request not in order to approach faith by way of reason but in order to delight in the comprehension and contemplation of the doctrines which they believe, as well as in order to be ready, as best they can, always to give a satisfactory answer to everyone who asks of them a reason for the hope which is in us.[2] Unbelievers habitually raise this particular problem as an objection to us, while derisively terming Christian simplicity a foolish simplicity; and many believers repeatedly mull over this same problem in their minds. I mean the following problem: For what reason and on the basis of what necessity did God become a man and by His death restore life to the world (as we believe and confess), seeing that He could have accomplished this restoration either by means of some other person (whether angelic or human) or else by merely willing it? Now, not only learned men but also many unlearned men ask about this problem and desire to know its solution. Many individuals, then, keep asking that this problem be dealt with; and in spite of the fact that the investigation seems very difficult, the solution is intelligible to everyone and is commendable because of the utility and the elegance of the reasoning. Therefore, even though the holy Fathers have said about this problem what ought to be adequate, nevertheless what God will deign to disclose to me about this topic I will endeavor to show to those who are inquiring.

Anselm of Canterbury

Now, issues which are examined by the method of question-and-answer are clearer, and so more acceptable, to many minds — especially to minds that are slower. Therefore, from among those who have been making this entreaty I shall take as my fellow-disputant the one who has been urging me to this end more insistently than the others, so that in the following way Boso may ask and Anselm answer.

Boso. Just as right order requires that we believe the deep matters of the Christian faith before we presume to discuss them rationally, so it seems to me to be an instance of carelessness if, having been confirmed in faith, we do not eagerly desire to understand what we believe. Indeed, assisted by the prevenient grace of God I am, it seems to me, holding so steadfastly to faith in our redemption that even if I were not in any respect able to understand what I believe, nothing could wrest me from firmness of faith. Accordingly, I ask you to disclose to me that which, as you know, many are asking about along with me: viz., for what reason and on the basis of what necessity did God — although He is omnipotent — assume the lowliness and the weakness of human nature in order to restore it?

Anselm. What you are asking of me exceeds my capacities. And so I fear to deal with matters too high for me,[3] lest perhaps when someone suspects or even observes that I do not give him a satisfactory answer, he may think that I have departed from true doctrine rather than that my intellect is not powerful enough to comprehend this truth.

B. You ought not so much to have this fear as you ought to remember that in a discussion of some problem it often happens that God discloses what at first was hidden. Moreover, you ought to hope from the grace of God that if you willingly share those things which you have freely received, you will merit the receiving of the higher things to which you have not yet attained.

A. There is another reason why it seems to me that we cannot at all — or else can only scarcely — deal amply with this matter now. For in order to do so we need an analysis of *ability* and *necessity* and *will* and of certain other notions which are so interrelated that no one of them can be fully examined apart from the others. And so to deal with these notions requires a separate work — one not easy [to compose], it seems to me, but nonetheless one not altogether useless. For an ignorance of these notions produces

Cur Deus Homo I

certain difficulties which become easy [to deal with] as a result of understanding these notions.

B. Where these notions become relevant you can speak briefly about them, so that we may have the knowledge which is adequate for the present work but may postpone to another time[4] the additional points which need to be discussed.

A. I am also very reluctant to honor your request both because the topic is very important and because just as it deals with Him who is beautiful in appearance above the sons of men,[5] so it is also adorned with a rationale which exceeds human understanding. Hence, I fear that just as I am accustomed to become indignant with untalented artists when I see the Lord Himself portrayed with an uncomely countenance, so I may provoke indignation if I presume to explore such an elegant topic by an inelegant and contemptible discourse.

B. This fear ought not to deter you, since just as you permit whoever can to say these things better, so you forbid no one who does not like your discourse from writing more beautifully. But so that I may exclude all your excuses: [remember that] what I am asking of you, you will be writing not for the learned but for me and for those who are seeking this solution together with me.

Chapter Two: How the things to be said are to be construed.

A. I observe your importunity and the importunity of those who with you seek this solution out of love and religious desire. Therefore, to the best of my ability, and assisted by God and by means of your prayers, I will attempt not so much to exhibit the solution you are seeking as to seek it with you. (In requesting this solution, you have often promised these prayers to me, who was requesting them for this same end.) But I want everything that I say to be accepted in the following manner:[6] If I say something which a greater authority does not confirm, then even though I seem to prove it rationally, it should be accepted as certain only in the sense that it appears to me for the time being to be thus, until God somehow reveals the matter to me more fully.[7] But if to some extent I am able to give a satisfactory answer to your question, then assuredly it must be the case that one who is wiser than I would be able to give a more fully satisfactory answer.

Indeed, we must realize that no matter what a man can say about this topic, the deeper rationale for so important a doctrine will still remain hidden.

Chapter Three: The objections of unbelievers and the replies of believers.

B. Allow me, then, to use the words of unbelievers. For since we are fervently seeking the rational basis of our faith, it is fair that I should present the objections of those who are altogether unwilling to approach our faith without rational argumentation. Although they seek a rational basis because they do not believe whereas we seek it because we do believe, nevertheless it is one and the same thing that both we and they are seeking. And if you give any reply to which Sacred Authority seems opposed, let me exhibit this Authority so that you may disclose how it is not really opposed.

A. Say what seems [right] to you.

B. The unbelievers who scoff at our simplicity raise against us the following objection: that we dishonor and affront God when we maintain that He descended into the womb of a woman, that He was born of a woman, that He grew, being nourished by milk and food for human beings, and — not to mention many other things which seem to be unsuitable for God — that He experienced weariness, hunger, thirst, scourging, and (in the midst of thieves) crucifixion and death.

A. We do not dishonor or affront God; instead, we give Him thanks from our whole heart, and we laud and proclaim the ineffable depth of His mercy. For the more miraculously and wondrously He has restored us from such grave and such deserved evils in which we found ourselves — restored us to such great and such undeserved goods which we had lost — the more He has demonstrated the greater degree of His love and graciousness toward us. Indeed, if unbelievers would carefully consider how appropriately the restoration of human nature was obtained in this manner, they would not deride our simplicity but with us would praise God's wise loving-kindness. For it was fitting that as death had entered into the human race by the disobedience of man, so life would be restored by the obedience of man.[8] And [it was fitting that] as the sin which was the cause of our condemnation had its beginning from a woman, so the Author of our justification and salvation would be born from a woman. And [it was fitting that] the Devil, who had conquered man by persuading him to taste of the tree, would be conquered by man through the suffering-on-the-tree which he himself inflicted. There are also many other things which when carefully examined manifest a certain inexpressible beauty in the fact of our redemption's having been accomplished in this manner.

Chapter Four: These answers seem to unbelievers to lack cogency and to be pictures, as it were.

B. All of these things must be acknowledged to be beautiful and to be pictures, as it were. However, if there is not a solid foundation upon which they rest, they do not seem to unbelievers to suffice for showing why we ought to believe that God was willing to suffer these things of which we are speaking. For someone who wants to paint a picture choses something solid upon which to paint, in order that what he paints may remain. No one paints on water or in the air, because no traces of the picture would remain there. Hence, when we exhibit to unbelievers these considerations of fittingness which you say are pictures, as it were, of a real event, then since they regard what we believe as a fiction rather than as a real event, they think that we are painting on a cloud, so to speak. Therefore, first of all we must exhibit the truth's firm rational foundation, i.e., the cogent reasoning which proves that God should or could have humbled Himself to [undergo] those things which we proclaim. Next, so that this body-of-truth, so to speak, may shine even more splendidly, these considerations of fittingness must be set forth as pictures of this body-of-truth.

A. Do not the following considerations seem to constitute a very cogent argument for why God ought to have done those things about which we are speaking?: viz., that the human race — His very precious work — had utterly perished; and it was not fitting that God's plan for man should be completely thwarted; and this plan of God's could not be carried out unless the human race was set free by its very Creator.

Chapter Five: The redemption of man could not have been accomplished through any other person than a divine person.

B. If this liberation were said to have been accomplished in any manner at all through a person — whether an angel or a man — other than a divine person, the human mind would find this view much more tolerable. For God could have created another man who had no sin and who was not from the sinful mass and who — as He created Adam — was not even from another man; and through this man, it seems, God's work could have been accomplished.

A. Don't you realize that man would rightly be deemed to be the servant of whatever other person would redeem him from eternal death? And if so, then man would not at all have been restored to the dignity which he would have had if he had not sinned. For man, who was meant to be the servant only of God and meant to be equal in every respect to the good angels,[9] would become the servant of him who is not God and whom the angels do not serve.

Chapter Six: How unbelievers find fault with our saying that God has redeemed us by His death, that in this way He has shown His love for us, and that He came to vanquish the Devil on our behalf.

B. What especially astounds unbelievers is that we call this liberation *redemption*. Indeed, they ask: "In what captivity, in which prison, or in whose power were you being held from which God could free you only by redeeming you through so much effort and, in the end, through His own blood?" We answer: He has redeemed us from sins and from His own wrath and from Hell and from the power of the Devil, whom He came to vanquish on our behalf because we ourselves were unable to conquer him; moreover He has bought back the Kingdom of Heaven for us. And because He has done all these things in this way, He has manifested how much He loves us.

Cur Deus Homo I

But when we make this reply to them, they retort: "If you maintain that God, whom you say created all things by His command, was unable solely by His command, to do all the things [you have just mentioned], then you contradict yourselves, because you make Him powerless. On the other hand, if you say that He was able [to do these things solely by His command] but willed [to do them] only in the above manner, then how can you argue for the wisdom of this one whom you claim willed to suffer so many unbecoming things for no reason at all? For all the things which you set forth depend upon His will. Indeed, God's wrath is nothing other than His will-to-punish. Therefore, if He does not will to punish men's sins, man is free from sins; and He is free from God's wrath and from Hell and from the power of the Devil, all of which he suffers because of his sins; and he receives those goods of which he is deprived because of his sins. For who has power over Hell or the Devil, or who possesses the Kindgom of Heaven, except Him who created all things? Thus, whatever things you fear or desire are subject to His will, which nothing can resist. Therefore, if He was unwilling to save the human race except in the way that you state, although He was able to do so by His merely willing to, then (to put it mildly) look at how you impugn His wisdom. For if for no reason at all a man were to do with great strain that which He could have done effortlessly, he would surely not be judged by anyone to be wise. Indeed, your saying that God showed in this manner how much He loves you is not at all defensible unless you show that He could not at all have saved man in any other way. For if He could not have saved man in some other way, then perhaps it might have been necessary that He manifest His love in this way. But since, indeed, He could have saved man by another means, why is it that in order to show His love He endured and performed those things which you have mentioned? Does He not show the good angels how much He loves them even though He does not endure such things for them? Now, as for your saying that He came to vanquish the Devil on your behalf: how is it that you dare to make this claim? Does not God's omnipotence reign everywhere? How is it, then, that God needed to descend from Heaven in order to conquer the Devil?"

These objections unbelievers seem to be able to raise against us.

Chapter Seven: The Devil had no just claim against man. Why the reason for God's liberating man in this manner seems to have been based in the Devil.

B. Now, we regularly make the following claim:[10] "In order to free man, God was required to deal with the Devil in terms of justice rather than dealing with him in terms of power — so that when the Devil killed Him who was God and in whom there was no reason for death, the Devil justly lost the power which he had over sinners. Otherwise God would have done unjust violence to the Devil. For the Devil justly possessed man, whom he had not seized by force; rather, man had freely delivered himself to the Devil." But I do not see what cogency this claim has. For if the Devil or man belonged to himself, or if he belonged to someone other than to God, or if he remained in some power other than God's, perhaps this claim might rightly be made. However, since neither the Devil nor man does belong to anyone except to God, and since neither of them exists outside the domain of God's power, how ought God to have dealt justly with one of His servants, regarding another of His servants, in an affair that was His own, except by punishing His servant who had persuaded a fellow-servant of God to forsake their common Lord and to come over to him, and who as a traitor had received a fugitive, and as a thief had received a thief together with what he had stolen from the Lord. Both of them were thieves, since under the persuasion of the one the other stole himself from his Lord. Now, if God were to deal in this way with His servant, what could be done more justly? Or if God (who is the judge of all) were to deliver man (who in the above way had come into captivity) from the power of the one who was unjustly holding him captive — no matter whether God would deliver him in order to punish him otherwise than at the hands of the Devil or in order simply to spare him from punishment — why would this be unjust? For although man was justly tormented by the Devil, the Devil was unjustly tormenting man. For man deserved to be punished — and by no one more fittingly than by him to whom he had consented in sinning. But the Devil was not entitled to punish man; indeed, the more he was driven to this end by a malicious impulse rather than drawn by a love for justice, the more unjust it was for him to be administering punishment. For he did not administer punishment by the command of God but by the permission of God's incomprehensible wisdom, by which God arranges even evil things for good.

Moreover, I think that those who believe that the Devil had some just claim to possessing man are led to this conclusion by the following consideration: They see that man is justly subjected to torment by the Devil and that God justly permits this tormenting; and so they suppose that the Devil justly inflicts it. Now, it sometimes happens that some *one* thing is both just and unjust in different respects, and that for this reason the thing is judged to be either just or unjust as a whole by those who do not examine the matter carefully. For example, it happens that someone unjustly strikes an innocent man and hence himself justly deserves to be struck. However, if the one who has been struck ought not to avenge himself but nonetheless does strike the one who struck him, he does so unjustly.[11] Therefore, this beating is unjust with respect to the man administering it, because he ought not to have avenged himself; but it is just with respect to the one who has received it, because by unjustly delivering a blow he justly deserved to receive one. Accordingly, from different viewpoints this very same action is both just and unjust; but it can happen that it is judged by one person only as just and by another person only as unjust. Hence, in this manner the Devil is said to torment man justly, because God justly permits this tormenting and because man justly suffers it. But regarding even the fact that man is said to suffer justly: he is said to suffer justly not because he himself is just but because he is punished by the just judgment of God.

But suppose that the handwriting of the decree which the apostle declares[12] to have been against us and to have been blotted out by the death of Christ is alluded to. And suppose someone thinks that the apostle's reference to handwriting signifies that prior to the suffering of Christ the Devil, as if by an agreement in writing, justly required man to continue sinning — this requirement being the interest due on the first sin which he persuaded man to commit, as well as being the penalty for this first sin. If hereby someone supposes himself to establish the Devil's just claim over man, I do not regard his interpretation as at all correct. For that handwriting, to be sure, is not the Devil's because it is called "the handwriting of the decree." And that decree was not the Devil's decree but God's. For by the just judgment of God, it was decreed and confirmed, as if in writing, that man, who had freely sinned, would not be able by himself to avoid either sin or the penalty for sin. For man is a "wind that departs and does not return."[13] And "he who sins is a servant of sin."[14] Now, he who sins ought not to be let-off unpunished — unless mercy spares the sinner and frees him and restores him. Therefore, we ought not to believe that by reference to this handwriting some justice on the Devil's part can be found in his tormenting of man. Indeed, even as in a good angel there is no injustice at all, so in an evil angel there is no justice at all. Therefore, there was in the Devil no reason why God ought not to use His power against him in order to liberate man.

Chapter Eight: How although the lowly things which we affirm of Christ do not apply to His divinity, nonetheless to unbelievers it seems unfitting that these things are affirmed of Him with respect to His humanity. Why it seems to them that this man did not undergo death willingly.

A. When God does some thing, then even though we do not see why He wills [to do it], His will ought to suffice us as a reason. For the will of God is never unreasonable.

B. True — Provided one is sure that God wills the thing in question. For if reason seems to oppose [God's willing something], many persons do not at all admit that He wills it.

A. When we say that God willed those things which we believe regarding His incarnation, what seems to you to go against reason?

B. To put it briefly: that the Most High descends to such lowly things, that the Almighty does something so laboriously.

A. Those who say this do not understand what we believe. For without doubt we maintain that the divine nature is impassible — that it cannot at all be brought down from its exaltation and cannot labor in what it wills to do. And we affirm that the Lord Jesus Christ is true God and true man — one person in two natures, and two natures in one person. Therefore, when we state that God undergoes some lowliness or weakness, we understand this to be in accordance with the weakness of the human substance which He assumed, not in accordance with the sublimity of His impassible [divine] nature. Accordingly, no rational considerations are recognized to oppose our faith. For by the above statement we do not signify any abasement of the divine substance; rather we declare the personal unity of the divine nature and the human nature. Therefore, we do not understand any abasement of the divine substance to have occurred in the incarnation of God; instead, we believe that the human nature was exalted.

B. So be it. Let nothing which is affirmed of Christ in accordance with the weakness of His human nature be attributed to His divine nature. But how can we show the justice or the reasonableness of God's having thus treated, or having permitted to be thus treated, that man whom the Father called His beloved son in whom He was well-pleased,[15] that man whom the Son caused Himself to become? And what justice is there in delivering up unto death, in place of a sinner, the most just of all men? What man would not be adjudged worthy of condemnation if he were to condemn an innocent party in order to free a guilty one? The conclusion seems to come to the same incongruity which was mentioned above.[16] For if God was not able to save sinners otherwise than by condemning a just man, where is His omnipotence? On the other hand, if He was able to but did not will to, how shall we defend His wisdom and justice?

A. God the Father did not treat *that* man as you seem to think He did, nor did He hand over someone innocent in the place of someone guilty-of-death. The Father did not force the Son to die against His will; nor did He permit Him to be put to death against His will. Instead, that man willingly underwent death in order to save men.

B. Even if [the Father did not compel Him to die] against His will — since He consented to the Father's will — nevertheless, in a certain respect the Father does seem to have compelled Him [to die], in that He commanded Him [to undergo death]. For it is said that Christ "humbled Himself and became obedient to the Father unto death, even unto death on the cross; for this reason God has also exalted Him."[17] And [we read] that "He learned obedience by the things which He suffered,"[18] and that "the Father spared not His own son but delivered Him up for us all."[19] And the Son Himself says: "I have not come to do my will but to do the will of Him who sent me."[20] And approaching the time of His crucifixion He said: "As the Father has given me commandment, so I do."[21] And again: "Shall I not drink of the chalice which my father has given me?"[22] And elsewhere: "Father, if it be possible, let this chalice pass from me; nevertheless not as I will but as You will."[23] Also: "Father, if this chalice cannot pass from me except I drink of it, Your will be done."[24] According to all of these passages Christ seems to have undergone death more because He was compelled by obedience than because He was committed by free will.

Chapter Nine: He died willingly. The meaning of the following texts: "He became obedient unto death"; "For this reason God has also exalted Him"; "I have not come to do my will"; "God spared not His own son"; "Not as I will but as You will."

A. As I see it, you are not distinguishing clearly between (1) that which He did because obedience required it and (2) that which, happening to Him because He remained obedient, He underwent even though obedience did not require it.

B. I need to have you explain this more clearly.

A. Why did the Jews persecute Him to the point of death?

B. For no other reason than that He held unwaveringly to justice and truth in His deeds and words.

A. I think that God requires this of every rational creature and that every rational creature owes this to God as a matter of obedience.

B. Yes, we ought to admit it.

A. Therefore, *that* man[25] owed this obedience to God the Father; and His humanity owed it to His divinity; and the Father required it of Him.

B. No one doubts this point.

A. Here, then, you have what He did because obedience required it.

B. That's true. And I now begin to see what He underwent,

having had it inflicted on Him because He persevered in obedience. For because He remained steadfast in obedience, death was inflicted on Him and He underwent death. But I do not understand how it is that obedience did not require Him to die.

A. If man had never sinned, ought he to have undergone death, or ought God to have required him to do so?

B. As we believe, man would not have died, nor would dying have been required of him. But I want to hear from you the rationale for this belief.

A. You do not deny that the rational creature was created just and was created for the purpose of being happy in the enjoyment of God.

B. No.

A. Now, you will not in the least suppose it to befit God to compel a creature, whom He had created just and for the purpose of happiness, to be unhappy through no fault of his own. But for a man to encounter death against his will constitutes a form of unhappiness.

B. It is evident that if man had not sinned, God ought not to have required him to die.

A. Therefore, God did not compel Christ to die, for in Christ there was no sin. Instead, Christ willingly underwent death — not by obeying a command to give up His life, but by obeying the command to keep justice. For He persevered so steadfastly in justice that He incurred death as a result.

But it can also be said that the Father commanded Christ to die when He commanded the thing in consequence of which Christ incurred death. In this sense, then, He did as the Father gave Him commandment;[26] and He drank of the chalice which the Father gave;[27] and He became obedient to the Father unto death;[28] and thus He learned obedience — i.e., He learned the extent to which obedience ought to be kept — by the things which He suffered.[29] But the phrase "He learned," which is used in the text, can be interpreted in two senses. Either "He learned" is used in place of "He caused others to learn," or else it is used because He learned in terms of experience that which He already knew-about in terms other than experience. Now, after the apostle had said "He humbled Himself and became obedient unto death, even the death of the cross,"[30] he added: "For this reason God has also exalted Him and given Him a name which is above every name"[31] (to which the words of David are similar: "He drank of the stream in the way; therefore, he lifted up his head").[32] This addition was not meant in the sense (1) that Christ could not at all have arrived at this exaltation except by obedience unto death and (2) that this exaltation was conferred only as a reward for this obedience. (For even before Christ had suffered, He said that all things had been given to Him by the Father,[33] and that all the Father's possessions were His[34] as well.) Rather, the additon was meant in the sense that the Son, together with the Father and the Holy Spirit, had decreed that He Himself would manifest to the world, in no other way than by dying, the loftiness of His omnipotence. Indeed, when this manifestation-of-loftiness which was decreed to occur only by means of His death does occur by means of His death, is it not unfittingly said to occur *because of* His death.

Suppose that we intend to perform some action but that we decide to do beforehand another action by means of which the intended action will be done. Now, if we do the intended action after having done the action which we willed to do beforehand, the intended action is rightly said to be done because of the fact that the preceding action, on account of which the intended action was delayed, has occurred; for we decided to do the intended action only by means of the preceding action. For example, suppose that I can cross a certain river either by horse or by boat. And suppose that I decide to cross the river only by boat, and so I postpone crossing because no ship is available. If I do cross the river after a boat has become available, then it is right to say of me: "A ship was ready; therefore he crossed over." And we speak in this manner not only when we determine to do something else *by means of* a thing which we will to occur beforehand but also when we determine to do something else only *subsequent to* the preceding thing and not by means of it. For example, suppose someone postpones eating because of the fact that on that day he has not yet attended the celebration of mass. After he has done this thing which he willed to do first, it is appropriate to say to him: "Eat something now, *because* you have done the thing on account of which you postponed eating." Therefore, it is an even less unusual expression to say that Christ was exalted *because* He underwent death, for He decreed to make Himself exalted both *after* death and *by means of* death. This expression can also be construed in the sense in which Christ the Lord is read to have advanced in wisdom and in grace with God[35] (i.e., not in the sense that it was really true but in the sense that He conducted Himself *as if* it were true). For after His death He was exalted *as if* this exaltation had occurred *because* of His death.

But His statement "I have not come to do my will but to do the will of Him who sent me"[36] is similar to His statement "My doctrine is not mine."[37] For what someone has from God rather than from Himself he ought to speak of as more God's than His own. Now, no man has from himself either the truth which he teaches or a just will; instead, he has these from God. Therefore, Christ came not to do His own will but to do the will of the Father, because the just will that He possessed derived not from His humanity but from His divinity. But [the text] "God spared not His own son but *delivered* Him up for us"[38] means nothing other than that God did *not liberate* Him.[39] For many statements of this type are found in Sacred Scripture. However, where He says "Father, if it be possible, let this chalice pass from me; nevertheless not as I will but as You will,"[40] and "If this chalice cannot pass from me except I drink of it, Your will be done":[41] by the reference to His own will He signifies His natural desire for security — a desire in terms of which His human flesh shunned the pain of dying. But He speaks of the Father's will not in the sense that the Father willed the Son's death rather than the Son's life, but in the sense that the Father was unwilling for the human race to be restored unless man performed some deed as great as Christ's death was to be (for reason did not demand what no man could perform). Therefore, the Son says that the Father wills His death, which He, the Son, prefers to undergo rather than to see the human race not be saved. It is as if He were to say: "Since You, Father, *do not will* that the reconciliation of the world be accomplished in any other way, I say that in this sense You *will* my death. Therefore, let this will of Yours be done — i.e., let my death occur — so that the world may be reconciled to You." For we often say that someone *wills* something because he does *not will* something else which, were he to will it, then that thing which he is said to will would not occur. For example, we say of someone who does *not will* to close a window through which a draft enters and extinguishes a lamp, that he *wills* to extinguish the lamp. In this sense, then, the Father *willed* the Son's death because He did *not will* for the *world* to be saved otherwise than by man's performing some very great deed, as I mentioned. Since no other man was able to perform this great deed: for the Son to will the salvation of men was tantamount to the Father's having commanded Him to die. Therefore, He did as the Father gave Him commandment, and He drank of the chalice which the Father gave Him, being obedient unto death.

Chapter Ten: How these same texts can rightly be interpreted in another way.

A. We can also rightly make the following interpretation: [in giving] the gracious will by which the Son willed to die for the salvation of the world, the Father gave the Son commandment (without, however, compelling Him), and gave Him the chalice of suffering, and did not spare Him but delivered Him up for us, and willed His death; and [in keeping this will] the Son was obedient unto death and learned obedience by the things He suffered. For even as with respect to His humanity He did not have from Himself the will to live justly but, rather, had it from the Father, so also He could not have had the will by which He willed to die (in order to perform such a good deed) except from the Father of lights, from whom comes every best gift and every perfect gift.[42] And as the Father is said to *draw* someone when He bestows this will upon him, so it is not inappropriate to say that He *moves* him. For just as the Son says with regard to the Father "No one comes to me unless the Father draws him,"[43] so He could have said ". . . unless the Father moves him." Similarly, He could also have said: "No one hastens to his death for my name's sake unless the Father moves or draws him." For since each man's will draws or moves him toward that which he wills unwaveringly, God is not inappropriately said to draw him or to move him when He gives him such a will. By this drawing or moving, no compelling force is signified; instead, there is signified a voluntary and devoted retaining of the good will which has been received. Therefore, if in this respect we cannot deny that the Father drew and moved the Son toward death when He gave Him that willingness, who cannot see that in this respect the Father gave Him commandment to undergo death voluntarily, and gave Him the chalice of which He would drink willingly?

Cur Deus Homo I

And if the Son is correctly said not to have spared Himself but to have delivered Himself up willingly for us, who would deny it to be correctly said that the Father, from whom the Son possessed such a willingness, did not spare the Son but delivered Him up for us and willed His death? And in this same sense, when the Son freely and unwaveringly kept the will which He had received from the Father, He became obedient to the Father unto death and He learned obedience by the things which He suffered — i.e., He learned how great is the work which needed to be accomplished by means of obedience. For simple and true obedience occurs when rational nature freely and without necessity keeps the will which it has received from God.

Although the foregoing ways are able to suffice, we can also correctly interpret in other ways the statement that the Father willed the Son's death. For just as we say "He wills" of that man who causes another to will, so we also say "He wills" of that man who does not cause another to will but merely approves of his willing.[44] (For example, suppose we see someone will to endure affliction bravely in order to accomplish what he is rightly willing. Even though we state that we are willing for him to endure that affliction, what we will and like is not his torment but his willingness.) We are also accustomed to say of someone who can prevent something but does not prevent it, that he wills what he does not prevent.[45] Therefore, since the Son's will pleased the Father, and since the Father did not prevent Him from willing what He did will or from carrying out what He willed, the Father is rightly said to have willed that the Son undergo death so graciously and beneficially — even though the Father did not delight in the Son's torment. However, the Son said that the chalice could not pass from Him except He drink of it. This He said not because He was unable to avoid death if He had willed to, but because (as I said) it was impossible for the world to be saved in any other way, and because the Son unwaveringly willed to undergo death rather than to leave the world unsaved. He spoke these words, then, in order to teach that the human race could not be saved otherwise than by means of His death; He did not speak them in order to indicate that He could not at all avoid death. Now, whatever things are said about Him which are similar to what has been said must be construed in such way that He is believed to have died not of necessity but of free will. For He was omnipotent; and we read of Him that "He was offered because it was His own will."[46] And He says, "I lay down my life in order to take it up again. No one takes it from me, but I lay it down of myself. I have the power to lay it down, and I have the power to take it up again."[47] Therefore, that which He does by His own will and power He is not at all rightly said to be compelled to do.

B. The mere fact that God permits Him to be thus treated, even though He was willing [to be thus treated], does not seem to befit such a father in regard to such a son.

A. On the contrary! It is altogether appropriate that such a father give his consent to such a son if this son wills something in a way that commends God's honor and conduces to man's salvation, which could not be accomplished otherwise.

B. Regarding this last point we are still concerned with how His death can be shown to be reasonable and necessary; for if it cannot be, then it seems that the Son ought not to have willed His death and that the Father ought neither to have required it nor permitted it. For the question is, why was God unable to save man in any other way? Or if He was able, why did He will to do so in the above manner? It does not seem fitting for God to have saved man in this manner; nor is it clear what Christ's death accomplishes with regard to man's salvation. For it would be strange if God so delighted in, or so needed, the blood of an innocent man that He either would or could only spare the guilty by means of this innocent man's being put to death.

A. Since in this inquiry you are assuming the role of those who prefer to believe nothing except what has been established in advance by reason,[48] I would like for us to agree to accept, in the case of God, nothing that is in even the least degree unfitting and to reject nothing that is in even the slightest degree reasonable unless something more reasonable opposes it. For in the case of God, just as an impossibility results from any unfittingness, however slight,[49] so necessity accompanies any degree of reasonableness, however small, provided it is not overridden by some other more weighty reason.

B. In this discussion I accept nothing more readily than [the proposal] that we both adhere to this agreement.

A. We are dealing only with God's incarnation and with the things which we believe regarding the assumed man.[50]

B. That's right.

A. Therefore, let us suppose the incarnation of God and the things we say about *that* man never occurred. And let us agree that (1) man was created for happiness, which cannot be possessed in this life, that (2) no one can attain happiness unless his sins have been forgiven, and that (3) no man passes through this present life without sin. And let us agree about the other things which we must believe if we are to have eternal salvation.

B. All right. For in no respect do these seem either impossible for God or unbefitting to Him.

A. Therefore, in order for man to attain happiness, the remission of his sins is required.

B. So we all believe.

Chapter Eleven: What sinning and making satisfaction for sin are.

A. Therefore, we must ask on what basis God forgives men their sins. To do this more clearly, let us first see what sinning and making satisfaction for sin are.

B. It is up to you to explain and up to me to pay attention.

A. If angels and men always rendered to God what they ought to, then they would never sin.

B. I cannot contradict this.

A. Therefore, to sin is nothing other than not to render to God what is due.

B. What is the debt which we owe to God?

A. The will of every rational creature ought to be subordinate to the will of God.

B. Nothing is truer.

A. This is the debt which angels and men owe to God. No one who pays this debt sins; and everyone who does not pay it does sin. This is the justice-of-will, or uprightness-of-will, which makes men just, or upright, in heart (i.e., in will).[51] This is the sole and complete honor which we owe to God and which God demands from us. For only such a will, when it is able to act, does works which are acceptable to God; and when it is not able to act, it alone is acceptable in itself, since without it no work is acceptable to God. Whoever does not pay to God this honor due Him dishonors Him and removes from Him what belongs to Him;

and this removal, or this dishonoring, constitutes a sin. However, as long as he does not repay what he has stolen, he remains guilty. But it is not enough for him merely to repay what has been stolen; rather, because of the wrong which has been inflicted, he ought to repay more than he has stolen. For example, if someone who injures another's health restores it, his doing so is insufficient payment unless he also gives some compensation for the painful wrong that was inflicted. Similarly, he who violates another's honor does not sufficiently repay this honor unless, in proportion to the injury caused by the dishonoring, he makes some restitution which is acceptable to the one whom he has dishonored. We must also note that when someone repays what he has unjustly stolen, he ought to return that which could not be exacted from him had he not stolen what belonged to another. Accordingly, then, everyone who sins is obliged to repay to God the honor which he has stolen. This [repayment of stolen honor] constitutes the satisfaction which every sinner is obliged to make to God.[52]

B. Since we have proposed to follow reason, I have nothing which I can say against you on all these matters, even though you alarm me a bit.

Chapter Twelve: Whether it is fitting for God to forgive sin out of mercy alone, apart from any payment of the debt.

A. Let us go back and see whether it is fitting for God to forgive sin out of mercy alone, apart from any repayment of the honor stolen from Him.

B. I see no reason why it is not fitting.

A. To forgive sin in this manner is identical with not punishing it. Now, in the absence of satisfaction, to order sin rightly is only to punish it; therefore, if sin is not punished, something disordered is forgiven.

B. What you say is reasonable.

A. But it is not fitting that God should forgive something that is disordered within His kingdom.

B. If I wished to say anything different, I fear that I would be sinning.

Cur Deus Homo I

A. Therefore, it is not fitting that God should forgive sin that goes thus unpunished.

B. This follows.

A. There is also something else which follows if sin that goes thus unpunished is forgiven: viz., God would be dealing with the sinner and the nonsinner in the same way — something which is unsuitable for Him [to do].

B. I cannot deny it.

A. Also consider the following point: Everyone knows that human justice is subject to law, so that God deals out the measure of recompense according to the degree of justice.

B. This is what we believe.

A. But if sin were neither paid for nor punished, it would be subject to no law.

B. I cannot think differently.

A. Therefore, if injustice is forgiven out of mercy alone, then injustice is more at liberty than is justice — something which seems especially unfitting. Moreover, this unfittingness is so extensive that it makes injustice resemble God, for as God is subject to no one's law, neither would injustice be.

B. I cannot oppose your reasoning. However, since God commands us to forgive completely those who sin against us,[53] it seems inconsistent that He commands us to do what it is unfitting for Him to do.

A. There is no inconsistency here, because God gives us this command so that we should not arrogate to ourselves His prerogative. For to take vengeance belongs to no one except to Him who is Lord of all.[54] Now, when earthly potentates rightly exercise retribution, the Lord Himself does it; for they have been ordained by Him to this end.[55]

B. You have eliminated the inconsistency which I thought was present in [your argument]. But there is something else to which I want to have your answer. God is so free that He is subject to no law and to no one else's judgment; and He is so kind that nothing more kind can be thought. Moreover, nothing except what He wills is right or fitting. Therefore, it seems strange for us to say either that He is altogether unwilling, or else that He is forbidden, to forgive a wrong done to Him; for from Him we regularly ask forgiveness for the wrongs we do to others.

A. What you say about His freedom, will, and kindness is

true. Yet we ought to explicate these notions so in accordance with reason that we do not seem to oppose His dignity. For there is freedom only with respect to what is advantageous or what is fitting;[56] and "kindness" which performs some work unbefitting to God must not be called kindness. But as for the statement that what God wills is just and what He does not will is not just: we must not interpret this to mean that if God were to will any kind of unfittingness, it would be *just* simply because He willed it. For the supposition "God wills to lie" does not warrant the inference "Lying is just," but, instead, warrants the inference "This being is not really God." For no will can at all will to lie except a will in which the truth has been corrupted — or better, a will which has become corrupted by abandoning the truth. Therefore, when we say "If God wills to lie," this means "If God is of such a nature as to will to lie. . . ." And so "Lying is just" is not inferable therefrom — unless we interpret the if-then statement as an example of our saying about two impossibilities "If this is true, then that is true," although neither the one nor the other is true. For example, someone might say "If water is dry, then fire is wet," neither of which component statements is true. Therefore, "If God wills such-and-such, then it is just" can be said truly only of those things which it is not unfitting for God to will. If God wills that it rain, it is just that it rain; and if God wills that some man be killed, it is just that he be killed. Therefore, if it is not fitting that God do something unjustly or inordinately, it does not pertain to His freedom, or kindness, or willingness that He forgive — without punishing him — a sinner who does not repay to Him what he has stolen.

B. You remove from me all the objections which I thought could be raised against you.

A. Consider still another reason why it was not fitting for God to do this.

B. I will gladly listen to whatever you say.

Chapter Thirteen: Nothing ought less to be tolerated in the order of things than that the creature remove the honor owed to the Creator and not repay what he removes.

A. Nothing ought less to be tolerated in the order of things than

Cur Deus Homo I

that the creature remove the honor owed to the Creator and not repay what he removes.

B. Nothing is clearer than this.

A. Now, nothing would be more unjustly tolerated than would be that thing than which nothing ought less to be tolerated.

B. This also is not unclear.

A. Therefore, you will not say, I believe, that God ought to tolerate that thing than which nothing is tolerated more unjustly, viz., that the creature not repay to God what he removes from Him.

B. Indeed, I see that it must not at all be said.

A. Likewise, if nothing is greater or better than God, then Supreme Justice (which is identical with God Himself) keeps nothing more justly than God's honor in regard to the governance of things.

B. Nothing is clearer than this either.

A. Therefore, God keeps nothing more justly than the honor of His dignity.

B. I have to admit it.

A. Do you think that God would keep His honor intact if He permitted it to be removed from Him in such way that neither did the thief repay it nor did God punish him?

B. I dare not say so.

A. Therefore, it is necessary either for the honor that has been removed to be repaid or else for punishment to result. Otherwise, either God would not be *just* to Himself or else He would not have the power[57] to do the one or the other — heinous things even to think.

Chapter Fourteen: How the punishment of a sinner honors God.[58]

B. I think that nothing more reasonable can be said. But I want to hear from you whether the punishment of a sinner is an honor for God — or, rather, what kind of honor it is. For if the punishment of a sinner is not an honor for God, then when a sinner does not repay what he has stolen but is punished instead, God loses His honor irrecuperably. But this consequence seems inconsistent with what has already been said.

A. It is impossible for God to lose His honor. Either the sinner freely repays what he owes or else God takes it from him against his will. For either a man willingly exhibits due subjection to God (be it by not sinning or be it by making payment for his sins), or else God subjects him to Himself against his will by tormenting him and in this way demonstrates that He is his master — a fact which the man refuses to acknowledge voluntarily. In this case, we must notice that as a man by sinning seizes what is God's, so God by punishing takes what is man's. Indeed, not only is that which someone already possesses said to be his own[59] but so is that which it is in his power to possess. Therefore, since man was created in such way that he would be able to possess happiness if he did not sin: when because of his sin he is deprived of happiness and of every good, he is repaying from his own possession (although against his will) what he has seized. For although what God removes from him He does not convert to His own advantageous use (as a man converts to his own use the money which he takes away from someone else), nevertheless what God takes away conduces to His honor simply by virtue of His taking it. For by taking it away He shows that the sinner and his possessions are subject to Him.

Chapter Fifteen: Whether God lets His honor be violated even slightly.

B. What you say is agreeable. But there is also another question to which I request your answer. If God ought to maintain His honor in the way you are establishing, why does He allow it to be even slightly violated? For that which is in any way allowed to be injured is not maintained wholly and perfectly.
A. Nothing can be added to or subtracted from His honor, considered in itself. For His honor is, in itself, incorruptible and altogether immutable. But when each single creature keeps, either by nature or by reason, its proper place [in the order of things] — a place prescribed for it, so to speak — it is said to obey God and to honor Him. And this [holds true especially for] a rational nature, which has the gift of understanding what it ought to do. When a rational nature wills what it ought to, it honors God

Cur Deus Homo I

— not because it confers anything on Him but because it willingly submits itself to His will and governance.[60] And, as best it can, it stays in its proper place in the universe and preserves the beauty of the universe. But when it does not will what it ought, then it dishonors God as much as lies in its power to do so. For it does not willingly submit itself to His governance; and it disturbs (as much as lies in its power to do so) the order and the beauty of the universe — even though it does not at all injure or tarnish God's power or dignity.

If those things which are encircled by the heavens wished not to continue to exist beneath the heavens, or wished to get away from the heavens, they would nonetheless be able to exist only beneath the heavens and be able to go away from the heavens only by coming toward them. For no matter from what place or to what place or by what route they would go, they would still be circumscribed by the heavens. And the farther they would get from any one part of the heavens, the closer they would get to the opposite part. Similarly, even though men and evil angels do not want to submit to the divine will and ordinance, they are unable to escape from it. For if they want to get out from under God's directive will, they run beneath His punitive will. And — if you ask about the route they traverse — they make their way only under His permissive will. And that which they perversely will or do is redirected by Supreme Wisdom towards the order and beauty of the aforementioned universe. Indeed, the voluntary making of satisfaction for wickedness, and the demand for punishment of anyone who does not make satisfaction — to pass over the fact that God causes, in many ways, good things to come from evil things — retain, in the universe, their proper place and preserve the beauty of its order. If where wickedness tries to disturb right-order Divine Wisdom did not provide for the making of satisfaction and the exacting of punishment, then in the universe (which God ought to order) there would occur a certain marring as a result of the violation of the order's beauty; and God would seem to fail in His governance. Just as these two results are unfitting, so they are impossible;[61] therefore either satisfaction or punishment must follow upon every sin.

B. You have satisfactorily answered my objection.

A. Therefore, it is evident that no one can honor or dishonor

God as He is in Himself; but someone seems to do so, to the extent he can, when he subjects his will to the will of God or withdraws it from the will of God.

B. I do not know what I can say against this conclusion.

Chapter Sixteen: The reason that the number of angels who fell is to be made up from among human beings.

A. Let me add still another point.

B. You may keep talking until listening begins to weary me.

A. It is evident that God planned to make up — from human nature, which He created without sin — the number of angels who had fallen.[62]

B. We believe it; but I would like to have a reason for it.

A. You are misdirecting me. For we planned[63] to deal only with the incarnation of God, and you are interposing other questions for me.

B. Don't be angry, for "God loves a cheerful giver."[64] And no one evidences that he cheerfully gives what he promises to, more than does someone who gives more than he promises to. So answer my question gladly.

A. We must not doubt that those rational natures which are or will be happy in the contemplation of God were foreknown by God to exist in a calculable and perfect number, so that it is not fitting that this number be greater or lesser. For either God does not know in what number it is more suitable that these natures be created — an alternative which is false — or else, if He knows, He will create rational natures in the number which He knows to be the most suitable for His purpose. Therefore, either the angels who fell were created to be within this number, or else because they could not remain in excess of it, they fell of necessity — an absurd thing to suppose.

B. What you say is clearly true.

A. Therefore, since they ought to have been within that number: either their number must be made up, or else rational natures which are foreknown to exist in a perfect number will remain in an imperfect number — something which cannot be the case.

B. Without doubt they are to be replaced.

A. Therefore, it is necessary that they be replaced from human nature, since there is no other nature from which they can be replaced.

Chapter Seventeen: Other angels cannot be substituted for fallen ones.

B. Why cannot fallen angels be restored? Or why cannot other angels be substituted for them?

A. When you perceive the difficulty of our restoration, you will discern the impossibility of their reconciliation.[65] However, the reason other angels cannot be substituted for them — not to speak of how this [creation and substitution of other angels] seems to be inconsistent with the perfection of the original creation — is the following: Other angels ought not to be substituted unless they could be such as fallen angels would have become had they not sinned. If [they had not sinned], they would have persevered without having witnessed any punishment of sin; but after their fall this state would have been impossible for the other angels who would be substituted for them. For if both the one who is not aware of any punishment for sin and the one who always gazes upon eternal punishment remain standing in the truth, they are not equally praiseworthy.[66] Indeed, the good angels must be thought to have been confirmed [in goodness] as a result of their own merit and not at all because of the fall of the evil angels. For if the good angels had sinned together with the evil angels, they would have been condemned with them; similarly, if the unjust angels had remained standing together with the just angels, they too would have been confirmed. Assuredly, if some of the angels were to be confirmed only because of the fall of the others, then either none of them would ever have been confirmed or else it would have been necessary for one of them to fall so that he would be punished in order for the others to be confirmed. Now, both of these consequences are absurd. Consequently, the angels who remained standing were confirmed in the way in which all of them alike would have been confirmed if they had remained standing. I discussed this way, as best I could, when I dealt with the reason why God did not give the Devil perseverance.[67]

B. You have proved that the evil angels are to be replaced from human nature. And from your reasoning it is evident that the number of elect men will not be less than the number of reprobate angels.[68] But show, if you can, whether the number of elect men will be greater [than the number of reprobate angels].

Chapter Eighteen: Whether there will be more holy men than there are evil angels.

A. If angels were present in the perfect number (of which we have been speaking) before some of them fell, then human beings were created only as substitutes for lost angels and, clearly, they will not be more numerous than fallen angels. On the other hand, if that number was not exhausted by all the angels, then both what perished and what was originally lacking were to be completed from among human beings; and there will be more elect men than there are reprobate angels; and so we shall say that human beings were created not only for replenishing the diminished number but also for filling up the still unfilled number.

B. Which alternative ought rather to be maintained?: that the angels were originally created in the perfect number, or the contradictory?

A. I will tell you my view.

B. I cannot demand more from you.

A. If man was created after the fall of the evil angels, as some people interpret the text in Genesis, then I do not see how I can thereby prove either alternative decisively. For it seems to me to be possible that the angels were already present in perfect number and that afterwards man was created in order to restore their diminished number. And it [also seems] possible that angels were not present in perfect number, because God was delaying (as He still is) the fulfillment of that number, since He was going to create human nature at a fitting time. Thus, either He would simply fill up that still incomplete number, or else if the completed number had been diminished, He would restore it.

However, if the entire creation was created at once, and if those days, in terms of which Moses seems to say that our world was not created at once, are to be interpreted otherwise than as we experience days in which we live, then I cannot see how angels could have been created in that completed number. Indeed, if they were so created, then I think that either some angels or human beings were going to fall of necessity or else there would be more persons in the Heavenly City than the fittingness of the perfect number would require. Therefore, if all things were created at once, then angels and the first two human beings seem to have been so present in an imperfect number that if no angel were to fall, then only what was lacking would be filled up from human beings; on the other hand, if an angel were to perish, then also what fell would be replaced from human beings. And human nature, which was weaker, would "acquit" God of blame and would confound the Devil should he try to attribute his fall to his weakness; for human nature, though weaker, would stand steadfast. But even if human nature were to fall, it would much more greatly vindicate God against itself and the Devil, since — though created mortal and much weaker — it would (in the elect) ascend from such weakness to a place higher than that from which the Devil had fallen. Indeed, it would ascend as much higher as the good angels (equality with whom would be its due) advanced (because they persevered) after the downfall of the evil ones.

For these reasons it seems to me more likely that angels were not present in the perfect number with which the Heavenly City will be filled. For this view is possible if man was not created at the same time as the angels; and it seems to be necessary if man and angels were created at the same time. (Many regard this simultaneous creation as more likely, since we read: "He who lives forever created all things together.")[69] But even if the perfection of the created world is to be construed as referring not so much to the number of individuals as to the number of natures, it is necessarily the case that human nature was created either to complement the perfection of creation or to be superfluous to it. Now, we dare not make the latter statement with regard to even the smallest worm's nature. Hence, human nature was created to occupy its own place in the created world and not merely to replace individuals of a different nature. Therefore, it is evident that even if no angel had perished, human beings would have had a place of their own in the Heavenly City. Thus, it follows that angels, before some of them fell, were not present in that perfect number. Otherwise, either men or some angels would have had to fall, since no one could have remained in that city in excess of the perfect number.

B. You have accomplished a great deal.

A. There is also another reason, it seems to me, which strongly favors the view that angels were not created in a perfect number.

B. State it.

A. If angels were created in that perfect number, and if human beings were created only as substitutes for lost angels, then it is clear that unless angels had fallen from their happiness human beings would not ascend to it.

B. This is evident.

A. Suppose, then, someone says that elect men will rejoice as much over the loss of the angels as over their own elevation since without doubt the latter would not occur unless the former had occurred. [In that case] how could men be protected from this perverse joy, or how would we say that fallen angels will be *replaced* by human beings? For if these angels had not fallen, they would have remained free of this fault (i.e., free of rejoicing over the fall of others); but men could not be free of it. Or, indeed, what kind of happiness would men with this fault deserve? Finally, how presumptuous it would be of us to say that God would not or could not bring about this substitution apart from this fault!

B. Does not a similar thing happen in the case of the Gentiles, who have been called to faith because the Jews have rejected it?

A. No. For if all the Jews had believed, the Gentiles would still have been called, since "in every nation he who fears God and works justice is acceptable to Him."[70] But since the Jews spurned the Apostles, their contempt was the occasion of the Apostles' having turned to the Gentiles.

B. In no respect do I see anything that I can say against this.

A. Why does this joy over another's fall seem to you to come to each man?

B. Why except that each would know that he would not at all be positioned where he will be unless another had fallen from this position?

A. Therefore, if no one had this assurance, there would not be any basis for anyone to rejoice over another's downfall.[71]

B. So it seems.

A. On the assumption that elect men will be much more numerous than the angels who fell, do you think that anyone of these elect men would have this assurance?

B. I cannot at all believe that he would have it or should have it. For with regard to the [perfect] number required for establishing that city: how could anyone know whether he was created for replenishing what was diminished or for filling up what was not yet completed? All would be certain, however, that they were created for completing that city.

A. Therefore, if there will be more human beings than reprobate angels, no one could or should know that he has been elevated to the Heavenly City only because of another's fall.

B. This is true.

A. Therefore, no one will have reason to rejoice over another's perdition.

B. So it follows.

A. We see, then, that if there will be more elect men than reprobate angels, there does not follow that unfittingness which is bound to follow on the assumption that there will not be more [elect men than reprobate angels]. Accordingly, since it is impossible for there to be any unfittingness in that city, it seems necessary that angels were not created in that perfect number and that there will be more blessed men than there are wretched angels.

B. I do not see how this can be denied.

A. I think that still another argument can be given for this same conclusion.

B. You ought to expound this one as well.

A. We believe that the physical mass of the world is to be transformed[72] for the better and that this will not occur until the number of elect men is filled up and the Blessed City completed. Moreover, [we believe that] upon completion of this city, the transformation will no longer be delayed. Hence, we can infer that from the beginning God planned to perfect both [this world's physical nature and that city of rational natures] at the same time. Thus, the inferior nature, which did not sense God, would not be perfected before the superior nature, which ought to enjoy God. And in its own way the inferior nature, having been changed for the better, would "rejoice" in the perfecting of the superior nature. Indeed, every creature — each in its own way rejoicing eternally in its creator, itself, and its fellow-creatures — would rejoice over its own so glorious and so marvellous perfectedness. Thus, that which the will freely causes in rational nature, this the unsensing creature would also naturally display as a result of the governance of God. (For we are accustomed to share joyfully in the exultation of our ancestors — for example, when on the "birthdays"[73] of saints we delight in festive celebration, rejoicing over their glory.) Now, the view under discussion seems to be supported by the following consideration: viz., that if Adam had not sinned, God would still have delayed the completion of that city until human beings were transformed into immortal immortality (so to speak) of their bodies, upon completion of that number-of-men which God was awaiting. For in Paradise human beings had a kind of immortality — viz., an ability not to die. But this ability was not "immortal" because it was able to "die," with the result that human beings would be unable to keep from dying.

But if the foregoing view is true — viz., that from the beginning God planned to perfect at one and the same time that rational, blessed city and this natural, insensible world — then [one of the following alternatives] seems to hold: (1) Before the downfall of the evil angels that city was not complete in its number of angels; rather, God was planning to complete it from human beings at the time He would change, for the better, the physical nature of the world. Or (2) if that city was complete in its number, it was not complete in its confirmation; and its confirmation was to be delayed even if no one within that city were to sin in the period up until the world's renewal, which we await. Or (3) if the confirmation was to be delayed no longer, the renewing of the world was to be hastened so that it would occur together with the confirmation. (~3) But it is altogether unreasonable [to suppose] that God purposed to renew immediately a newly created world and to destroy — at the very beginning, before the reason for their having been created was evident — those things which will not exist after this renewal. Consequently, then, it is not the case that angels were so present in a perfect number that their confirmation was no longer delayed; for the renewal of the new world would have had to occur immediately — a consequence which is unfitting. (~2) But that God willed to delay the confirmation until the future renewal of the world also seems unfitting —

especially since He had accomplished this confirmation so soon in some beings, and since it is plausible that in the case of the first human beings He would have accomplished this confirmation at the time of their sin if they had not sinned, just as He did in the case of the persevering angels. It is true that men were not yet elevated to that equality-with-the-angels to which they were going to come when the number of them who would be elevated would be complete. Nonetheless, it seems that if they had conquered, and thus had not sinned when tempted, then with all their offspring they would have been so confirmed in the justice in which they dwelt that they would not be able to sin any more — just as because they sinned and were conquered, they are so weak that as far as their own power goes they cannot exist without sin. For who would venture to say that injustice is more able to bind in servitude a man who consents to its first enticement than justice is able to confirm in freedom a man who adheres to it at the time of this first temptation? Now, since human nature was present as a whole in our first parents, it *was conquered* as a whole in them, with the result that it sinned (the sole exception being *that* man whom God was able to keep separate from the sin of Adam, even as He was able to create Him from a virgin and without recourse to the seed of a male). Similarly, human nature would have *conquered* as a whole in our first parents if they had not sinned. Therefore, the [first] alternative remains: viz., that the Heavenly City was not filled up by the original [undiminished] number of angels but was to be completed from human beings. If these considerations are correct, then there will be more elect men than there are reprobate angels.

B. What you say seems very reasonable to me. But how shall we interpret the text that God "appointed the bounds of people according to the number of the children of Israel"?[74] Because the words "angels of God" are [sometimes] found in place of "children of Israel," some people interpret this text in such way that the number of elect men to be elevated is construed as [exactly] corresponding to the number of good angels.

A. This interpretation is not opposed to the foregoing view provided it is not true that as many angels have fallen as have remained standing. For on the assumption that there are more elect angels than reprobate ones: it is both necessary that elect men replace reprobate angels and also possible for elect men to be equal in number to the happy angels; and so there will be a greater number of just men than there are of unjust angels.

But remember the proviso with which I began[75] to deal with your perplexity: viz., that if I say something which a greater authority does not confirm, then even though I seem to prove it rationally, it should be accepted with no other degree of certainty than that it appears this way to me for the time being, until God somehow reveals the matter to me more fully. For if I say something that unquestionably contradicts Sacred Scripture, I am certain that it is false; and I do not want to hold that view if I know it [to be false]. But there are matters, concerning which, different beliefs can be entertained without danger. For example, the topic we are now discussing is of this sort. (For in case we do not know whether or not the number of men to be elected is greater than the number of lost angels, and in case we deem one of these alternatives to be better than the other, there is no danger to the soul, it seems to me.) Now, if in matters of this kind we so interpret the divine sayings that they seem to favor different views, and if no other passage is found where they determine what must assuredly be held to, then I do not think we ought to be reproached.

As for your having cited the verse[76] "He appointed the bounds of people," or nations, "according to the number of the angels of God" — a verse which in another translation reads "according to the number of the children of Israel": both translations have either the same meaning or else different but compatible meanings. Therefore, both "angels of God" and "children of Israel" must be construed to signify good angels only or else elect men only or else both angels and elect men together — i.e., the Heavenly City as a whole. Or else, "angels of God" [signifies] the holy angels only, and "children of Israel" [signifies] just men only. Or else, "children of Israel" [signifies] angels only, and "angels of God" [signifies] just men only. Now, if both expressions designate good angels only, then this amounts to the same thing as if only "angels of God" [had been used]. But if [both designate] the Heavenly City as a whole, then the meaning is that people (i.e., multitudes of elect men) will continue to be taken up, or that there will continue to be people in our world, until the predetermined but not yet completed number of that city becomes completed from among men.

Presently, I do not see how "children of Israel" would signify either angels alone or both angels and holy men together. But it would not be strange for *holy men* to be called "children of Israel," even as they are called "children of Abraham."[77] They can also rightly be called angels-of-God by virtue of the following considerations: (1) They imitate angelic life; (2) likeness to and equality with the angels is promised them in Heaven; (3) all who live justly are "angels" of God (and hence are called confessors or martyrs; for one who bears witness to, and confesses, the truth of God is His messenger, i.e., His "angel." Moreover, if an evil man is called a devil — as the Lord says[78] about Judas because of the similarity of his malice [to a devil's] — then why shall not a good man be called an angel because of his imitation of justice?). Therefore, it seems to me, we can say that God has appointed the bounds of people according to the number of *elect men*; for in our world there will continue to be people and human procreation until the number of elect men is completed; and once this number is completed, the human reproduction which occurs in the present life will cease.

But if we interpret "angels of God" to indicate holy angels only and interpret "children of Israel" to indicate just men only, then "God appointed the bounds of people according to the number of the angels of God" can be construed in two ways: viz., either in the sense that as many people — i.e., as many human beings — as there are holy angels of God will be elevated; or in the sense that there will continue to be people until the number of the angels of God is filled up from among men. However, "God appointed the bounds of people according to the number of the children of Israel" can be interpreted in only one way, it seems to me: viz., in the sense that (as has been stated above) there will continue to be people in the present world until the number of holy men is elevated. Now, from either translation we may infer that as many men will be elevated as angels will remain standing. From this inference, however, there does not follow — even though lost angels are to be replaced from among men — that as many angels fell as persevered. Nonetheless, if anyone makes this latter claim, he will have to find missteps in the above-given arguments which seem to show (1) that angels, before some of them fell, were not present in that perfect number

Anselm of Canterbury

(which I referred to above) and (2) that there will be more elect men than there are evil angels.

B. I do not regret having made you say these things about angels, for you have not done it in vain. Return now to the point from which we digressed.

Chapter Nineteen: Man cannot be saved without satisfaction for sin.

A. It has been established[79] that God planned to replace from among men the angels who fell.

B. This point is certain.

A. Therefore, in the Heavenly City the men who will be elevated thereto in place of angels ought to be such as those whom they will there replace were going to be — i.e., [they ought to be] such as the good angels now are. Otherwise, it would not be the case that those who have fallen are *replaced*, and consequently God either could not complete the good work He began or else He would regret having begun such a good work — both of which alternatives are absurd.

B. Truly, [elect] men ought to be equal to the good angels.

A. Have the good angels ever sinned?

B. No.

A. Can you think that a man who has once sinned and has never made satisfaction to God for his sin, but is simply let-off unpunished, would be equal to an angel who has never sinned?

B. I can think and say these words, but I can no more grasp their intelligibility than I can rightly think a falsehood to be a truth.[80]

A. Therefore, in the absence of satisfaction it is not fitting for God to elevate sinful man to the places of lost angels, since truth does not permit a sinful man's being elevated to equality with the happy angels.

B. Reason demonstrates this.

A. Consider also whether in the case of man alone — disregarding the fact that he ought to be equal to the angels — God ought to elevate him in this way to any happiness, even to the kind of happiness which he possessed before he sinned.

B. State your view, and I shall examine it as best I can.

Cur Deus Homo I

A. Let us suppose that some rich man is holding in his hand a pearl of great value which no impurity has ever touched, and which no one else can remove from his hand unless he permits it. And let him be intending to hide it away in his treasury, where his most cherished and most valuable possessions are located.

B. I am imagining this just as if it were before us.

A. What if, even though he could prevent it from happening, he were to permit some envious person to knock this pearl from his hand into the mire? And what if afterwards he were to take it from the mire and store it, still dirty and unwashed, in some clean and costly receptacle, intending to treasure it henceforth in this condition? Would you think him wise?

B. How could I think this? For would it not be much better for him to retain and safeguard, as clean, the pearl which is contaminated?

A. Would not God have been doing a similar thing if without there being any cleansing (i.e., without there being any satisfaction) He had brought man — stained by the mire of sin and going to remain in this condition forever — back at least into Paradise, from which he had been cast out? For in Paradise man, who was to join the company of the angels, was originally being held sinless in God's hand, as it were. And God permitted the Devil (for if God had willed to prevent the Devil, the Devil would not have been able to tempt man), incited by envy, to thrust man (who nevertheless consented) into the mire of sin.

B. I dare not deny that there would be a similarity if God were to do this. Hence, I do not grant that He can do it. For [if God were to do this], it would seem that either He was unable to complete what He had planned or else He regretted His good plan. And neither of these possibilities can befall God.

A. Therefore, believe most assuredly that without satisfaction (i.e., without voluntary payment of the debt) God cannot forgive unpunished sin and the sinner cannot arrive at happiness — not even such happiness as he had before he sinned. For without satisfaction it would not be the case that man is really restored — not even restored to such a state as that in which he was existing prior to his sin.

B. I cannot at all refute your arguments. But why is it that we pray to God "Forgive us our debts"?[81] And why does every nation beseech the god in whom it believes to forgive its sins?

For, on the one hand, if we pay [to God] what we owe, why do we ask Him to forgive us? Is God unjust, so that He demands again what has already been paid? On the other hand, if we do not pay it, why do we pray in vain for Him to do what He cannot do, seeing that it is unfitting?

A. He who does not make payment says in vain "Forgive me." But he who does make payment also makes this supplication; for this making-of-supplication belongs to the payment. For God does not owe anything to anyone; but every creature is indebted to God. Accordingly, it is not expedient for man to deal with God as an equal with an equal. Regarding this issue it is not necessary to give you an answer now. For when you come to learn why Christ died, perhaps you will detect by yourself the answer you are seeking.

B. Well, then, the answer you have given to my perplexity satisfies me for now. The following point, however, you have demonstrated so clearly that even if I wanted to I could not doubt[82] its truth: viz., that no man can arrive at happiness if he is sinful or can be freed from sin if he does not repay what he seized by sinning.

Chapter Twenty: Satisfaction ought to be proportional to the measure of the sin. Man cannot make satisfaction by himself.[83]

A. I think you will also not doubt that satisfaction ought to be proportional to the measure of the sin.

B. Were it not so, sin would to some extent remain unordered — something which cannot be the case if God leaves nothing unordered in His kingdom. Now, it has already been established[84] that even the slightest unfittingness is impossible in the case of God.

A. Tell me, then: what will you pay to God in proportion to your sin?

B. Penitence, a contrite and humbled heart, fasting and a variety of physical toil, the mercy of giving and forgiving, as well as obedience.

A. In all these cases what are you giving to God?

B. Do I not honor God when out of fear of Him and love for

Cur Deus Homo I

Him I in contrition of heart cast aside temporal mirth, when in fasting the toil I tread under foot the pleasures and repose of this life, when in giving and forgiving I generously bestow my possessions, and when in obedience I subject myself to Him?

A. When you render something which you would owe to God even if you had not sinned, you ought not to reckon it as payment of the debt which you owe for your sin. Now, you owe to God all of the things you have just mentioned. For in this mortal life there ought to be so much love, and so much desire to arrive at that end for which you have been created (an arrival whereunto prayer is relevant), and so much sorrow because you are not yet there, and so much fear lest you not arrive, that you ought to experience joy only over those things which give you either assistance in arriving or the hope thereof. For you do not deserve to have what you do not love and desire in proportion to[85] its nature, and over which you do not grieve because you do not yet possess it but are still in such great danger as to whether or not you will ever possess it. To possess this, it is also a prerequisite to flee from the repose and worldly pleasures (except insofar as you know them to conduce to your aspiration to arrive at this possession) which call the soul away from that true rest and delight. Moreover, you ought to consider that you are required to give — even as you recognize that what you give, you have not from yourself but from Him whose servant both you and the one to whom you give are. And nature teaches you to deal with your fellow-servant (i.e., one man dealing with another) as you would want to be dealt with by him,[86] and teaches that anyone who is unwilling to give of what he has ought not to receive what he does not have. Now, regarding forgiveness I will say briefly that vengence does not at all belong to you (as I stated earlier),[87] since you are not your own[88] and he who has wronged you is neither yours nor his own; rather you are both servants of one Lord and have both been created by Him out of nothing. Moreover, if you avenge yourself on your fellow-servant, you haughtily presume to exercise over him the judgment which is the prerogative of the Lord and Judge of all. Finally, in the case of obedience, what do you give to God that you do not already owe Him, to whose command you owe all that you are, all that you have, and all that you can do?

B. I now do not dare to say that in all these cases I am giving to God something which I do not owe to Him.

A. Therefore, what do you pay to God according to the measure of your sin?

B. If even had I not sinned I would — in order to keep from sinning — owe to God myself and whatever I can do, I have nothing with which to make payment for my sin.

A. What, then, will become of you? How will you be able to be saved?

B. If I take seriously your arguments, I do not see how. But if I have recourse to my faith, then in the Christian faith, which works through love,[89] I have the hope that I can be saved. For we read: "If the unjust be converted from his injustice and do justice,"[90] all his injustices are forgotten.

A. This is said only to those who either looked forward to Christ before He came or believe on Him after He comes. But when we proposed to examine by reason alone whether His coming was necessary for man's salvation, we hypothesized that Christ and the Christian faith had never existed.[91]

B. So we did.

A. Therefore, let us proceed by reason alone.

B. Although you lead me into difficulties, I greatly desire for you to proceed just as you have begun.

Chapter Twenty-one: How grave sin is.

A. Let us assume that you do not owe all those things which you have just supposed you could render as payment for your sin. And let us see whether they can avail to making satisfaction for even one very small sin — such as taking a single look which is contrary to God's will.

B. Except for the fact that I hear you calling this sin into question, I would think that I could blot it out by a single act of remorse.

A. You have not yet considered how grave sin is.

B. Show me this now.

A. Suppose you were to find yourself in the presence of God and someone were to give you the command: "Look in that direction." And suppose that, on the contrary, God were to say: "I am absolutely unwilling for you to look." Ask yourself in your heart what there is, among all existing things, for the sake of which you ought to take that look in violation of God's will.

B. I find nothing for the sake of which I ought to do this — unless perhaps I were caught in the necessity of having to commit either this sin or some greater one.

A. Exclude this necessity, and consider with regard only to the sin in question whether you could [legitimately] commit it for the sake of saving your life.

B. I see clearly that I could not.

A. So as not to make you tarry longer: what if it were necessary either for the whole world and whatever is other than God to perish and be reduced to nothing or for you to do so small a thing which is contrary to the will of God?

B. When I consider the action itself, I see it to be something trifling. But when I reflect upon the fact that it is contrary to the will of God, I recognize that it is something extremely grave and comparable to no loss. However, we are often irreproachable in acting against someone's will, so that his possessions are safeguarded; afterwards, our having done this pleases the one against whose will we have acted.

A. This happens to a man who sometimes does not understand what is useful to him, or who cannot replace what he loses; but God has no needs, and even as He has created all things, so He could also replace them if they were to perish.

B. I must admit that even for the sake of preserving the whole of creation, it is not the case that I ought to do something which is contrary to the will of God.

A. What if there were more than one world, full of creatures, just as this world is?

B. If there were an infinitely multiple number of worlds and they too were exhibited to me, I would still give the same answer.

A. You can do nothing more rightly. But if it were to happen that contrary to the will of God you were to take that look, consider as well what you would be able to render as payment for this sin.

B. I do not have anything more than what I have already mentioned.[92]

A. By comparison, then, this is how gravely we sin whenever we knowingly do something, however small, contrary to the will of God. For we are always in His presence, and He always commands us not to sin.

B. As I see it, we are living in very great danger.

A. It is evident that God demands satisfaction in proportion to the extent of the sin.

B. I cannot deny it.

A. Therefore, you do not make satisfaction unless you pay something greater than is that for whose sake you ought not to have sinned.

B. I see both that reason requires this and that it is altogether impossible.

A. And God cannot elevate to happiness anyone who is at all obligated by the debt for sin, because God ought not to do so.[93]

B. This verdict is exceedingly grave.

Chapter Twenty-two: How when man permitted himself to be conquered by the Devil he did an injury to God for which he is unable to make satisfaction.

A. Listen to still another reason why it is no less difficult for man to be reconciled to God.

B. Unless faith consoled me, the previous reason by itself would make me despair.

A. Listen anyhow.

B. Go on speaking.

A. Man, who was created without sin, was placed in Paradise with an inclination toward God — placed between God and the Devil, as it were — in order that he would conquer the Devil by not consenting to his inducement toward sin. [This conquest would] vindicate and honor God as well as confound the Devil, since man, weaker [than the Devil], would not sin on earth when tempted by the Devil, who, stronger [than man], had sinned in Heaven untempted by anyone. And although man was easily able to succeed at this, he freely permitted himself — merely because of the temptation and without being compelled by any force — to be conquered according to the Devil's will and contrary to the will and honor of God.

B. What are you getting at?

A. Judge whether it is not against the honor of God for man — still having to his discredit the slanderous injury he inflicted on God — to be reconciled to God without first honoring God by defeating the Devil, just as he dishonored God when he was defeated by the Devil. But the victory ought to be such that even as man, who was strong and potentially immortal, readily consented to the Devil so as to sin (for which reason he justly incurred the penalty of mortality), so being now weak and mortal (as he has made himself), he will defeat the Devil through the impediment of death so as not at all to sin. But man cannot do this as long as, from the wound of the first sin, he is conceived and born in sin.[94]

B. I repeat: what you say is, on the one hand, proved by reason and, on the other, impossible.

Chapter Twenty-three: What it was that man, when he sinned, removed from God and cannot repay.[95]

A. Listen to one more thing without which man cannot be justly reconciled and which is no less impossible.

B. You have already placed before us so many things required for us to do that whatever you add to them cannot more greatly frighten me.

A. Listen anyhow.

B. I am listening.

A. When he permitted himself to be overcome by the Devil, what did man take away from God?

B. You tell me, as you have been doing; for I do not know what man could have added to the evils which you have already indicated.

A. Did he not remove from God whatever God had purposed to do with human nature?[96]

B. It cannot be denied.

A. Attend to strict justice, and judge in accordance with it whether man makes to God satisfaction equal to his sin unless by conquering the Devil he restores to God exactly what he removed from God by letting himself be conquered by the Devil. The result would be that as by man's having been defeated the Devil seized what was God's and God lost it, so by man's triumphing the Devil loses what was God's and God regains it.

B. Nothing can more strictly or more justly be thought.

A. Do you suppose that Supreme Justice can violate this justice?

B. I do not dare to think so.

A. Therefore, man neither can nor ought, in any respect, to receive from God what God planned to give him — unless he returns to God all that he took away from Him, so that as God lost something because of man, He will also regain it because of man. This can only happen in the following way: Just as by man's defeat the whole of human nature became corrupted[97] and leavened, as it were, with sin — and no one who is sinful is elevated by God to complete the Heavenly City — so by man's triumphing, as many men are justified from sin as were going to fill up that number which man was created to complete. But sinful man cannot at all accomplish this justification, because a sinner cannot justify a sinner.

B. Nothing is more just and nothing is more impossible. But from all these considerations it seems that, as far as regards the happiness for which man was created, God's mercy and man's hope vanish.

Chapter Twenty-four: As long as man does not pay to God what he owes, he cannot be happy and is not excused because of his inability.

A. Wait a little longer.

B. What further points do you have?

A. If we call unjust a man who does not pay to another man what he owes, then it is much more the case that a man who does not pay to God what he owes is unjust.

B. If a man is able to pay but does not do so, he is indeed unjust. But if he is unable to pay, how is it that he is unjust?

A. If he is not at all the cause of his inability, perhaps he can to some extent be excused. But if he is to blame for his inability, then even as the inability does not lighten the weight of his sin, so it does not excuse him from not paying his debt.[98] Suppose that a master enjoins a task upon his servant and instructs him not to cast himself into a pit which the master points out to him and from which the servant would not at all be able to get out. And suppose this servant, spurning the command and the admonition of his master, voluntarily puts himself into the indicated pit, with the result that he is altogether unable to accomplish the work assigned to him. Do you think that his inability would serve to any extent as an excuse for his not performing the assigned task?

B. Not at all. Rather, it would serve to increase his blameworthiness, since he would have brought his inability upon himself. Indeed, he would have sinned in two ways — because he would not have done what he was instructed to do, and he would have done what he was instructed not to do.

A. So, too, man is inexcusable. For he voluntarily became obligated to that debt which he is unable to pay, and through his own doing he lapsed into his inability, so that he is unable to pay either what he owed before sinning — viz., that he keep from sinning — or what he owes because he has sinned. Indeed, this inability is blamable, because he is not obliged to have it; rather, he is obliged not to have it. For just as not having what one ought to have is blamable, so having what one ought not to have is blamable. Therefore, as man is blameworthy for not having the ability which he received in order to be able to avoid sin, so he is blameworthy for having the inability by which he is unable either to retain justice and avoid sin or to pay what he owes for his sin. For he freely did that thing because of which he lost this ability and came into this state of inability. (For not having an ability which one ought to have is identical with having an inability which one ought not to have.) Therefore, the inability to pay to God what he owes — an inability which is the cause of his not paying — does not excuse a man if he does not make payment, since an effect of sin does not excuse a sin which he commits.

B. This [verdict] is exceedingly grave, but it must be true.

A. Therefore, a man who does not pay to God what he owes is unjust.

B. This is surely true. He is unjust because he does not make payment; and he is unjust because he is unable to make payment.

A. Now, no one who is unjust will be admitted to the state of happiness; for even as happiness is a state of sufficiency in which nothing needed is lacking, so it befits only him in whom justice is so pure that there is no injustice in him.

B. I do not dare to believe otherwise.

A. Therefore, he who does not pay to God what he owes will not be able to be happy.

B. I cannot deny, either, that this consequence follows.

A. But suppose you wanted to say: "The reason that God, who is merciful, forgives the debt of one who humbly beseeches Him is that this man is unable to pay this debt." Well, God can be said to forgive only one of two things: (1) that which man ought voluntarily to pay but cannot (viz., that which can make payment for a sin which ought not to have been committed even for the sake of preserving everything that is not God); (2) that which, by punishing man, God was going to take away from man against man's will, viz., happiness (as I mentioned above).[99] Now, on the one hand, if God forgives what man ought willingly to pay — forgives it simply because man is unable to pay it — what does this amount to other than that God forgives what He cannot obtain? But it is a mockery to attribute this kind of mercy to God. On the other hand, if God forgives what He was going to take away from man against man's will — forgives it because of man's inability to pay what he ought willingly to pay — God lightens the punishment and makes a man happy *because* of his sin, and *because* he has what he ought not to have. For man ought not to have this inability; and so, as long as he has it without there being satisfaction, he is sinful. But this kind of divine mercy is utterly contrary to God's justice, which allows only for punishment to be requited for sin. Therefore, as it is impossible for God to be at odds with Himself, so it is impossible for Him to be merciful in this way.

B. I see that a divine mercy different from this kind must be sought.

A. Assume that the reason why God forgives someone who does not pay what he owes is that he is unable [to pay it].

B. I wish it were so.

A. Now, all the while that this person would not make payment, either he would be willing to make payment or he would not be willing. If he willed [to pay] what he was unable to [pay], he would be unsatisfied. On the other hand, if he were unwilling [to pay what he was not able to pay], he would be unjust.

B. Nothing is clearer than this.

A. Now, whether unsatisfied or unjust, he would be unhappy.

B. This is also clear.

A. Therefore, as long as he did not make payment, he could not be happy.

B. If God is guided by the principle of justice, then there is no way for this unhappy, insignificant man to escape; and the mercy of God seems to vanish.

A. You have asked for a reason; listen to this one. I do not deny that God is merciful, for He saves men and beasts, as He has multiplied His mercy.[100] However, we are speaking about that ultimate mercy, by which He makes a man happy after this life. And I think that by the previously given arguments I have adequately established (1) that this happiness ought to be given only to him whose sins have been completely forgiven, and (2) that this forgiveness ought to occur only after payment of the debt which is owed for sin — owed in proportion to the magnitude of the sin. If you think that there can be some objection to the previous arguments, you ought to say so.

B. To be sure, I do not see that any of your arguments can at all be called into question.

A. I do not think [they can be] either — provided they are carefully examined. Nevertheless, if even one of all these arguments which I have given is confirmed by irrefutable truth, that ought to be sufficient. For whether the truth is irrefutably proven by one argument or by more than one argument, it is equally well safeguarded from all doubt.

B. So it is indeed.

Chapter Twenty-five: Necessarily, man is saved through Christ.

B. How, then, will man be saved if he does not pay what he owes and if he ought not to be saved unless he pays it? Or how can we impudently maintain that God, who is rich in mercy beyond human understanding, cannot bestow this mercy?

A. At this point you ought to ask those who believe that Christ is not necessary for man's salvation — those in whose place you are speaking — to explain how man can be saved apart from Christ. However, if they cannot at all do so, then let them stop scoffing at us, and let them come near and join themselves to us, who do not doubt that man can be saved through Christ; or else let them give up the hope that man's salvation can somehow occur. But if they dread doing so, let them believe with us in Christ, so that they can be saved.

B. Let me ask you, just as I did at the beginning, to show me in what way man is saved through Christ.

A. Since even unbelievers admit that man can in some way be made happy, and since we have demonstrated adequately that man's salvation can by no means occur if we assume that Christ does not exist: has not the possibility of man's being saved through Christ been sufficiently proved? For it is possible for man to be saved either by means of Christ, or else by some other means, or else by no means. Therefore, if it is false that man's salvation can by no means occur, and false that it can occur by some other means, it is necessary that it occur by means of Christ.

B. Suppose someone perceives the reason why man's salvation cannot occur in some other manner but does not understand how it can occur through Christ. And suppose he wants to claim that it cannot occur either by means of Christ or by any other means. What answer shall we give him?

A. What answer ought to be given to someone who affirms of what must occur that it cannot occur— his reason being simply that he does not know how it occurs?

B. That he is foolish.

A. Therefore, what he says must be treated with contempt.

B. That's true. But he ought to be shown how the thing he thinks to be impossible does really occur.

A. From what I have already said, do you not realize that it is necessary for some men to attain happiness? For if it is unfitting for God to bring a man having any stain to that end for which He created him free of every stain — lest [by so doing] He should seem either to regret the good work He had begun or to be unable to fulfill His purpose — then, much more, because of this same unfittingness, it is impossible that no man whatsoever be elevated to the end for which he was created. Therefore, either the kind of satisfaction-for-sin which I earlier showed[101] to be required must occur outside the context of the Christian faith — something which no sound reasoning can demonstrate — or else satisfaction-for-sin must assuredly be believed to occur within the context of the Christian faith. For that which on the basis of rational necessity is inferred really to be the case ought not to be called into any doubt, even if the reason why it is true is not discerned.

B. What you say is true.

A. So what more are you asking?

B. I have not come for you to remove from me doubts about my faith but for you to show me the rational basis of my certainty. Therefore, just as you have led me rationally to the place where I can see that for his sin sinful man owes to God what he cannot pay, and that unless he pays [what he owes] he cannot be saved, so I want you to lead me to the place where on the basis of rational necessity I understand the following points: viz., (1) that all those things which the Catholic faith commands us to believe about Christ if we want to be saved must be true; (2) how they avail to man's salvation; and (3) how it is that God saves man by mercy although He forgives man's sin only if man pays what he owes on account of his sin. In order that your arguments may be the more certain, begin so basically that you establish them on a firm foundation.

A. May God continue to aid me now. For you do not at all spare me or take into account the weakness of my knowledge when you impose upon me so difficult a task. Nevertheless, trusting in God rather than in myself, I shall make the attempt (since I have already commenced); and with God's help I shall do the best I can. But lest because of too lengthy a sustained-presentation weariness should arise in him who is willing to read these things, by making another beginning let us distinguish what is still to be presented from what has already been said.

BOOK II

Chapter One: Man was created *just* in order to be happy.

A. We ought not to doubt that God created rational nature *just* in order for it to be happy through enjoying Him.[1] Indeed, the reason it is rational is in order to discriminate between what is just and what is unjust, between what is good and what is evil, between what is a greater good and what is a lesser good.[2] Otherwise [i.e., could rational nature not make these discriminations], it would be the case that it was created rational in vain. But God did not create it rational in vain. Therefore, there is no doubt that it was created rational for the foregoing purpose. Similar reasoning proves that rational nature received the ability to make these discriminations in order that it would hate and shun evil, and love and choose good, and more greatly love and choose a greater good [than love and choose a lesser good]. For otherwise, it would be the case that God bestowed in vain upon rational nature this ability-to-discriminate, because rational nature would discriminate in vain if it did not love and shun in accordance with its discrimination. But for God to have bestowed in vain such a great capability would not be fitting. Thus, it is certain that rational nature was created for the purpose of loving and choosing the Supreme Good above all other things — loving and choosing it for its own sake and not for the sake of anything else. (For if [rational nature loves the Supreme Good] for the sake of something else, it really loves not the Supreme Good but this other thing.) But rational nature is able to do this only if it is just. Therefore, so that it would not be rational in vain, it was created both rational and just at once. Now, if it was created *just* in order to love and choose the Supreme Good, then it was created just either for the further purpose of one day attaining what it loves, and has chosen, or else not for this purpose. But if it were not the case that rational nature was created *just* for the further purpose of attaining the thing it justly loves and chooses, then its having been created such as justly to love and choose this thing would have been in vain, and there would be no reason why rational nature ought ever to attain this thing. The consequence would be that as long as rational nature would do just works by loving and choosing the Supreme Good, for which it was created, it would be unhappy; for against its will it would be in a state of deprivation, since it would not possess what it desired. But this view is utterly absurd. Consequently, rational nature was created *just* in order to be happy through enjoying the Supreme Good, viz., God. Accordingly, man, who is rational in nature, was created *just* in order to be happy through enjoying God.

Chapter Two: Man would not have died if he had not sinned.

A. The fact that man was created in such a state as not to have to die is easily proven from the following consideration: It is opposed to God's wisdom and justice (as I said earlier)[3] that He compel to undergo death someone blameless, whom He created just, for the purpose of becoming eternally happy. Consequently, if man had never sinned, he would never have died.

Chapter Three: Man will be resurrected with the body in which he lives during this present life.

A. From the above considerations the eventual future resurrection of the dead is clearly proven. Indeed, if man is to be perfectly restored, he ought to be restored to such a state as he would have been in had he not sinned.
B. It cannot be otherwise.
A. Therefore, just as had man not sinned he was to have been transformed[4] into incorruptibility with the body he had, so it ought to be the case that when he will be restored he will be restored with the body in which he lives during this present life.
B. What answer shall we give if someone claims that this ought to occur in the case of those in whom the human race will be restored but that it need not occur in the case of reprobate men?
A. Nothing can be thought to be more just or fitting than the

Anselm of Canterbury

following: The whole man (i.e., consisting in a soul and a body) would have been eternally happy if man had persevered in justice; correspondingly, the whole man will be eternally unhappy if man continues in injustice.

B. On these matters you have satisfied me with terse answers.

Chapter Four: God will accomplish with human nature that which He began.

A. From the foregoing considerations the following point is easy to recognize: Either God will accomplish with human nature that which He began, or else He has created in vain so sublime a nature for [receiving] so great a good. But if God is recognized to have created nothing more precious than rational nature, for the purpose of rejoicing in Him, then He is very far from allowing any rational nature to perish completely.[5]

B. A rational mind cannot think otherwise.

A. Therefore, it is necessary that God will accomplish with human nature what He began. But this accomplishment can occur, as I said,[6] only by means of complete satisfaction for sin. And no sinner can make complete satisfaction.

B. I now understand the necessity of God's accomplishing what He began — in order that He not seem, contrary to what is fitting, to fail in what He has undertaken.

Chapter Five: Although [what God began] must be accomplished, nevertheless He will not accomplish it under the constraint of necessity. There is a necessity which diminishes or eliminates gratitude, and there is a necessity which increases it.

B. But if [the previous statement] is true, then the necessity of avoiding unfittingness seems to "constrain" God, so to speak, to procure man's salvation. How, then, can we deny that He does this more for His own sake than for our sake? And if it is true [that He does this more for His own sake than for ours], what gratitude do we owe Him for that which He does for His own sake? And how will we [be able to] attribute our salvation to His grace if He saves us out of necessity?

A. There is a necessity which diminishes or eliminates gratitude to a benefactor; and there is a necessity in terms of which a greater gratitude is owed for a benefit. For example, when because of the necessity to which someone is subject he confers a benefit against his will, little or no gratitude is owed to him. But when he willingly submits himself to the necessity of doing a good work, and does not merely endure this necessity against his will, surely he deserves greater gratitude for his good work. For this "necessity" ought not really to be called a necessity but [ought to be called] a grace, since he voluntarily incurred it or holds to it, without anyone constraining him. For suppose you willingly promise today to bestow a gift tomorrow; and tomorrow you do bestow it with this same willingness. Although it is necessary that, if you can, you do tomorrow give what you have promised (or else be caught in a lie), nonetheless the one to whom you give this benefit is no less indebted to you for the bestowal of it than if you had not made a promise. The reason for his indebtedness is that you did not hesitate to make yourself indebted to him prior to the actual giving. The case is similar when someone freely vows to enter monastic life. For although, necessarily, he is obliged to keep his vow after having made it (on pain of incurring condemnation as an apostate), and although he can be compelled to keep it if he is unwilling to, nonetheless if he does willingly keep what he has vowed, he is more (rather than less) pleasing to God than if he had not made a vow. For it is for God's sake that he has renounced not only ordinary life but even ordinary life's being permitted to him. And he must not be said to live a monastic life out of necessity but [must be said to live it] by reason of the same freedom by which he vowed it. Therefore, it is much more the case that if God does for man the good work which He began, then even though it is not fitting for Him to leave unfinished the good work He has undertaken, we ought to attribute the entire good work to grace; for He began this work for our sake and not for His own, since He Himself needs nothing. When He created man, He was not ignorant of what man was going to do. And, nevertheless, by creating man by His own goodness, He freely bound Himself, as it were, to accomplish the good which He had undertaken. In last analysis, God does nothing by necessity, because He is not in any way compelled to do anything or prevented from doing anything.[7] And when we say that God does something as if under the necessity of avoiding dishonor (which, surely, He is in no danger of encountering) we must, rather, interpret this to mean that He does it under the necessity of maintaining His honor. Indeed, this necessity is nothing other than the immutability of His honor — an immutability which He has from Himself and not from another, and which therefore is improperly called necessity. Nevertheless, let us say that it is necessary that God's goodness — on account of its immutability — accomplish with man what it began, even though the entire good which it does is by grace.

B. I grant it.

Chapter Six: Only a God-man can make the satisfaction by means of which man is saved.

A. But this work can only be accomplished if there is someone who pays to God, for man's sin, something greater than every existing thing besides God.

B. This has been proven.[8]

A. Moreover, whoever can give to God something of his own which surpasses everything that is less than God must be greater than everything that is not God.

B. I cannot deny it.

A. Now, nothing except God surpasses everything that is not God.

B. This is true.

A. Therefore, only God can make this satisfaction.

B. This follows.

A. But only a man ought to make this satisfaction. For in any other case it would not be man who makes it.

B. Nothing seems more just.

A. Therefore, if (as has been established)[9] it is necessary that the Heavenly City be completed from among men, and if this completion can occur only if the aforementioned satisfaction is made, and if only God can make this satisfaction and only a man ought to make it: it is necessary that a God-man make it.

B. "Blessed be God."[10] Now we have discovered a major

point regarding the topic we are investigating. Therefore, proceed as you have begun. For I hope that God will continue to aid us.

Chapter Seven: It is necessary that one and the same [individual] be fully divine and fully human.

A. We must now investigate the manner in which a God-man can exist. For it is not the case that the divine nature and the human nature can be changed into each other so that the divine nature becomes human or the human nature becomes divine; and it is not the case that they can be so mingled that from these two natures there is formed a third nature which is neither fully divine nor fully human. Indeed, if it were possible for the one nature to be changed into the other, then the result would be only someone who is divine and not someone who is human, or else only someone who is human and not someone who is divine. Or if they were so mingled that from the two corrupted natures a third nature were formed (as from two individual animals — one male and one female, but of different species — a third animal is born, which does not retain fully either the nature of the father or the nature of the mother but receives a third nature, which is a mixture of the two), then the result would be neither someone who is human nor someone who is divine. Therefore, the God-man[11] about whom we are asking cannot be made from a divine nature and a human nature either by the transformation of the one into the other or by the corrupt mingling of both into a third. For these things cannot happen; or if they can happen, they do not apply to what we are investigating.

But if these two integral natures are said to be conjoined in some manner such that, nevertheless, the human nature is distinct from the divine nature and the one who is divine is not identical with the one who is human, then it is impossible for either one to do what must be done. For the one who is divine will not do it, because He will not be under obligation to do it; and the one who is human will not do it, because he will not be able to do it. Hence, in order that a God-man will do this, it is necessary that one and the same [individual] be fully divine and fully human, so as to make this satisfaction. For only one who is truly divine can make satisfaction, and only one who is truly human ought to make it. Therefore, since it is necessary to find a God-man who retains the integrity of both natures, it is no less necessary that these two integral natures conjoin in one person (just as a body and a rational soul conjoin in one man); for otherwise it is impossible that one and the same [individual] be fully divine and fully human.

B. All that you say pleases me.

Chapter Eight: God ought to assume a human nature from the race of Adam and from a virgin woman.

A. It now remains to ask from where and in what way God will assume a human nature. Either He will take it from Adam or He will create a new human being from no other human being — as He created Adam. But if God were to create a new human being, not of Adam's race, then this human being would not belong to the race of men who are born from Adam. Therefore, it would not be the case that he ought to make satisfaction for Adam's race, because he would not descend from it. For just as it is right that human nature make satisfaction for human nature's guilt, so it is necessary that the one who makes satisfaction be either the sinner himself or someone of his race. Otherwise, neither Adam nor his race would make satisfaction for themselves. Therefore, just as from Adam and Eve sin was transmitted unto all men, so only they themselves or someone descended from them ought to make satisfaction for men's sin. Consequently, since they themselves are unable to [make satisfaction], it is necessary for the one who will do this to derive from them.

Moreover, just as, had Adam not sinned, he and his entire race would by themselves have remained standing, without the assistance of another creature, so if Adam's race rises after the fall, it should rise and be lifted up by its own efforts. For no matter through whom it is restored unto its own place, assuredly it will stand because of him through whom it will recover its place. Moreover, when God first created human nature in Adam alone and willed to create a woman (in order for human beings to be reproduced from the two sexes) only from Adam, He showed clearly that He willed to create only from Adam that which He was going to create from human nature. Therefore, if the race of

Cur Deus Homo II

Adam were restored through a man who is not from the Adamic race, it would not be the case that [it is restored] unto the dignity that would have been its possession had Adam not sinned. And, thus, it would not be fully restored; and God's plan would seem to be a failure. But both of these consequences are unfitting. Therefore, the human nature [of the man] through whom Adam's race is to be restored must be assumed from Adam.

B. If we follow reason, as we proposed to, then this conclusion must, inescapably, be true.

A. Let us now look into whether God ought to assume a human nature (1) from a father and a mother (as do other human beings) or (2) from a man without a woman or (3) from a woman without a man. For no matter in which one of these three ways the human nature is assumed, it will be from Adam and from Eve — from whom derives every human being of either sex. Moreover, it is not the case that one of the three ways is easier for God than are the other two so that a human nature ought more fittingly to be assumed in this one way.

B. You are proceeding commendably.

A. But not much effort is required to show that *that* man would be begotten more purely and more honorably from a man alone or from a woman alone than from a union of the two, as are all other offspring of human beings.

B. This point is clear enough.

A. Therefore, His human nature was taken either from a man alone or from a woman alone.

B. It cannot be taken from anywhere else.

A. God can create a human being in either of four ways: viz., (1) from a man and a woman (as constant experience shows); (2) neither from a man nor from a woman (as He created Adam); (3) from a man without a woman (as He created Eve); (4) from a woman without a man (something which He had not yet done). Therefore, in order for Him to prove that even this fourth way is subject to His power and was reserved for this very purpose, nothing is more fitting than that He assume from a woman without a man *that* man about whom we are inquiring. Now, we need not discuss whether this would be done more worthily from a virgin or from a nonvirgin; instead, we must affirm, without any doubt, the fittingness of the God-man's being born from a virgin.

B. You speak in accordance with my heart's sentiment.

A. Is what we have said something solid? Or is it, like a cloud, the empty kind of thing for which you said unbelievers reproach us?[12]

B. Nothing is more solid.

A. Therefore, do not paint on an empty fiction but paint on the solid truth, and affirm that the following is especially fitting: As the sin of man and the cause of our condemnation took its beginning from a woman, so the remedy for sin and the cause of our salvation is born from a woman.[13] And in order that women not despair of belonging to the company of the blessed (since it was from a woman that so great an evil proceeded), it is fitting that so great a good proceed from a woman, in order to reestablish women's hope. And paint the following: If a virgin was the cause of all the evil to the human race, then it is much more fitting that a virgin would be the cause of all the good for the human race. And paint this too: If the woman whom God created from a man without a woman was created from a virgin, then it is also especially fitting for the man who would be made from a woman without a man to be made from a virgin. But for now let these be enough examples of the pictures which can be painted on the truth that the God-man ought to be born from a virgin woman.

B. These pictures are very beautiful and reasonable.

Chapter Nine: It is necessary that the Word alone and a human nature conjoin in one person.

A. We must now also ask in which one of His persons God, who is three persons, would assume a human nature. For a plurality of the persons cannot assume one and the same human nature into a unity of person. Therefore, it is necessary that this assumption take place with respect to only one [of the three] persons. Now, in the letter *On the Incarnation of the Word*, addressed to Lord Pope Urban, I have spoken — to an extent that I regard as sufficient for the present investigation — about this personal unity of the divine nature and a human nature,[14] and have said for which person of God this most fittingly occurs.[15]

B. Nevertheless, do mention briefly here why the person of the Son ought to become incarnate rather than the person of the Father or the person of the Holy Spirit.

A. If either of the other persons were to become incarnate, there would be two sons in the Trinity: viz., (1) the Son-of-God, who is the Son even before the incarnation, and (2) the one who by virtue of the incarnation would be the son of the virgin. And between these two persons who ought always to be equal there would be an inequality with respect to the dignity of their births. For the one who was begotten of God would have a more excellent birth than would the one who was begotten of the virgin. Likewise, if the Father were to become incarnate there would be two grandsons in the Trinity, because by virtue of the human nature that He assumed the Father would be the grandson of the parents of the virgin; and the Word, even though He would possess nothing from human nature, would nonetheless be the grandson of the virgin, since He would be the son of her son. Now, all these consequences are unfitting. But in the case of the incarnation of the Word none of them occur.

There is also another reason[16] why it is more fitting for the Son to become incarnate than it is for either of the other two persons: viz., it sounds more fitting for the Son to supplicate the Father than for another of the persons to supplicate either of the other two.

Furthermore, man (for whom the Son was going to pray) and the Devil (whom the Son was going to defeat) had, by virtue of an autonomous[17] willing, arrogated to themselves a false likeness to God. Therefore, they had sinned more specifically, so to speak, against the person of the Son, who is believed to be the true likeness of the Father.[18] Hence, the punishment or the remission of the guilt is more fittingly ascribed to Him to whom the wrong is more specifically done. Consequently, since reason leads us inescapably to conclude (1) that the divine nature and a human nature must join together in one person, and (2) that this union cannot occur with regard to a plurality of divine persons, and (3) that, obviously, the union occurs more suitably in regard to the person of the Word than in regard to either of the other two persons, it is necessary that the Divine Word and a human nature conjoin in one person.

B. The route by which you lead me is so completely fortified by reason that I do not see how I can veer from it either to the right or to the left.

A. I am not leading you; instead, He of whom we are speaking and without whom we can do nothing leads us both whenever we keep to the way of truth.

Chapter Ten: This man is not required to die. How He is able to sin and not able to sin. Why He and an angel ought to be praised for their justice even though they cannot sin.

A. However, we now ought to investigate whether this man would be required to die, just as all other men are required to die. Now, if Adam was not going to die had he not sinned, much more would not this man — in whom there could be no sin, because He would be God — be required to undergo death.

B. I want you to dwell awhile on this point. For whether He is said to be able to sin or not to be able to sin, in both cases a question of no small importance occurs to me. For if He is said not to be able to sin, then it seems that this view ought not to be readily believed. To speak for a moment not of one who has never existed (as we have been doing until now) but of one whom we know and whose deeds we know: would anyone deny that He was able to do many things which we call sins? Indeed — to mention only one — how would we say that He was unable to tell-a-lie, which is always a sin? He says to the Jews regarding the Father: "If I say that I do not know Him, I shall be a liar like you."[19] Now, in this sentence He says the words "I do not know Him." Therefore, who would deny that He was able to utter these five words without the others, so as simply to say "I do not know Him"? But if He were to do this, then as He Himself says, He would be a liar; and to be a liar is to be a sinner. Therefore, since He *was* able to do this, He was able to sin.

A. He was both able to make this statement and not able to sin.

B. Demonstrate this point.

A. All ability depends upon willing. For when I say "I am able to speak or to walk," the proviso "if I will to" is understood. For if willing is not included, then the ability is not really an ability but is a necessity. For when I say "I am able to be dragged off or to be overcome against my will," this is not an instance of my ability but is an instance of constraint and of another's ability. Indeed, "I am able to be dragged off or to be overcome'' means nothing other than "Someone else is able to drag me off or to overcome me."[20] Therefore, we can say of Christ, "He was able to tell a lie," provided "if He willed to" is understood. And since He was not able to lie against His will and was not able to will to lie, He can equally well be said not to have been able to lie. So, then, He was able to lie and not able to lie.

B. Let us now return to making our investigation about Him as if He did not yet exist — just as we began to do. Accordingly, I say: if He were unable to sin because, as you say, He would be unable to will to sin, then He would keep justice of necessity. Therefore, He would not be *just* out of freedom of choice. Consequently, what esteem would be owed to Him for His justice? Indeed, we are accustomed to say that the reason God created angels and man to be such that they could sin was so that although they were able to forsake justice but kept it out of freedom of choice they would merit esteem and praise, which would not be their due if they were *just* of necessity.

A. Are not the angels who now cannot sin worthy of praise?

B. Indeed they are. For by virtue of having been able [to sin] but having willed not [to sin] they merited their present state of being unable [to sin].

A. What do you say about God, who is not able to sin but who did not merit this state by virtue of [having] an ability-to-sin, by means of which He, nonetheless, did not sin? Is He not worthy of praise for His justice?

B. Here I want you to answer for me. If I say that He ought not to be praised, I know that I am not telling the truth. But if I say that He ought to be praised, I am afraid of undermining the reason which I stated regarding the angels.

A. The reason that angels are to be praised for their justice is not that they were able to sin but is rather that thereby [i.e., because of having been able to sin] they, in a sense, have from themselves the fact that they are not able to sin.[21] (In this respect they are somewhat similar to God, who has from Himself whatever He has.) For one who does not remove something when he can is said to bestow it; and one who does not cause [something not to be], although he is able to cause it not to be, is said to cause something to be.[22] So, then, in the case where an angel was able to remove justice from himself but did not remove it, and was able to cause himself not to be just but did not do so, he is rightly said to have given himself justice and to have caused himself to be just. In this sense, then, he has justice from himself; for a creature is not able to have justice from himself in any other way. And, hence, an angel ought to be praised for his justice; and he is *just* not by necessity but in terms of freedom, since necessity is improperly called necessity in a case where there is neither compulsion nor prevention. Therefore, since whatever God has He has completely from Himself, He ought supremely to be praised for the goods which He possesses and keeps not because of any necessity but (as I said above)[23] by His own eternal immutability. So, then, since that man who will be identical with God will have from Himself every good which He will have, and will have it not by necessity but in terms of freedom, He will be *just* of Himself and hence will be worthy of praise. For although what His human nature will have, it will have from His divine nature, nevertheless He will have it from Himself, since His two natures will be one person.

B. You have satisfied me on this point; and I see clearly that He will not be able to sin and that, nevertheless, He will be worthy of praise for His justice.

But since God is able to make such a man, I think that it must now be asked why He did not create angels and the first two human beings to be such that they also would be unable to sin and worthy of praise for their justice.

A. Do you understand what you are saying?

B. I seem to myself to understand it, and hence I ask why He did not create them in such a state.

A. The reason is that it should not and could not have happened that any one of them would be identical with God, as we speak of that man as being. And if you ask why He did not do this for as many of them as there are divine persons, or at least for one of them, I reply: reason did not at all require that this be done at that time but (since God does nothing without a reason) completely excluded the possibility.

B. I am ashamed of having asked this question. Continue with what you were going to say.

A. Let us say, then, that He would not be required to die, since He would not be a sinner.

B. I must admit this.

Chapter Eleven: He dies of his own power. Mortality does not pertain to sinless human nature.

A. But it now remains to examine whether He would be able to die with respect to His human nature (for with respect to His divine nature it would always be the case that He is incorruptible).

B. Why should we be in doubt about this, since He would be a real man, and every man is naturally mortal?

A. I think that mortality pertains not to sinless human nature but to corrupt human nature. Indeed, if man had never sinned and if his immortality had been immutably confirmed, he would have been no less a real man; and when mortals will rise in incorruptibility, they will be, no less, real men. For if mortality pertained to the essence [*veritas*] of human nature, there could not at all be a man who was immortal. Therefore, neither corruptibility nor incorruptibility[24] pertains to the sinless state of human nature, since neither of these is essential to human nature;[25] rather, the one conduces to man's unhappiness, the other to his happiness. (But since there is no human being who does not die, the word "mortal" was included in the definition of "man" by the philosophers, who did not believe that human nature as a whole[26] ever could have been or ever can be immortal.) Therefore, the fact that that man would be a real man does not suffice to show that He ought to be mortal.

B. Then, look for another reason; for I do not know, if you do not, the reason which proves that He can die.

A. There is no doubt that as He will be God, so He will be omnipotent.

B. This is true.

A. Therefore, if He wills to, He shall be able to lay down His life and take it up again.[27]

B. If He cannot do this, it seems that He is not omnipotent.

A. Therefore, if He wills to, He shall be able never to die; and, [if He wills to], He shall be able to die and to arise. But as far as His power is concerned, it does not matter whether He lays down His life without anyone else serving as a cause thereof or whether, with His permission, someone else is a cause of the fact that He lays it down.

B. There is no doubt about this.

A. Therefore, if He is willing to permit it, He will be able to be killed; and if He is unwilling to permit it, He will not be able to be killed.

B. Reason leads us unswervingly to this conclusion.

A. Reason has also taught us[28] that He ought to have something greater than whatever is inferior to God — something which He would give to God willingly and not out of debt.

B. This is true.

A. But this gift can be found neither beneath Him nor beyond Him.

B. This is true.

A. Therefore, it must be found in Him.

B. This follows.

A. Therefore, He will give either Himself or something belonging to Himself.

B. I cannot think otherwise.

A. It must now be asked what kind of giving this ought to be. For since every creature is God's, it is not the case that He will be able to give to God — as if it were to one who did not already have this as his own — either Himself or anything belonging to Himself.

B. True.

A. Therefore, this giving must be interpreted as follows: In some way in which He will not be required to, He will offer, for the honor of God, either Himself or something belonging to Himself.

B. This follows from the things already said.

A. If we say that He will give Himself in the sense of obeying God, so that by perseveringly keeping justice He will surrender Himself to God's will, this would not be a case of giving what God does not already exact from Him as a debt. For every rational creature owes this obedience to God.

B. This cannot be denied.

A. Therefore, He must in some other way give to God either Himself or something belonging to Himself.

B. Reason drives us to this conclusion.

A. Let us see whether perhaps this giving is the giving of His

Cur Deus Homo II

life, or the laying down of His life, or the handing Himself over to death, for the honor of God. For God does not exact His life from Him as something owed. Indeed, since there will be no sin in Him, He will not be required to die, as I said.[29]

B. I cannot think otherwise.

A. Let us consider, in addition, whether this view agrees with reason.

B. You continue to speak, and I shall continue to listen willingly.

A. If man sinned through pleasure, is it not fitting that he make satisfaction through distress? And if (with the result that he dishonored God by sinning) he was conquered by the Devil so easily that it could not happen more easily, is it not *just* that in making satisfaction for sin man should (for the honor of God) conquer the Devil by such a difficult means that it could not be done by any means more difficult? And is it not fitting that man, who by sinning so stole himself from God that he cannot remove himself to any greater extent, should by making satisfaction so give himself to God that he cannot give himself to any greater extent?

B. There is not anything more reasonable.

A. Now, for the honor of God, a man can willingly and out of no obligation suffer nothing more harsh and difficult than death; and a man cannot at all give himself to God to any greater extent than when he hands himself over to death for the honor of God.

B. All of this is true.

A. Therefore, He who shall will to make satisfaction for man's sin ought to be such that He can die if He wills to.

B. I see clearly that that man about whom we are inquiring ought to be such that He will not die of necessity (because He will be omnipotent) and will not die out of obligation (because He will never be a sinner) and yet will be able to die of His own free will (because it will be necessary [that he be able to die freely]).

A. There are also many other reasons why it is especially fitting for that man to be like men and to dwell among them, yet without sin. These reasons stand out, of themselves, more readily and more clearly in His life and deeds than they can be demonstrated by reason alone, independently of experience. For who will explain how necessarily and how wisely it happened that He who was going to redeem men and to lead them back, by His teaching, from the way of death and perdition to the way of life

Anselm of Canterbury

and eternal happiness associated[30] with men and in this association (although He taught them by word how they ought to live) presented Himself as an example? But how could He give Himself as an example to weak and mortal men, so that they would not depart from justice on account of wrongs or insults or pain or death, if they did not know that He Himself experienced all these things?

Chapter Twelve: Although He shares our misfortunes, He is not unhappy.

B. All of these considerations show plainly that He ought to be mortal and ought to share our misfortunes. Yet all of these misfortunes contribute to our unhappiness. Will He, therefore, be unhappy?
A. By no means. For as something-beneficial which someone possesses against His will does not conduce to his happiness, so to experience something-detrimental wisely and willingly, without being compelled to, is not [a cause of] unhappiness.
B. This point must be granted.

Chapter Thirteen: It is not the case that along with our other infirmities He has ignorance.

B. But in regard to this likeness which He ought to have to men, state whether He would have ignorance, even as He would have our other infirmities.
A. Why do you doubt whether God is all-knowing?
B. Well, because *that* man will be mortal with respect to His human nature, even though He will be immortal with respect to His divine nature. So why will He not likewise be able to be genuinely ignorant, even as He will be genuinely mortal?
A. The assumption of a human nature into the unity of a divine person will be done only wisely by Supreme Wisdom. And so Supreme Wisdom will not assume into its human nature that which is not at all useful (but is, in fact, very harmful) to the work which this man is going to do. Now, to be sure, ignorance would be of no use to Him; instead, it would be of much harm. For

Cur Deus Homo II

without great wisdom how would He do the very numerous and very great works which He was going to do? Or how would men believe Him if they knew that He was ignorant? Or even if they did not know [this about Him], of what use would His ignorance be? Furthermore, if only what is known is loved, then just as there would not be any good which He did not love, so there would not be any good which He did not know. But only one who knows how to discern good from evil has a complete knowledge of good. And no one who does not know evil knows how to make this distinction [between good and evil]. Therefore, just as the one of whom we are speaking will have complete knowledge of every good, so He will not be ignorant of any evil. Therefore, He will know everything, even though He will not publicly display all of His knowledge in His association with other men.

B. In the case of His adult life the fact of the matter seems to be as you say it is. But in the case of His infancy: just as infancy would not be a fitting time for wisdom to appear in Him, so it would not be necessary — as well as not fitting — for Him to have wisdom then.[31]

A. Did I not say that the incarnation would be accomplished wisely? Indeed, God will assume mortality wisely; and He will use mortality wisely because He will use it very usefully. But He would not be able to assume ignorance wisely, because ignorance is never useful but is always harmful (except perhaps in the case where an evil will — which would never be in Him — is kept from its evil effect because of ignorance). For even if ignorance would never be harmful in any other respect, it would be harmful merely in that it would prevent the benefit of knowledge. Moreover — to resolve your puzzle briefly — from the very moment that that man will exist He will always be fully divine, just as He is fully human. Hence, He will never exist without His power, might, and wisdom.

B. Although I did not doubt that this was always the case with Christ, nevertheless I asked to hear the reason for it. For often we are certain that something is the case but nevertheless do not know how to prove it rationally.

Chapter Fourteen: How His death outweighs the number and the magnitude of all sins.

B. I ask you now to teach me how His death outweighs the number and the magnitude of *all* sins — seeing that you have shown[32] *one* sin which we regard as trifling to be so infinite that if an infinite number of worlds were exhibited, each as full of creatures as is our world, and if these worlds could be kept from being reduced to nothing only on the condition that someone would take a single look contrary to the will of God, this look ought, nonetheless, not to be taken.

A. Suppose *that* man were present, and you knew who He was, and someone said to you: "Unless you kill this man this whole world and whatever is not God will perish." Would you do this for the sake of preserving every other creature?

B. I would not do it even if an infinite number of worlds were exhibited to me.

A. What if you were then told: "Either kill this man or all the sins of the world will come upon you"?

B. I would reply that I would prefer to bear all other sins — not only those which have been committed and will be committed in this world, but also whatever sins can be thought of, in addition to these — than to commit this one sin. And I think that I ought to give the same answer not only for the case of slaying Him but also for the case of the slightest harm which would touch Him.

A. You think correctly. But tell me why your mind judges that one sin which harms this man is more dreadful than all other sins which can be conceived; for no matter what sins are committed, they are all sins against Him.

B. The reason is that a sin which is committed against His person surpasses, incomparably, all conceivable sins which are not against His person.

A. What will you say about the fact that often someone voluntarily endures harm against his person in order not to suffer greater harm in regard to his possessions?

B. [I will say] that God does not have need of this longsuffering; for all things are subject to His power, as you mentioned previously[33] in reply to one of my questions.

Cur Deus Homo II

A. You give a good answer. We see, then, that no magnitude nor multitude of sins which are not against the person of God is comparable to [the sin of] harming the physical life of this man.

B. This is very clear.

A. In your opinion how great a good is [the life] of Him whose being-put-to-death is so evil?

B. If every good is as good as its destruction is evil, then [His life] is a good incomparably greater than the evil of those sins which His being-put-to-death immeasurably surpasses.

A. You speak the truth. Reflect also upon the fact that sins are as detestable as they are evil; and the life of this man is as lovable as it is good. Hence, it follows that His life is more lovable than sins are detestable.

B. I cannot fail to understand this.

A. Do you think that such a great and lovable good can suffice to pay what is owed for the sins of the entire world?

B. Indeed, it can [suffice to pay] infinitely more [than that].

A. Therefore, you see how His life would overcome all sins if it were given for them.

B. Clearly.

A. Therefore, if to give one's life is to accept death, then just as the giving of His life outweighs all men's sins, so too does His acceptance of death.

B. This is plainly the case regarding all sins which do not touch the person of God.

Chapter Fifteen: How His death blots out even the sins of those who put Him to death.

B. But now I see another point that must be questioned. If to put Him to death is as evil as His life is good, how can His death overcome and blot out the sins of those who have put Him to death? Or if it blots out the sin of one of them, how can it blot out any of the sins of other men as well? For we believe that many of the former have been saved and that countless other men are saved.

A. This question is answered by the apostle who said that "if they had known it, they would never have crucified the Lord of Glory."[34] For a sin done knowingly and a sin done in ignorance are so different from each other that the evil which these men could never have done knowingly, because of its enormity, is venial because it was done in ignorance. For no man could ever will, at least knowingly, to kill God;[35] and so those who killed Him in ignorance did not rush forth into that infinite sin with which no other sins are comparable. Indeed, in order to ascertain how good His life was, we considered the magnitude of this sin not with respect to the fact that it was committed in ignorance but as if it were done knowingly — something which no one ever did or ever could have done.

B. You have shown rationally that the slayers of Christ were able to obtain pardon for their sin.

A. For what more do you now ask? Assuredly, you see how rational necessity shows that the Heavenly City is to be completed from among men and that this completion can be effected only through the forgiveness of sins — a forgiveness which no man can have except through a man who is himself God and who by his death will reconcile sinful men to God. Plainly, then, we have found Christ, whom we confess to be divine and human, and to have died for us. But now that we know this fact without any doubt, we also must not doubt the truth of all the things He says (since God cannot lie) and the wisdom of all the things He did (even though we may not understand the reason for them).

B. What you say is true. And I do not at all doubt that what He said is true or that what He did was done reasonably. But I have the following request: Disclose to me in what way there ought and can occur that thing whose occurrence unbelievers regard as unseemly or impossible in the Christian faith. Disclose this not in order to confirm me in faith but in order to make me, already so confirmed, joyful in the understanding of this truth.

Chapter Sixteen: How God assumed from the sinful mass a sinless human nature. The salvation of Adam and of Eve.

B. Therefore, just as you have disclosed the rationale of the points which have been stated above, so I ask you to disclose the rationale of the points about which I am still going to ask. First of all, how did God assume from the sinful mass — i.e., from the

Cur Deus Homo II

human race, which was completely contaminated with sin — a sinless human nature (as something unleavened from something leavened)? For although the conception of this man was clean and was free from the sin of carnal delight, nevertheless the virgin from whom He was assumed was conceived in iniquities, and her mother conceived her in sins; and this virgin was born with original sin, since she sinned in Adam, in whom all have sinned.[36]

A. Now that it has been established that that man is God and is the Reconciler of sinners, there is no doubt that He is completely sinless. However, this sinlessness is not possible unless He was assumed sinless from the sinful mass. But if we cannot comprehend in what way the wisdom of God accomplished this sinless assumption, we ought not to be astonished; rather, we ought reverently to tolerate the fact that within the mystery of so deep a matter there is something which we cannot know. Indeed, God has restored human nature in a more miraculous manner than He created it; for it is just as easy for Him to do the one as the other. Now, it is not the case that before human nature existed it sinned and, as a result, ought not to have been created. But after it was created, it did merit, through sinning, the loss of what it was created as being and of the end for which it was created. Nonetheless, in order that it would exist to be punished or to be the object of God's mercy (neither of which could occur if it were reduced to nothing), it did not completely lose what it was created as being. Therefore, God restored human nature so much more miraculously than He created it — inasmuch as He restored it from someone sinful and while it was undeserving, but created it neither from anyone sinful nor when it was undeserving. Moreover, how miraculous it is for the divine nature and a human nature so to conjoin in one [individual] that the integrity of each nature is preserved and the same [individual] who is divine is also human! Therefore, who would presume even to suppose that the human intellect would be able to discern how wisely and how miraculously so inscrutable a work was done?

B. I agree that in this life no man can completely disclose so deep a mystery. And I do not ask you to do what no man can do but to do only as much as you can. For you will be more persuasive that deeper reasons lie hidden in this matter if you show that you see some rationale in it than if, by saying nothing, you evidence that you discern none at all.

Anselm of Canterbury

A. I see that I cannot be free of your urging. But if to some extent I can demonstrate what you are asking, let us give thanks to God. However, if I cannot, let those points which have already been proved suffice. For since it has been established that God ought to become a man, there is no doubt that He did not lack the wisdom and the power to do this without sin.

B. I gladly accept this point.

A. Surely, it was fitting that the redemption made by Christ was beneficial not only to those who then existed but also to others as well. For suppose that the following were true:

> There is a king against whom all the inhabitants of one of his cities — except for one sole inhabitant, who is nevertheless of their race — so sinned that none of them is able to perform that [meritorious work] in virtue of which he would escape condemnation to death. But this inhabitant who alone is innocent has such great favor with the king that he is able — and has such great love for the guilty ones that he is willing — to bring about reconciliation for all who will trust in his plan. He will reconcile them by means of a service which will be especially pleasing to the king; and he will do this on the day determined in accord with the king's will. Now, not all who are to be reconciled are able to be present on that day. Therefore, because of the magnitude of this service, the king grants absolution from all past guilt to all those who either before or after that day acknowledge their desire both to obtain pardon on the basis of the work done on that day and to assent to the agreement then contracted. And [the king grants that] if they sin again after this pardon, they will be pardoned anew through the efficacy of this agreement, provided they are willing to make an acceptable satisfaction and thereafter to mend their ways. Nevertheless, [all of this occurs] in such way that no one may enter his palace until after the execution of the service on the basis of which his guilt is pardoned.

By comparison, since not all men who were to be saved were able to be present when Christ made that redemption, there was so much efficacy in His death that the effect of His death extends even to those who are absent in space and time. Moreover, from the following fact we easily recognize that His death ought not to be of benefit only to those then present: there could not have been present at His death as many [men] as are necessary for establishing the Heavenly City — even if all the men who existed everywhere at the time of His death were admitted to that redemption. For there are more evil angels than there were men (from whom the number of evil angels is to be restored) living on that day.

We must not believe that there was any time — from the point of man's creation — in which this present world with the creatures created for men's use was so empty that in it there was no member of the human race who shared in the end for which man was created. For it seems unfitting that God would even for a moment have permitted the human race (and those things which He created for the use of men, from among whom the Heavenly City is to be completed) to have existed in vain, so to speak. For to some extent these men would seem to exist in vain as long as they did not seem to exist for that end for which they were especially created.

B. By a fitting reason to which nothing seems opposed you show that there was never a time — from the point of man's creation — when no man at all shared in that reconciliation in whose absence every man would have been created in vain. We can conclude that this view is not only fitting but also necessary. For if this view is more fitting and more reasonable than the view that at some time there was no one concerning whom God's purpose in creating man was being accomplished, and if nothing opposes this reasoning, then necessarily there was always someone who shared in the aforementioned reconciliation. Hence, we must not doubt that Adam and Eve shared in that redemption, even though Divine Authority does not openly state this.

A. Moreover, since God created them and immutably planned to create from them all other men, whom He was going to take into the Heavenly City, it also seems incredible that He would exclude these two from His plan.

B. Indeed, we ought to believe that He created them especially for the following purpose: viz., that they would be in the company of those for whose sake they were created.

A. You are thinking correctly. Nevertheless, no soul was able to enter the heavenly paradise before the death of Christ, just as I stated above about the palace of the king.

B. We hold this belief.

A. But the virgin from whom that man (of whom we are speaking) was taken belonged to the class of those who through Him were cleansed from their sins before His birth; and He was taken from her in her purity.

B. What you say would please me greatly except for the fact that, although He ought to have His purity from sin from Himself, He would seem to have it from His mother and to be pure through her rather than through Himself.

A. It is not so. Rather, since His mother's purity (by means of which He is pure) came only from Him, He was also pure through Himself and from Himself.

B. You are right about this. But still another question must be raised, it seems to me. For earlier[37] we said that He was not going to die by *necessity*. And now we see that His mother was pure through His future death; and unless she had been pure, He would not have been able to exist from her. Why, then, is it not the case that He died of necessity, since He was able to exist only because He was going to die? For if He had not been going to die, the virgin from whom He was taken would not have been pure, since her purity could not at all have occurred except by her faith in His actual death; and He could not have been taken from her unless she were pure. Therefore, if He did not have to die after having been taken from the virgin, then it could have happened that He was not taken from the virgin after He had in fact been taken from her — something which is impossible.

A. If you had carefully considered what was said earlier, you would have recognized, I think, that the solution to this problem is already contained in those statements.[38]

B. I do not see how.

A. When we asked whether He could have told a lie, did we not show[39] that in the case of lying there are two abilities?: viz., an ability to will to lie and an ability to lie. And [did we not prove that] although He had the ability to lie, still since He had from Himself the fact that He could not will to lie, He must be praised for His justice, by which He kept the truth.

B. This is true.

A. Likewise in the case of preserving one's life: there is an ability to will to preserve it and an ability to preserve it. Therefore, when we are asked whether this God-man was able to preserve His life, so as never to die, we must not doubt that He always had the ability to preserve [His life], even though He was not able to will to preserve it so as never to die. And since He had from Himself the fact that He was not able to will [to preserve His life], He laid down His life not by necessity but by free ability.

B. The ability to tell a lie and the ability to preserve His life were not completely similar in Him. For in the case of the former it follows that if He were to will to, He would be able to tell a lie; but in the case of the latter it seems that even if He had willed not to die, He would no more have been able to avoid dying than He would have been able not to be what He was. For the reason He was a man was in order to die; and on account of the virgin's faith in His future death He was able to be taken from her — as you have just said.

A. Even as you suppose that He was not able not to die (or that He died of necessity) because He was not able not to be what He was, so you can assert that He was not able to will not to die (or that of necessity He willed to die) since He was not able not to be what He was. For it is no more true that He became a man for the purpose of dying than [it is true that He became a man] for the purpose of willing to die. Therefore, just as you ought not to say that He was not able to will not to die (or that of necessity He willed to die), so we must not say that He was not able not to die (or that He died of necessity).

B. On the contrary. Since both of these — viz., to die and to will to die — are subject to the same rationale, they *both* seem to have been characteristic of Him by necessity.

A. Who [was it who] freely willed to become a man in order (by this same immutable will) to die, and in order that the virgin from whom that man was taken would be purified by faith in the certainty of His death?

B. God — i.e., the Son of God.

A. Was it not shown earlier[40] that when the will of God is said to do something of necessity, it is not really compelled by any necessity but instead maintains itself by its own free immutability?

B. Yes, this has been demonstrated. But we see, on the other hand, that what God immutably wills is not able not to occur but instead is necessary to occur. Therefore, if God willed for that man to die, He was not able not to die.

A. From the fact that with the intention of dying the Son of God assumed a human nature, you infer that that man was not able not to die.

B. This is the way I understand the matter.

A. Was it not also clear from what has already been said[41] that the Son of God and the assumed man are one person, so that the same [individual] is divine and human, Son of God and Son of the Virgin?

B. This is true.

A. Therefore, of His own volition that man died and was not able not to die.

B. I cannot deny it.

A. Therefore, since the will of God does not do anything of necessity but does everything of its own power, and since that man's will was God's will, He did not die of necessity but died only of His own power.

B. I cannot refute your arguments. For I cannot at all fault either the statements you premise or the inferences you draw. Nevertheless, the point I have made keeps occurring to me: viz., that even if He had willed not to die, He would no more have been able to avoid dying than [He would have been able] not to be what He was. For, indeed, it was true that He was going to die, because if it had not been true that He was going to die, then the faith in His future death would not have been true faith — through which faith both the virgin from whom He was born and many others as well were cleansed from sin. Now, if this faith had not been true faith, then it could not have been of any benefit.[42] Therefore, if He had been able not to die, He would have been able to cause not to be true what was true.

A. Before He died why was it true that He was going to die?

B. Because with an unchangeable will He freely willed to die.

A. Therefore, if, as you say, He was not able not to die because it was true that He was going to die, and if it was true that He was going to die because He freely and unalterably willed to die, then it follows that He was not able not to die only because He willed — with an unalterable will — to die.

B. This is correct. But whatever the cause was, it is nevertheless true that He was not able not to die (and that it was necessary that He die).

A. You are grasping at straws and, as the saying goes, are looking for a knot on a bulrush.[43]

B. Have you forgotten what I said at the beginning[44] of our discussion, in objection to your excuses?: viz., that what I was asking of you, you would do not for the learned but for me and for those making this request with me. Therefore, bear with the fact that I am raising questions commensurate with the slowness and dullness of our intellects, so that even in the case of our puerile questions you may continue to give satisfactory answers to myself and to these others — just as you did at the beginning.

Chapter Seventeen: In God there is neither necessity nor impossibility. There is a necessity which compels and a necessity which does not compel.

A. As I have already pointed out,[45] it is improper to say that God cannot do something or that He does something by necessity. Indeed, all necessity and impossibility are subject to His will; but His will is not subject to any necessity or to any impossibility. For a thing is necessary or impossible only because He wills it to be so; but it is far from being true that He wills or does not will some thing because of a necessity or an impossibility. Therefore, since He does (*facit*) all the things He wills and only the things He wills: just as no necessity or impossibility precedes His willing or not willing, so [no necessity or impossibility precedes] His doing or not doing, although He immutably wills and does many things. Moreover, when God causes (*facit*) something, then once it has happened it is no longer able not to have happened; instead, it is henceforth always true that it has happened. Nevertheless, it is not right to say that it is impossible for God to cause what is past not to be past; for in this case what is operative is not the necessity of not doing something or the impossibility of doing something but only the will of God, who, since He is the Truth, wills that the truth always be immutable, just as it *is* [always immutable]. Similarly, if God unalterably plans to do something in the future, then even though, prior to its occurrence, what He plans to do is not able not to occur in the future, nevertheless in Him there is not any necessity to do it or any impossibility not to do it, since in Him only the will accomplishes this. For whenever we say "God is not able," we are not denying His ability but are signifying His insuperable ability and power.[46] For nothing else is meant except that no thing can make Him do what He is said to be unable to do. (This kind of expression is often used; and so, frequently, the reason a thing is said to-be-able is not because there is any ability in it but because there is an ability in some other thing, and [the reason a thing is said] not-to-be-able is not because there is any inability in it but because there is an inability in some other thing.[47] For, in fact, we say "This man is able to be overcome" in place of "Someone is able to overcome this man"; and [we say] "That man is not able to be overcome" in place of "No one is able to overcome that man." For to be able to be overcome does not constitute an ability but constitutes an inability; and not to be able to be overcome does not constitute an inability but constitutes an ability.) And our reason for saying that God does something by necessity is not that there is some necessity in Him but that there is some necessity in some other thing — just as I said about His "inability," in a case where He is said not-to-be-able. Indeed, all necessity is either a compulsion or a prevention. These two kinds of necessity are mutually convertible contraries, just as are the necessary and the impossible. For whatever is compelled to be is prevented from not being; and what is compelled not to be is prevented from being — just as what is necessary to be is impossible not to be, and as what is necessary not to be is impossible to be (and conversely).[48] However, when in the case of God we say that something is necessary to be (or not to be) this statement does not mean that there is in Him a necessity which compels (or prevents); rather we mean that in all other things there is a necessity which prevents them from doing — and compels them not to do — anything contrary to that which is being [improperly] stated of God. For example, when we say "It is necessary that God always speak the truth" and "It is necessary that God never tell a lie," nothing else is meant except that in God the steadfastness for maintaining the truth is so great that it is necessary that no thing can cause Him not to speak the truth or can cause Him to tell a lie.[49]

Therefore, when we say that that man (who according to a unity of person, as was said above,[50] is identical with the Son of God and is Himself God) was not able not to die (or was not able to will not to die) after He was born from the virgin: we do not signify in Him any inability to keep (or any inability to will to keep) His immortal life. Rather, [we signify] the immutability of the will by which He freely became a man in order (while persevering in this will) to die; and [we signify] that no thing was able to change this will. For it would be an inability rather than an ability, if He were able to will to lie, or to will to deceive, or to will to change the decision which He previously willed to be immutable. Moreover, as I said earlier,[51] when someone freely plans to do a good deed and — subsequently and with this same willingness — does perform the deed he planned to, then even though if he were unwilling to keep his promise he could be compelled to do so, he ought not to be said to do by necessity that which he does. Rather, [he ought to be said to do it] by the free will in terms of which he set out to do it. For a thing ought not to be said to be done or not done by necessity or by inability in a case where the will — and not the necessity or the inability — performs something. Now, if this point holds for men, then it is much more the case that necessity and inability must not at all be ascribed to God, who does nothing except what He wills, and whose will is not able to be compelled or restrained by any force. In Christ the diversity of natures and the unity of person served the following end: If the human nature was not able to do what was required to be done for restoring men, then the divine nature would do it; and if [what was required] did not at all befit the divine nature, then the human nature would do it. And not two different [individuals] but one and the same [individual], existing perfectly in two natures, would pay through His human nature what this nature ought to pay and would be able through His divine nature to do what was required.[52] In fact, the virgin who was purified by faith in order that He could be taken from her, believed that He would die only because He would will to — just as she had learned from the prophet who said of Him: "He was offered because it was His own will."[53] Therefore, since her faith was true faith, it was necessary that the [object of her faith] would be as she believed [it would be]. But if you are once again disturbed by my saying "It was necessary. . . ," then remember that the truth of the virgin's faith was not the cause of His dying freely, but that her faith was true faith because He was going to die freely. Accordingly, if someone says "It was necessary that He die only of His own will because the faith (or because the prophecy) which preceded the event was true," then this amounts to nothing other than if you were to say: "It was necessary for it to be going to happen in this manner because it was going to happen in this manner." But this kind of necessity does not compel a state of affairs to occur; rather, the existence of the state of affairs causes the existence of the necessity.

For there is a necessity which precedes and is the cause of a thing's being the case; and there is a necessity which succeeds and is caused by the thing's being the case.[54] When the heavens are said to revolve because it is necessary for them to revolve, then this is a necessity which precedes and efficiently causes. But when I say that because you are speaking, you are — necessarily — speaking, this is a necessity which is subsequent and does not efficiently cause anything but, instead, is caused. For when I make this statement, I signify that nothing can cause it to be the case that while you are speaking you are not speaking; I do not signify that anything is compelling you to speak. For although the force of their natural state compels the heavens to revolve, no necessity causes you to speak. Now, wherever there is antecedent necessity there is also subsequent necessity; but it is not the case that where there is subsequent necessity there must be antecedent necessity. For example, we can say "Because the heavens are revolving, they are — necessarily — revolving"; but it is not also true that you are speaking because it is necessary for you to speak.[55]

Subsequent necessity applies to all tenses, in the following manner: Whatever has been, necessarily has been; whatever is, necessarily is and necessarily was going to be; whatever is going to be, necessarily is going to be. This is the necessity which (when Aristotle deals with singular and future propositions) seems to deny that there are real alternatives and to affirm that all things occur of necessity. Since the faith (or the prophecy) concerning Christ was true faith (or true prophecy) *because* He was going to die of His own will and not by necessity: it was necessary — in terms of the necessity which is subsequent and which does not efficiently cause anything — that His death would occur voluntarily. In terms of this necessity, He became a man; in terms of this necessity He did and suffered whatever He did and suffered; in terms of this necessity He willed whatever He willed. For because these things were going to occur, necessarily they did occur; and because they occurred, necessarily they were going to occur; and because they occurred, necessarily they occurred. And if you wish to know the true necessity of all the things He did and suffered, know that they all occurred of necessity simply because He willed them. However, no necessity preceded His willing. Therefore, if they occurred only because He willed them, then if He had not willed them they would not have

Cur Deus Homo II

occurred. Accordingly, then, no one took His life from Him, but He Himself laid it down and took it up again because He had "the power to lay down His life and to take it up again," as He says.[56]

B. You have satisfied me that He cannot be proved to have died because of any necessity; and I do not regret having urged you to make this investigation.

A. I have presented, it seems to me, a reliable account of how it is that God assumed a sinless human nature from the sinful mass. Nevertheless — aside from the consideration that God can do what human reason cannot comprehend — I think we ought not at all to deny that there is still another account [*ratio*] in addition to the one I have given. But the present rationale [*ratio*] seems to me to be able to suffice. Moreover, if I now wanted to investigate the other rationale it would be necessary to examine what original sin is and how from our first parents it is imparted unto the whole human race (except for that man of whom we are now speaking). And it would be necessary to touch upon some other issues which require a treatise of their own. Therefore, being content with the argument we have articulated, let us pursue what remains of the task we have begun.

B. As you will — but with the proviso that at some future time you fulfill your "obligation" [to expound], with God's help, the other rationale which you shun examining now.

A. Since I know that I have this willingness, I do not deny your request. But because I am uncertain about future events, I dare not make you a promise. Instead, I entrust the matter to the disposition of God.[57]

Chapter Eighteen: How the life of Christ is paid to God for the sins of men. The sense in which Christ ought, and the sense in which He ought not, to have suffered.

A. But tell me now what you think must still be resolved regarding the problem you set forth at the beginning — because of which problem many other topics intruded themselves.

B. The crux of the problem was why God became a man in order to save mankind through His death, although He was apparently able to accomplish man's salvation in some other way.[58]

Responding to this problem, you showed by many compelling reasons that the restoration of human nature ought not to be left undone, and yet could not be done unless man paid what he owed to God for his sin. This debt was so great that only God was able to pay it, although only a man ought to pay it; and, thus, the same [individual] who was divine was also human. Hence, it was necessary for God to assume a human nature into a unity of person, so that the one who with respect to his nature ought to make payment, but was unable to, would be the one who with respect to his person was able to. Next, you showed that that man who was God had to be taken from a virgin by the person of the Son of God; and you showed how He could be taken sinless from the sinful mass. You proved very clearly that the life of this man was so sublime and so precious that it can suffice to make payment for what is owed for the sins of the whole world — and even for infinitely more [sins than these]. Therefore, it now remains to show how His life is paid to God for the sins of men.

A. If He allowed Himself to be killed for the sake of justice, did He not give His life for the honor of God?

B. Even though I do not see how He could reasonably have done this — since He was able to keep justice unwaveringly and His life eternally — nevertheless, if I can understand a thing which I do not doubt, I will admit that He freely gave to God, for God's honor, some such gift to which whatever is not God is not comparable in value, and which can make recompense for all the debts of all men.

A. Do you not realize that when He endured with patient kindness the injuries, the abuses, the crucifixion among thieves — which were all inflicted upon Him (as I said above)[59] for the sake of the justice which He obediently kept — He gave men an example,[60] in order that they would not, on account of any detriments they can experience, turn aside from the justice they owe to God? He would not at all have given this example if, as He was able to do, He had turned aside from the death that was inflicted upon Him for such a reason.[61]

B. It seems that it was not necessary for Him to give this example, since we know that many people before His coming — and John the Baptist after His coming and before His death — sufficiently gave this example by bravely enduring death for the sake of the truth.

Cur Deus Homo II

A. Except for Him, no human being through his death ever gave to God what he was not necessarily going to lose at some time or other, or ever paid what he did not already owe. But that man freely offered to the Father what He was never going to lose as a result of any necessity; and He paid on behalf of sinners that which He did not already owe for Himself. Therefore, it is much more the case that He gave an example, in order that no single human being would hesitate (when reason demands it) to render to God on behalf of himself that which one day he will summarily lose. For although He did not at all need to do so for Himself, and although He was not at all compelled to do so for others to whom He owed only punishment, He gave with such great willingness so precious a life — indeed, His own self — i.e., so great a person.

B. You are coming very close to satisfying me. But bear with my asking a question which although you may think it foolish to ask, nevertheless I would not readily know what to answer if it were asked of me. You say that when He died, He gave what He was not obliged to.[62] But no one will deny that when He gave this example in such a way, He did something better (and that His doing it was more pleasing to God) than if He had not done it. And no one will say that He was not obliged to do what He understood to be better and to be more pleasing to God. Therefore, how can we maintain that He did not owe to God the deed He performed — i.e., the deed He knew to be better and to be more pleasing to God — especially since a creature owes to God all that he is, all that he knows, and all that he can do?

A. Although a creature has nothing from himself,[63] nevertheless when God grants him the right to do or not to do something, He gives him both prerogatives in such way that although the one alternative is the better, neither alternative is definitely required. Rather, whether he does what is the better or whether he does the alternative, we say that he ought to do what he does. And if he does what is the better, he should have a reward, because He voluntarily gives what belongs to him. For example,[64] although the state of virginity is better than the marital state, neither of these is definitely required of a man. Instead, we say both of him who prefers to marry and of him who prefers to keep his virginity that he ought to do what he does. For no one claims that virginity ought not to be chosen or that marriage ought not to be chosen.

Rather, we say that before a man has decided upon either of these, he ought to do the one which he prefers; and if he keeps his virginity, he looks forward to a reward for the voluntary gift which he offers to God. Therefore, when you say that a creature owes to God what he knows to be the better and what he is able to do, then if you mean "[He owes it] as a debt" and do not add "provided God commands it," [your claim] is not in every case true. For, indeed, as I said, a man does not owe virginity as a debt; but if he prefers, he ought to marry.

Now, perhaps the word "ought"[65] troubles you, and perhaps you cannot understand it apart from [its signifying] a debt. If so, then be aware that just as *ability* and *inability* and *necessity* are sometimes ascribed not because they are in the things to which they are ascribed but because they are in something else,[66] so it also happens in the case of *ought to*. Indeed, when we say that the poor *ought* to receive alms from the rich, this statement means nothing other than that the rich ought to give alms to the poor. For this obligation ought to be exacted not of the poor but of the rich. We also say that God *ought* to rule over all things — not because He at all owes anything but because all things ought to be subject to Him.[67] And [we say that God] ought to do what He wills, since what He wills ought to occur. Likewise, when a creature wills to do what it is his prerogative to do or not to do, we say that he ought to do it, since what he wills ought to occur. Hence, when the Lord Jesus, as I said,[68] willed to endure death: since it was His prerogative to undergo death or not to undergo death, He *ought* to have done what He did, because what He willed ought to have been done; and He *ought not* to have done it, because [He was] not [obliged to do it] out of debt.[69]

Assuredly, the Lord Jesus was divine and human. Therefore, in accordance with His human nature (from the time that He was a man) He so received from His divine nature (which is different from His human nature) to have as His prerogative whatever-He-had that He was not obliged to give anything except what He willed to. And in accordance with His person He so possessed from Himself what He possessed, and was so completely sufficient unto Himself, that He was not obliged to make any recompense to anyone else and did not need to give anything in order to be recompensed.

B. I now see clearly that it was not in any respect out of debt that He gave Himself over to death for the honor of God (as my argument seemed to show), and that nevertheless He ought to have done what He did.

A. Surely, that honor belongs to the whole Trinity. Therefore, since He Himself is God — viz., the Son of God — He offered Himself to Himself (just as to the Father and the Holy Spirit) for His own honor. That is, [He offered] His humanity to His divinity, which is one and the same divinity common to the three persons. Nevertheless, in order to say more clearly what we mean, while still abiding within this truth, let us say (as is the custom) that the Son freely offered Himself to the Father. For in this way we speak most fittingly. For by reference to one person [viz., the Father] we understand it to be God as a whole to whom the Son offered Himself according to His humanity; and through the name "Father" and the name "Son," an enormous devotion is felt in the hearts of those listening when the Son is said to entreat the Father for us in this way.

B. I accept this most gladly.

Chapter Nineteen: How very reasonable it is that human salvation results from his death.[70]

A. Let us see now, as best we can, how very reasonable it is that human salvation results from His death.

B. My mind strives toward this end. Now, although I think that I understand this point, I want you to produce the structure of the argument.

A. It is not necessary to discuss how great is the gift which the Son freely gave.

B. This is [already] sufficiently clear.[71]

A. But you will not suppose that he who freely gives to God so great a gift ought to go unrewarded.

B. On the contrary, I recognize that it is necessary for the Father to reward the Son. Otherwise, the Father would seem to be either unjust, if he were unwilling [to give a reward], or powerless, if He were unable [to give a reward]. And both of these features are foreign to God.

A. One who rewards another either gives what the other does not already have or else remits what can be exacted from the other. Now, even before the Son performed so great a deed, everything that was the Father's was also the Son's;[72] and the Son never owed anything that could be remitted. Therefore, what will be recompensed to one who needs nothing and to whom there is nothing that can be given or remitted?

B. On the one hand, I see the necessity for giving a reward — and, on the other, the impossibility thereof. For it is necessary that God pay what He owes; but there is not anything which He can pay.

A. If so great and so deserved a reward were not paid either to the Son or to someone else, then the Son would seem to have performed so great a deed in vain.

B. This is heinous to suppose.

A. Therefore, it is necessary that a reward be paid to someone else, since it cannot be paid to Him.

B. This follows inescapably.

A. If the Son wanted to give to someone else that which is owed to Himself, would the Father rightly be able either to prevent Him or to withhold the reward from the one to whom the Son would give it?

B. Indeed, I think it both just and necessary that the reward be paid by the Father to the one to whom the Son wanted to give it. For the Son is permitted to bestow what is His own; and only to someone other than to the Son can the Father pay what He owes.

A. To whom will the Son more fittingly give the fruit and the recompense of His death than to those for whose salvation He became a man (as sound reasoning has taught us), and to whom (as we said),[73] by dying, He gave an example of dying-for-the-sake-of-justice? Surely, they would imitate Him in vain if they would not share in His merit. Or whom will He more justly make to be heirs of the reward He does not need, and heirs of His overflowing fulness, than His own kinsmen and brethren (whom — bound by such numerous and great debts — He sees languishing with need in the depth of miseries), so that what they owe for their sins may be forgiven them and what they lack on account of their sins may be given to them?

B. The world can hear of nothing more reasonable, nothing more kind, nothing more desirable. Indeed, I receive so much confidence from this thought that right now I cannot say with how much joy my heart exults. For it seems to me that God rejects no human being who approaches Him under this name.

A. This is true — provided he approaches as he ought. Sacred Scripture everywhere teaches us how we are to approach the participation in such great grace and how we are to live under this grace. Sacred Scripture is founded upon the solid truth, as upon a firm foundation; and with God's help we have perceived this truth to some extent.

B. Truly, whatever is erected upon this foundation is established upon a solid rock.[74]

A. I think that I have now to some extent satisfactorily answered your question — even though someone better than I can do this more fully, and even though the reasons for this matter are deeper and more numerous than my intelligence (or any mortal's intelligence) can comprehend. It is also clear that God did not at all need to do what we have been discussing; rather the immutable truth required it. For although on account of a unity of person God is said to have done the thing which that man did, nevertheless God did not need to come down from Heaven in order to overcome the Devil. And [God did not need] to act against the Devil by means of justice in order to free man. Rather, God demanded of man that he overcome the Devil and that, having offended God by his sin, he make satisfaction by his justice. Indeed, God did not owe anything to the Devil except punishment; and man did not [owe the Devil anything] except to conquer him in return for having been conquered by him. But man owed to God, not to the Devil, whatever was required of him.[75]

Chapter Twenty: How great and how just the mercy of God is.

A. We have discovered that God's mercy — which, when we were examining God's justice and man's sin, seemed to you to perish — is so great and so harmonious with His justice that it cannot be conceived to be greater or more just. Indeed, what can be thought to be more merciful than for God the Father to say to a sinner, condemned to eternal torments and having no way to redeem himself: "Receive my only begotten son and render him in place of yourself," and for the Son to say "Take me and redeem yourself' "? For the Father and the Son do make these respective statements, as it were, when they call and draw us to the Christian faith. And what is more just than that He to whom is given a reward greater than every debt should forgive every debt if it is presented to Him with due affection?[76]

Chapter Twenty-one: It is impossible for the Devil to be reconciled.

A. But if you will carefully consider human reconciliation, then you will understand that the reconciliation of the Devil (about which you asked)[77] is impossible. For man was not able to be reconciled except through a God-man[78] who could die and by whose justice there would be restored to God what He had lost by man's sin. Similarly, condemned angels cannot be saved except through a God-angel[79] who could die and who by his justice would restore to God what the sins of the other angels took away from Him. Moreover, even as man ought not to have been lifted up through another man who would not be of the same race (even though he would be of the same nature), so no angel ought to be saved through another angel (even though all angels are of one nature), since angels are not — as men are — of the same race. For it is not the case that all angels are descended from one angel as all human beings are descended from one human being.

Furthermore, the restoration of angels is prevented by the fact that as they fell without anyone's abetting their fall, so they ought to rise without anyone's assistance. (But this is impossible for them.) For otherwise[80] they cannot be restored to the dignity which they were going to have; for if they had not sinned they would without anyone else's assistance have remained standing in the truth by means of the ability they had received. Therefore, if anyone thinks that our Savior's redemption ought eventually to be extended even to fallen angels, reason proves that he is deceived by what is unreasonable. I say this not because the value of His death would not outweigh, by its magnitude, all the sins of men and angels, but because an immutable reason opposes the elevation of lost angels.

Cur Deus Homo II

Chapter Twenty-two: The truth of the Old and of the New Testament has been proved within the statements that have been made.

B. All the statements you make seem to me to be reasonable and to be statements which cannot at all be contradicted. And I recognize that whatever is contained in the Old and in the New Testament has been proved by the solution of the single problem which we have set forth. For you prove the necessity of God's becoming a man, and you do so in such way that even if the few things you have introduced from our books are removed (e.g., what you mentioned about[81] the three persons of God and about[82] Adam), you would satisfy not only the Jews but also the pagans by reason alone. Moreover, this very God-man has established the New Testament and confirmed the Old. Therefore, just as it is necessary to affirm that He was truthful, so no one can deny the truth of anything contained in these testaments.[83]

A. If we have said anything which ought to be corrected, I do not refuse correction if it is done in accordance with reason. But if that which we think we have rationally discovered is corroborated by truth's testimony, we ought to attribute this not to ourselves but to God, who is blessed forever. Amen.

THE VIRGIN CONCEPTION
AND ORIGINAL SIN
(De Conceptu Virginali et Originali Peccato)

CHAPTER TITLES

1. What original and personal justice, and original and personal injustice, are.
2. How human nature was corrupted.
3. Sin is present only in a rational will.
4. Except for justice or injustice nothing is just or unjust in itself; and nothing is punished except the will.
5. The evil which is identical with sin or injustice is nothing.
6. Nevertheless, when God punishes for sin, He does not punish for nothing.
7. How the seed of man is said to be unclean and to be conceived in sins, even though there is no sin in it.
8. In the seed taken from the Virgin there is neither sin nor the necessity for future sin.
9. Why the sin by which the human race is condemned is imputed to Adam rather than to Eve, even though he sinned after her and because of her.
10. Why men who were not conscious of Adam's sin are nonetheless weighed down by it.
11. Propagation from the Virgin is not subject to the law and merits of natural propagation. There are three orders of events.
12. It would not be right for Adam's evils to be transmitted to that man.
13. Even if [that man] were not God but were a mere man, still it would be necessary that he be like the first man was created to be.
14. Its being written that men are conceived from unclean seed and in iniquities does not oppose our proposed argument, even though these texts properly apply to some cases.
15. How the sinful mass is not sinful as a whole.
16. Why John [the Baptist] and others who were likewise conceived miraculously are not originally free from sin.

De Conceptu Virginali

17. Why God became incarnate even though He was able to make from Adam as many sinless and nondivine beings as was sufficient [to complete the Heavenly City].
18. God was conceived from a *just* virgin — not out of necessity, as if He could not be conceived from a sinful virgin, but rather because such a conception was fitting.
19. How the argument here and the one given there are alike, and how they differ.
20. He who was born of the Virgin had original justice in place of original sin.
21. Why He could not have had personal injustice.
22. The magnitude of original sin.
23. Why and how [sin] is transmitted to infants.
24. The sins of ancestors after Adam are not reckoned in the original sin of their descendants.
25. How [the sins of ancestors] harm the souls of their [descendants].
26. How, nevertheless, everyone bears his own sin, not the sin of his father.
27. What original sin is. It is equal in all [human beings].
28. Against those who think that infants ought not to be condemned.
29. How the inability to have justice excuses infants after their baptism.

THE VIRGIN CONCEPTION AND ORIGINAL SIN[1]
(De Conceptu Virginali et de Originali Peccato)

Although if I am able to I wish on all matters to accommodate your religious desire, brother and most beloved son Boso, I certainly count myself especially indebted [to do so] when I understand that this desire is aroused in you by me. For I am certain that upon your reading in the book *Why God Became a Man* (which you more than the others urged me to write, and in which I have cast you in the role of my fellow-disputant) that, in addition to the rationale I offered there, another rationale[2] can be detected for how it was possible for God to assume a sinless human nature [*homo*] from the sinful mass of the human race, your alert mind comes to be greatly aroused to ask what this other rationale is. Accordingly, I fear that I may seem to you unjust if I conceal from you, my dear friend, what thoughts I have on this subject. Therefore, I shall briefly state my view in such way as neither to condemn the faithful opinion of anyone else regarding this matter nor stubbornly to defend my own opinion if it can be rationally proven to oppose the truth. Nevertheless, I still think that the account of this which I presented in that same small work[3] is altogether valid and adequate if it is carefully examined. Indeed, nothing prevents this matter from having more than one rationale, each of which can suffice by itself.

Chapter One: What original and personal justice, and original and personal injustice, are.

To see, then, how it was possible for God to assume from the sinful mass of the human race a sinless human nature, we must first inquire about original sin, because only this doctrine gives rise to the problem at hand. For if we see how Christ could not be subject to *original* sin, then it will be clear how the assumption or conception of this man was free from *all* sin.

Indeed, there is no doubt that the word "original" is derived from the word "origin." Hence, if original sin is present only in man, it seems to take its name either (1) from reference to the origin of human nature (i.e., from the beginning of human nature) — original in that this sin is contracted at human nature's origin — or else (2) from reference to the origin (i.e., to the beginning) of each person, because this sin is contracted at each person's origin. But this sin is seen not to stem from the beginning of human nature, since human nature's origin was *just*, for our first parents were created just and altogether sinless. Therefore, original sin seems to take the name "original" from reference to the origin of each human person. Yet, if anyone says that original sin is called original because of the fact that individuals acquire it from those from whom they received the origin of their *nature*, I will not object — provided he does not deny that original sin is contracted at the time of the origin of each *person*.

In each man are present together a *nature*, by which he is human, as are other men, and a *person*, by which he is distinguished from other men, as when he is called "this man" or "that man" or is called by his proper name (e.g., "Adam" or "Abel").[4] The sin of each man is in both his nature and his person; for example, the sin of Adam was in his humanity (i.e., in his nature) and in the one who was called Adam (i.e., in the person). Nevertheless, there is a sin which each man contracts together with his nature at the time of his origin, and there is a sin which he does not contract with his nature but which he commits after he is already a person distinct from other persons. Now, the sin which is contracted at the time of his origin is called original. (It can also be called natural — not because it comes from the essence of his nature but because it is received together with his nature because of the nature's corruption.) But the sin which each man commits after he is a person can be called personal, because it is committed through the fault of the person.

By similar reasoning justice can be called both original and personal. For indeed, Adam and Eve were *just* originally — i.e., at the time of their beginning, as soon as they existed as human

De Conceptu Virginali

beings and without any intervening time. But justice can be called personal when someone unjust receives the justice which he did not have at the time of his origin.

Chapter Two: How human nature was corrupted.

Therefore, if Adam and Eve had kept their original justice, those who were to be born of them would originally have been just, even as were Adam and Eve. But because Adam and Eve sinned personally — sinned even though originally they were strong and uncorrupted and had the ability always easily to keep justice — their whole being became weakened and corrupted. Indeed, the body [became weakened and corrupted] because after their sin it became like the bodies of brute animals, viz., subject to corruption and to carnal appetites. And the soul [became weakened and corrupted] because as a result of the bodily corruption and the carnal appetites, as well as on account of its need for the goods which it had lost, it became infected with carnal desires. And because the whole of human nature was in Adam and Eve, no part of it being outside of them, human nature as a whole was weakened and corrupted.[5]

Therefore, along with the corruption which human nature incurred as a result of sin, there remained in human nature both an obligation to have the perfect and pure justice it had received and an obligation to make satisfaction for having deserted justice.[6] Accordingly, even as human nature if it had not sinned would have been propagated in the same condition as it was created by God [viz., without corruption], so, having sinned, it is propagated in the condition it brought upon itself through sinning. Consequently, since human nature is unable[7] by itself either to make satisfaction for its sin or to recover its deserted justice, and since "the body which is corrupted burdens the soul"[8] (especially when the body is rather weak — e.g., in infancy or in the mother's womb), so that the soul cannot even understand justice, we see it to be necessary that in infants human nature is born with (1) the obligation to make satisfaction for the first sin, which it was able always to avoid, and with (2) the obligation to possess original justice, which it was able always to keep. Nor in the case of infants does human nature's inability excuse it for its failure in them to discharge its obligations. For human nature brought this inability upon itself by deserting justice in our first parents, in whom it was present as a whole, and it is always under obligation to have the ability that it received for the sake of always keeping justice. Original sin in infants can be seen to be this [condition of obligation and inability]. Let me also add thereto the sins of one's recent ancestors — sins that are reckoned "unto the third and the fourth generation."[9] For although it is possible to question whether or not all of these sins are to be understood as included in the notion of original sin, nevertheless so as not to seem to be minimizing the seriousness of original sin for the sake of the topic I am investigating,[10] I shall stipulate that original sin is so grave that no one can show it to be more so.

Chapter Three: Sin is present only in a rational will.

But whether original sin consists of all this[11] or whether it is something less, I think that original sin can in no way be asserted to be in an infant before he has a rational soul — even as justice [cannot be said] to have been in Adam before he became a rational man. Now, if while remaining sinless Adam and Eve had begotten offspring, justice would not and could not have been in the seed prior to the seed's having been formed into a living human being. Therefore, if the seed of a human being cannot admit of justice before becoming a human being, then the seed cannot be subject to original sin before becoming a human being.

Assuredly, we ought not to doubt that original sin is injustice. For if every sin is injustice and if original sin is a sin, then surely original sin is also injustice. But if someone says that not every sin is injustice, let him concede the possibility that a sin is present in someone while at the same time no injustice is there — a view seen to be preposterous. But what if someone says that original sin is not to be called a sin in an unqualified sense but is to be called a sin [only] in conjuction with the qualification "original" (just as a depicted man is not really a man but is a *depicted* man)? Then, to be sure, it would follow that (1) an infant who has no sin except original sin is free of sin, and (2) it is not the case that, among human beings, only the Son of the Virgin was without sin both in His mother's womb and when begotten of His mother,

De Conceptu Virginali

and (3) an infant who dies unbaptized and having no sin except original sin either is not condemned or else is condemned without sin. But we accept none of these consequences. Hence, every sin is injustice, and original sin is a sin in an unqualified sense. And from these two statements it follows that original sin is also injustice. Likewise, if God condemns a man only because of that man's injustice and if He condemns someone because of his original sin, then it follows that original sin is nothing other than injustice. But if this conclusion is true and if injustice is nothing other than the absence of required[12] justice (for injustice is seen to be only in a nature which does not have justice when it ought to), then assuredly [the concept of] original sin is included within the definition of "injustice."

But if justice is uprightness-of-will which is kept[13] for its own sake and if this uprightness can be present only in a rational nature, then it follows that even as no nature except a rational nature can admit of justice, so no nature except a rational nature ought to have justice. Therefore, since injustice can be present only where there ought to be justice, original sin — which is injustice — is present only in a rational nature. But only God, angels, and the human soul (by virtue of which a man is called rational, and without which he is not a man) are rational natures. Therefore since original sin is not present in God or in an angel, it is present only in the rational soul of a man.

We must also realize that if justice is uprightness-of-will kept for its own sake, then justice can be present only in a will. Therefore, injustice [can be only in a will]. For the absence of justice is called injustice only where justice ought to be. Thus, besides justice or injustice themselves, nothing is said to be just or unjust except either a will or else on account of a just or an unjust will. On account of the will we call a man or an angel just or unjust, and a soul or an action just or unjust.

Chapter Four: Except for justice or injustice nothing is just or unjust in itself; and nothing is punished except the will.

Considered in itself, not anything — whether it be a substance or an action or something else — is just except justice or is unjust, or a sin, except injustice. Not even the will, in which justice or injustice is present, [is just or unjust in itself]. For the power of soul by which the soul wills something and to which we give the name "will" is one thing. (This power can be called the instrument-for-willing, just as sight can be called the instrument-for-seeing.) And justice — by virtue of whose possession a will is called just, and by virtue of whose deprivation a will is called unjust — is another thing. The affections and uses of this instrument are also called wills; but it would take too long to elaborate these distinctions here.[14]

Considered in themselves, not even those appetites which the apostle calls both "the flesh which lusts against the spirit" and "the law of sin which is in our members, warring against the law of our mind"[15] are just or unjust. For they do not make just or unjust the man who experiences them; but they make unjust only the man who consents to them by an act of will when he ought not to. For the same apostle says, "There is no condemnation to those who are in Christ Jesus, who do not walk in accordance with the flesh" (Rom. 8:1) — i.e., who do not give consent-of-will to the flesh. Now, if these appetites were to make unjust the one who experienced them without consenting to them, then condemnation *would* result. Hence, it is not a sin to experience these appetites; rather, it is a sin to consent to them [when one ought not to]. For if in themselves these appetites were unjust, then every instance of consenting to them would be an instance when they caused the consenter to be unjust. But when irrational animals consent to them, they are not called unjust. Likewise, if the appetites were sins they would be removed at baptism, when every sin is washed away. But, clearly, this does not at all happen. Therefore, there is not any injustice in the essence of the appetites; rather, there is injustice in a rational will which complies inordinately with them. For when the will resists the appetites by "delighting in the law of God in accordance with the inner man,"[16] then the will is just. Now, the apostle calls the justice which the law commands both "the law of God," because it is from God, and "the law of the mind,"[17] because it is understood by means of the mind — just as the old law is called both "the law of God,"[18] because it is from God, and "the law of Moses,"[19] because it was delivered through Moses.

As for my having said that an action is called unjust not in itself

De Conceptu Virginali

but on account of an unjust will: the truth of this statement is evident in the case of those actions which can at times be done not unjustly — for example, killing a man (as did Phinehas)[20] or sexual intercourse (as within marriage or among irrational animals). However, the truth of my statement is not so easily recognized in the case of those actions which can never occur other than unjustly — for example, perjury and certain other things which ought not to be named.[21] Yet, consider a given action by which something is done — an action which exists only while that thing is being done and which upon completion of that thing passes away, so that it no longer exists. Or consider a work which is produced and which remains (for example, when we write what ought not to be written and the act of writing by which the letters are formed ceases but the letters themselves remain). Now, if the action were a sin, then when the action passed away so that it no longer existed, the sin would likewise pass away and no longer exist. Or if the work were a sin, then as long as the work [e.g., the letters] remained, the sin would not be removed. But we often see cases in which sins are not removed even though the action ceases, as well as cases in which sins are removed even though the work remains. Therefore, neither the action (which passes away) nor the work (which remains) is ever [in itself] a sin.

In fact, if the members and the senses are reproved for the voluntary actions which are unjustly done, the members and the senses by which they are done can reply: "God subjected us and the power that is in us to the will, so that in accordance with its command we cannot keep from moving ourselves and from doing what it wills. Indeed, the will moves us as its instruments, and *it* does the deeds which we seem to do. We cannot resist it by our own power, nor can the works that it does be prevented. Neither ought we nor can we disobey the master whom God has given us. When we obey this master, we are obeying God, who gave us this law." Therefore, what sin is committed by the members or the senses or their works — all of which God thus subjected to the will — if they conform to God's ordinance for them? Hence, whatever they do must be completely imputed to the will.

Since what I have just said is true, someone may possibly wonder why the members and the senses are punished for the will's fault. But in fact they are not punished for it, since only the will is punished. For only what is against one's will is for him a

Anselm of Canterbury

punishment;[22] and only something with a will experiences punishment. Now, the members and the senses will nothing by themselves. Therefore, just as the will acts in the members and the senses, so in them it is tormented or delighted. If someone rejects this statement, let him realize that only the soul (to which the will belongs) experiences and acts in the members and the senses, and so only the soul is tormented or delighted in them. However, we are accustomed to call the actions done by an unjust will sins, because in the will by which these actions are done sin is present. Now, to certain actions we give names which signify that the actions are done unjustly — e.g., the names "fornication" and "lying." Still, when we consider the action or the utterance, we understand one thing; and when we consider whether the action or the utterance is done justly or unjustly, we understand another thing.

Finally, every being comes from God, from whom there is nothing unjust.[23] Therefore, in itself no being is unjust.

Chapter Five: The evil which is identical with sin or injustice is nothing.

Injustice, however, is nothing at all, even as is blindness. For blindness is nothing other than the absence of sight where sight ought to be; and it is no more the case that this absence is something in an eye, where sight ought to be, than it is in a piece of wood, where sight ought not to be. For injustice is not the kind of thing which infects and corrupts the soul in the way that poison infects and corrupts the body; nor does it do something in the way that happens when a wicked man does evil deeds. When a savage beast breaks its bonds and rages about wildly, and when a ship — if the helmsman leaves the rudder and delivers the vessel to the wind and the waves — strays and is driven into dangers of one kind or another, we say that the absence of chains or of a rudder causes these events.[24] [We say this] not because their absence is something or does something but because if they had been present they would have caused the wild animal not to rage and the ship not to perish. By comparison, when an evil man rages and is driven into various evil deeds, which are a danger to his soul, we

De Conceptu Virginali

say that injustice causes these deeds.[25] [We say this] not because injustice is a being or does something but because the will (to which all the voluntary movements of the entire man are submitted), lacking justice, driven on by various appetites, being inconstant, unrestrained, and uncontrolled, plunges itself and everything under its control into manifold evils — all of which justice, had it been present, would have prevented from happening.

From these considerations, then, we easily recognize that injustice has no being, even though we are accustomed to give the name "injustice" to an unjust will's affections and acts, which, considered in themselves, are something. By this line of reasoning we understand evil to be nothing. For even as injustice is only the absence of required justice, so evil is only the absence of required good. But no being — even if it is called evil — is nothing; and for it to be evil is not the same thing as for it to be something. Indeed, for any being to be evil is simply for it to lack the good which it ought to have. But to lack the good which ought to be present is not the same as to be something. Therefore, for any being to be evil is not the same thing as for it to be something.

I have been briefly discussing an evil (viz., injustice) which without doubt is always nothing. But detriment is an evil (and hence things detrimental are called evil) which sometimes is nothing, as in the case of blindness and deafness, but which sometimes is seen to be something, as in the case of pain and grief.[26] However, in the discourse I wrote on *The Fall of the Devil* I have shown[27] adequately, it seems to me, that justice is uprightness-of-will kept for its own sake, that injustice is only the absence of required justice and has no being, and, furthermore, that every being is from God and that only good is from God. [I have discussed the notion of] justice more fully in the discourse I wrote *On Truth*.[28]

Chapter Six: Nevertheless, when God punishes for sin, He does not punish for nothing.

Certain people, when they hear that sin is nothing, are accustomed to ask: "If sin is nothing, then why does God punish a man

Anselm of Canterbury

for sin? — for no one should be punished for nothing." Although this is a lowly question, some answer must be briefly given to these people, because they do not know what they are asking.

Although the absence of justice is nothing both where justice ought to be and, alike, where it ought not to be, nevertheless God rightly punishes sinners for something and not for nothing. For, as I stated in the aforementioned book, God exacts from sinners against their wills the honor due Him which they were unwilling to pay freely,[29] and He separates them from the just by an appropriate arrangement, so that there is nothing disordered[30] in His kingdom. However, God does not punish for their lack of justice — i.e., for nothing — creatures in whom justice ought not to be; for there is not anything that He demands from them, and the fitting order of the universe does not require this punishment. So, then, when God punishes for sin, which is the absence of required justice — an absence which is nothing — He does not at all punish for nothing. And it is true that unless there is something because of which God ought to punish, He does not at all punish for nothing.

Chapter Seven: How the seed of man is said to be unclean and to be conceived in sins, even though there is no sin in it.

From the things already said it is now clear, I believe, that sin and injustice are nothing, that they are present only in a rational will, and that no being except a will is properly called unjust. Hence, an alternative seems to follow: Either from the very moment of his conception an infant has a rational soul (without which he cannot have a rational will), or else at the moment of his conception he has no original sin. But no human intellect accepts the view that an infant has a rational soul from the moment of his conception. For [from this view] it would follow that whenever — even at the very moment of reception — the human seed which was received perished before attaining a human form, the [alleged] human soul in this seed would be condemned, since it would not be reconciled through Christ — a consequence which is utterly absurd. Thus, this half of the alternative must be completely excluded. But if an infant does not have sin from the

De Conceptu Virginali

moment of his conception, then why does Job inquire of God: "Who can make him clean who was conceived from unclean seed? Is it not You, who alone are?"[31] And how is what David says true?: "I was conceived in iniquities, and in sins did my mother conceive me."[32] Therefore, if I am able I shall inquire as to how it is that infants — in spite of the fact that sin is not in them at the very moment of their conception — are said to be conceived from unclean seed and in iniquities and sins.

Indeed, often something not the case is asserted by Divine Scripture to be the case simply because its future occurrence is certain. Thus, in fact, God says to Adam regarding the forbidden tree: "On whatsoever day you shall eat of it, you shall surely die."[33] [God said this] not because on that day Adam was going to die bodily, but because on that day he was going to be placed under the necessity of someday dying. Similarly, because of the necessity of someday dying, Paul says: "If Christ is in you, however, the body is indeed dead because of sin, but the spirit is alive because of justification."[34] Now, the bodies of those to whom he was speaking were not dead; but they were going to die as a result of sin, because "by one man sin entered into this world, and as a result of sin [came] death."[35] Thus, when Adam sinned, we all sinned in him — not because at that time we ourselves who did not yet exist sinned, but because we were going to exist from Adam and because at the time of his sin there was produced the necessity that we would sin when we existed, since "through one man's disobedience many were made to be sinners."[36]

We can understand in a similar manner [the statement] that a man is conceived from unclean seed and in iniquities and sins — i.e., not in the sense that in the seed there is iniquity or sin or the uncleanness of sin, but in the sense that from the seed and from the conception from which a man begins to exist he receives the necessity that when he comes to possess a rational soul, he will have the uncleanness-of-sin, which is nothing other than sin and iniquity. For even if an infant be begotten by a corrupt concupiscence, there is no more fault in the seed than there is in the spittle or the blood should someone malevolently expectorate or malevolently shed some of his own blood. For what is at fault is not the spittle or the blood but the evil will. Therefore, it is clear both how there is no sin in infants from the moment of their conception and how those statements I adduced from Divine Scripture are true. Indeed, there is no sin in those infants, for they do not have a will, which is a necessary condition for the presence of sin. Nevertheless, sin is said to be in them, since in the seed they contract the necessity of sinning at the time when they will become human beings.

Chapter Eight: In the seed taken from the Virgin there is neither sin nor the necessity for future sin.

So if these conclusions are true, as I think they are, then because that which is taken into an offspring from a parent has no will, it has no sin. Hence, it is clear that the stain of sin could not at all have been present in that which the Son of God took into His own person from the Virgin. But I stated[37] that the seed contracted from parents is contracted with the necessity for sin at that future time when the seed will be enlivened by a rational soul. The only reasons for this necessity are the following: Human nature is born in infants, as I said,[38] with the obligation to make satisfaction for the sin of Adam and (in accordance with what I supposed)[39] of recent ancestors; but it cannot at all make this satisfaction, and as long as it does not do so it is sinning. Furthermore, human nature is not able by itself to reacquire the justice which it deserted; and the soul, which is burdened by the corrupted body,[40] is not able even to understand justice, which can be neither kept nor possessed without first being understood. Consequently, if the seed taken from the Virgin can be shown to be free of these constraints, we shall see clearly that it did not at all contract the necessity for sin.

If first we repel [from that seed] the necessity by which human nature seems to be obliged to make satisfaction for the sins of both its first and its recent ancestors, then because the assuming and the assumed natures are a unity of person, we can readily show that the following necessities are foreign to that seed: the necessity by which human nature is unable by itself to recover justice, and the necessity by which the corrupted body so burdens the soul that in the completely formed human being[41] the soul is unable without the assistance of grace to keep justice were it received, and in infants is unable even to understand justice.

De Conceptu Virginali

Now, if that seed can be understood to be free from the obligation of our first parents, then there will be no doubt about the fact that it incurs no obligation from its more recent ancestors. Therefore, with the help of God I will try to ascertain first of all how this point can be known, so that after I have established it, I will not have to go to much trouble to establish the other points.

Chapter Nine: Why the sin by which the human race is condemned is imputed to Adam rather than to Eve, even though he sinned after her and because of her.

To the above end, it seems to me especially necessary to ask why the sin by which the human race is condemned is more frequently and more particularly imputed to Adam rather than to Eve, even though Eve sinned before him and Adam sinned after her and because of her. For the apostle says: "But death reigned from Adam to Moses, even over those who did not sin according to the likeness of Adam's transgression."[42] There are also many other texts which are seen to incriminate Adam rather than Eve.

I think this imputation occurs because the whole of that union of two members is signified by the name of the principal member — just as we are accustomed to signify a whole by reference to one of its parts. Or else it occurs because even though Adam's rib was fashioned into a woman, still Adam and his rib together can be called Adam — just as we read that God "created them male and female and blessed them and on the day they were created called their name Adam."[43] Or it occurs because if Eve alone had sinned and Adam had not sinned, it would have been necessary only for Eve, and not for the whole human race, to be lost. For from Adam, in whom God had created the seed of all mankind, God was able to create another woman; and through her the plan[44] of God could have been brought to completion from Adam. For these same reasons I will refer to both of them by the name "Adam" except for times when it will be necessary to distinguish between them.

Chapter Ten: Why men who were not conscious of Adam's sin are nonetheless weighed down by it.

Indeed, every descendant of Adam is human by virtue of his creation and is Adam by virtue of his propagation and is a person by virtue of the individuation by which he is distinguished from others. Now, he has his humanity through Adam but not on account of Adam. For just as Adam did not make himself human, so he did not create in himself a reproductive nature; rather, God, who created him human, created this reproductive nature in him so that human beings might be propagated from him. But there is no doubt about why each of us is bound by the obligation we are discussing. The reason is not that each of us is human or that each of us is a person. For if each one were bound by this obligation because he is human or is a person, then it would have been necessary for Adam to have been bound by this obligation even before he sinned, since he was then both human and a person. But this consequence is utterly absurd. Hence, the remaining alternative is that each one is under this obligation only by virtue of the fact that he is Adam — yet, not simply by virtue of his being Adam, but rather by virtue of his being Adam the sinner. [For were it simply by virtue of being Adam], then, assuredly, it would follow that if Adam had never sinned, those propagated from him would nevertheless be born with this debt — an impious consequence.

It is not out of place to repeat here what I have already said,[45] viz., why because each man is propagated from Adam, each is weighed down by Adam's sin, or debt, even though not conscious of this sin. When God created Adam He created in him a reproductive nature which He subjected to Adam's power, so that Adam might use this nature in accordance with his will as long as he willed to be subject to God. For he would use it in accordance with a rational human will, not in accordance with irrational bestial pleasure. For even as it is proper to beasts to will nothing rationally, so it is proper to men to will nothing irrationally. Men ought always to will rationally, because Adam received and could always have kept the power to do so. Moreover, God gave Adam the following grace: Even as when without the operation of a

De Conceptu Virginali

reproductive nature or a creature's will God created Adam both rational and just together, so — provided Adam were not to sin — those whom Adam would beget through the operation of his will and reproductive nature would be *just* at the moment they had rational souls.

Indeed, the same reasoning which shows that rational nature was created just — reasoning which I developed in the aforementioned[46] short work — also proves that those who could have been propagated from sinless human nature would have to have had both justice and rationality alike. For, indeed, He who created the first man by means other than parental generation also creates those who are produced from the first man by means of the created reproductive nature. Hence, if there had been no prior sin, every man would have been both just and rational — even as was Adam. But since Adam was unwilling to be subject to the will of God, his reproductive nature, although not destroyed, was not subject to his will as it would have been had he not sinned. Moreover, he lost the grace which he was able to keep for those to be propagated from him; and all who are propagated by the operation of the nature that Adam had received are born obligated by his debt. Accordingly, since human nature (which as a whole was so present in Adam that none of it was present outside of him) dishonored God by uncoerced sinning and thus was unable to make satisfaction by itself, human nature lost the grace which it had received and which it was able always to keep for those to be propagated from it, and each time it is propagated by the bestowed reproductive nature, it contracts sin together with the accompanying penalty for sin.

Chapter Eleven: Propagation from the Virgin is not subject to the law and merits of natural propagation. There are three orders of events.

Now we must carefully consider whether or not this "inheritance," so to speak, of sin and of the penalty for sin is justly transmitted to the man propagated from Adam through the Virgin. It is certain, indeed, that Adam received a nature which reproduces itself only by means of a man and a woman together. For, indeed, it is not in human nature's power, and it is known to

Anselm of Canterbury

be impossible, that a man alone or a woman alone — simply by the working of his or her nature and will — could beget a human being. For just as the clay of the earth had not received a nature or a will by whose operation the first man would be produced from it (even though the clay was that from which the first man could be created by God), so it was not by the operation of human nature and the human will that a woman was made from a man's rib or that a man was made from a woman alone. Rather, God, by His own power and will, created one man from the clay, created another man from a woman alone, and created a woman from a man alone.

Now, although nothing happens except by the efficient or the permissive will of God, nevertheless (1) certain things are done by His power and will alone, (2) certain things are done by created nature, and (3) still other things are done by the will of the creature. But just as by itself created nature can do nothing except what it has received from the will of God, so by itself the creature's will can do nothing except what nature either assists in or concedes to.

(1) In the beginning, the will of God alone created the natures of things, giving to certain of them wills suitable to each, so that these natures and wills might accomplish their work in the course of things, doing so in accordance with that order which God prescribed for them. And the will of God continues to do many things when from these natures and wills it accomplishes what they themselves would not at all do in accordance with their appointed use and purpose. Indeed, it is the work of God's will alone when the sea offers to a people a dry path within itself, when the dead rise, when water is suddenly changed into wine, when the minds of men are taught by the Holy Spirit things which they did not know either by themselves or from another creature, when under the guidance of grace alone evil wills are converted from their evil impulses unto that which is beneficial, and when many other things are done which neither the creature nor the will of the creature would have done through its usual course of activity. (2) Nature draws what is heavy downward and what is light upward. Nature causes the earth to bring forth countless herbs and trees and causes these to bear fruit; sometimes nature does this by means of a [human] will that first plants and cultivates, and sometimes without the initial working of a will. And nature

De Conceptu Virginali

does many other things which we recognize more readily by witnessing than by being taught. (3) But things of the following kind are attributed to a will: traveling, building, writing, speaking, and similar things which only a will does.

Therefore, since careful examination shows that whatever occurs is done[47] either (1) by the will of God alone or (2) by nature in accordance with the power given to it by God or (3) by the will of a creature (and since things which are done neither by created nature nor by the will of a creature but solely by the will of God are always miracles), there appear to be three orders of events: viz., the miraculous, the natural, and the voluntary.

Indeed, the miraculous is not at all subject to the others or to their law but rules freely. Nor does it do violence to them when it is seen to oppose them; for they have nothing except what they have received from it, and it has given them nothing except what is subordinate to it. Therefore, since the propagation of a man from a virgin alone is neither natural nor voluntary but is miraculous (even as both the propagation which produced a woman from a man alone and the creation of a man from clay are miraculous), it is clear that this propagation is not at all subject to the laws and merits of propagation effected by both the will and nature, although separately. (For in this work the will does one thing and nature does another thing.) Nevertheless, Adam, [who was begotten] from no other human being, and Jesus, [who was begotten] from a woman alone, and Eve, [who was begotten] from a man alone, are all real human beings — just as any man or woman [who is begotten] from a man and a woman is a real human being. Now, every human being is either Adam or from Adam. But Eve is from Adam alone, and all others are from Adam and Eve. Now, since Mary, from whom alone Jesus is [begotten], is from Adam and Eve, Jesus must be from Adam and Eve. For in this way it was expedient that He who was going to redeem the human race would exist from, and be born from, the father and the mother of all [human beings].

Chapter Twelve: It would not be right for Adam's evils to be transmitted to that man.

So too, it is not difficult to understand why the Son of the Virgin is not subject to Adam's sin, or debt. For, indeed, Adam was created just — free from sin, its oft-mentioned debt, and its penalty. Moreover, he was created happy and with the ability always to keep the justice he had received. And by keeping justice he was able to keep that happiness and freedom[48] just mentioned. Accordingly, since he did not keep these goods for himself (although he was easily able always to do so), he removed[49] them from himself and subjected himself to their opposites. Thus, he became a servant of sin, or injustice, and of a debt he was unable to pay, and of an unhappiness consisting in the inability to recover the goods that had been lost. Therefore, just as he was able to remove from himself the goods which he had (and to bring upon himself the evils which he did not have) only by not keeping these goods for himself when he was able to, so he was able to remove these goods from another (and to bring evils upon another) only by not keeping these goods for him for whom he was able to keep them. Now, he was able to keep them only for those whose possibility of generation had been made subject to his will. Therefore, Adam could not transmit the aforementioned evils to any person (even though propagated from him) with respect to whose generation neither the reproductive nature given to Adam nor Adam's will accomplished or was able to accomplish anything. Therefore, it would be neither reasonable nor right for the aforesaid evils of Adam to be transmitted to the man conceived from the Virgin.

Chapter Thirteen: Even if [that man] were not God but were a mere man, still it would be necessary that he be like the first man was created to be.

Likewise, if with the pure gaze of reason we carefully examine the wise justice of God, we recognize that it would be utterly absurd for any necessity resulting from another's sin or debt or penalty to pass down to this man by way of that seed which is not produced or inseminated by any created nature, by any creature's will, or by any power given to anyone, but which God's own will alone separates from the Virgin in order by a new power to beget a man free of sin. [And this would hold true] even if the human nature were not assumed into the person of God but were made a

De Conceptu Virginali

mere man. Now, by means of the same reasoning which shows that God ought to have created Adam only just and unburdened by any debt or detriment, a rational mind recognizes clearly that the one whom God likewise begat by His own will and power ought not to be created already subjected to any evil. For it would be totally unbefitting to the omnipotent and wise goodness of God for God by His own will alone to create such a rational nature[50] from matter in which there is no sin. Anyone who does not understand this fact does not know what is unbefitting with respect to God. Therefore, even if God were thus to create a mere man (as I said), it would be necessary that he be endowed with no less justice and happiness than was Adam when he was first created.

Chapter Fourteen: Its being written that man is conceived from unclean seed and in iniquities does not oppose our proposed argument, even though these texts properly apply to some cases.

Now, I said[51] that in man's seed there is no sin before there is a rational soul, but that the seed can be called contaminated with sin and iniquity because of that future uncleanness when the seed will have developed into a completed human being. If anyone's mind fails to grasp my point and thinks that the seed is unclean in its conception — because of the fact that he reads: "Who can make him clean who is conceived from unclean seed?" and "I was conceived in iniquities, and in sins did my mother conceive me" (texts[52] which I have cited against myself) — I make no protracted effort here (because none is required of me) to get him to understand what he cannot comprehend. But I do ask him to attend to what I shall say briefly.

Assuredly, those who have written these texts meant them to be understood (1) of every man's seed or (2) only of that seed which is inseminated with the sense of pleasure that would have characterized only brute animals if man had not sinned. But if such great men meant these texts to apply to every man's seed, then they were maintaining that the seed taken from the Virgin herself was unclean — an impious belief. Hence, they were not writing these things about every man's seed. But if they were

Anselm of Canterbury

writing this about a man's seed in accordance with the second sense, then they wanted the texts to be understood only of that seed which is conceived with the aforementioned pleasure. But this sense does not at all oppose our argument, which asserts that the seed taken from the Virgin is clean, even though it is from the sinful mass.

Chapter Fifteen: How the sinful mass is not sinful as a whole.

Although a man is called blind, blindness is not in any part of him except in the eye, where sight ought to be; for blindness is not in the hand or in the foot. And when a man is called deaf, deafness is nowhere except in the ear. Similarly, even though the mass of the human race is called sinful, sin is not in any part of the human race except (as I have said)[53] in the will; and the seed is known not to have a will at the moment of human conception. Therefore, if the arguments given above are pondered, then since no true or seemingly true reasoning contradicts them, we can now freely conclude that no reason, no truth, and no understanding allows that anything pertaining to the sin of the sinful mass either could or should have affected the man who was conceived from the Virgin alone — even though He was assumed from the sinful mass and even were He not God.

Chapter Sixteen: Why John [the Baptist] and others who were likewise conceived miraculously are not originally free from sin.

But suppose that I am referred to John the Baptist and to others who were propagated from sterile parents and from parents in whom the reproductive nature was dead even before old age. And suppose that on account of an argument similar, as it were, to mine someone thinks that because these individuals were conceived miraculously they ought to have been born without sin and the penalty for sin. Assuredly, the argument which shows that the virgin conception was free from all necessity for sin must be understood to be completely irrelevant to the case of these individuals. For it is one thing to do something new and unexpected

De Conceptu Virginali

and unprecedented within nature; and it is another thing to heal a nature enfeebled by either old age or some defect and to recall it to its proper working. Now, if Adam had not sinned, then just as he would have remained unweakened by old age and by any infirmity, so the reproductive nature which had been created in him and (as I have already said)[54] placed in his power to use would not have been impeded from its natural course by any fall. Therefore, in the case of John and the others like him there is not something new given to Adamic nature, as there is in the case of the Son of the Virgin; in their case what was weakened by natural causes is known to have been restored. Therefore, since these individuals were begotten by means of the reproductive nature given to Adam, they neither can be nor ought to be at all likened — with respect to the miracle of conception, and in such way that they can be shown to be free from the bond of original sin — to Him of whom we are discoursing.

Chapter Seventeen: Why God became incarnate even though He was able to make from Adam as many sinless and nondivine beings as was sufficient [to complete the Heavenly City].

Perhaps someone will ask: "If, as you maintain, someone who was merely human without being also divine could have been made from Adam without any taint of sin, then why was it necessary that God be incarnated? For either God was able to redeem sinners through one such man who was without any sin, or else by a similar miracle God was able to create as many men as were necessary to complete the Heavenly City."

To this question I give the following brief response. God became a man because a man who was not God would not be able to redeem other men, as I have shown[55] in that oft-mentioned short work. Moreover, He did not create as many such men as were necessary, lest, if none of Adam's natural progeny would be saved, God would appear to have created Adam's reproductive nature in vain and to have corrected, so to speak, what He had created imperfectly. And it does not befit Supreme Wisdom to do this with regard to any nature.

A little ways back[56] I proposed to investigate how the seed taken from the Virgin — seed in which there was shown to be no sin — could be understood to be free from the aforesaid necessities in which I supposed all other men to be conceived. I was confident that if first of all the necessity for sin and the necessity of [having] the debt of Adam and of recent ancestors would be rationally excluded from that seed, then because that man was God His seed could be freed from the necessity by which human nature is unable by itself to recover the justice it has deserted, and from the necessity by which the "corrupted body burdens the soul,"[57] especially in the case of infants. Thus, I began by asking how that seed could be understood to be free from the necessity for sin and the necessity of [having] Adam's debt,[58] so that afterwards the answer I was seeking would be easier to ascertain with respect to the other necessities. And by the abundant grace of that man the sinlessness of whose conception we are discussing, the following result occurred: Not only was He recognized to be free from all sin and debt and from the aforementioned necessities, but in addition we even proved rationally that a man thus conceived — even were He not God but a mere man — ought to be endowed with no less justice and happiness than was characteristic of the state in which Adam was created. For, indeed, both of the following suppositions were seen to be equally unreasonable: (1) By means of such a propagation sin or the penalty for sin descends from any ancestors down to that man; and (2) God freely creates a rational nature unjust, or creates it unhappy when it does not merit unhappiness by virtue of being unjust.

Chapter Eighteen: God was conceived from a *just* virgin — not out of necessity, as if He could not be conceived from a sinful virgin, but rather because such a conception was fitting.

Although, then, the Son of God was most truly conceived from a most pure virgin, this was done not of necessity, as if it were rationally impossible for a just offspring to be begotten from a sinful parent by this kind of propagation. But [it was done] because it was fitting that the conception of that man be accomplished from a most pure mother. Assuredly, it was fitting that the

De Conceptu Virginali

Virgin be beautified with a purity than which a greater cannot be conceived, except for God's. For, toward her, God the Father was so disposed to give His only Son — whom He begot as equal with Himself and whom from His own heart He loved as Himself — that the Son was naturally one and the same common Son of God the Father and of the Virgin. And she was the one whom the Son chose to make substantially His mother. And with respect to her the Holy Spirit willed, and from her He was going to accomplish, that the very one from whom He Himself proceeded would be conceived and begotten. Now, I have already spoken[59] of how the Virgin was cleansed by faith before this conception; but there I presented a different argument concerning the topic being discussed here.

Chapter Nineteen: How the argument here and the one given there[60] are alike, and how they differ.

As I see it, either of these two arguments is sufficient by itself for [settling] the present question; but jointly they fully satisfy a mind that is seeking both rigor of reasoning and fittingness of action. Moreover, although the two arguments move toward the same conclusion, nevertheless they differ in the following respect: The one which I have here presented shows (without being contradicted by any other considerations) that since sin is nowhere in man's nature except in the will, by such a propagation God ought to produce even from the substance of a sinful virgin a just offspring (indeed, only a just offspring); but the other argument proves that even if sin were in the entire being of the Virgin, nevertheless (regarding the purity of such a conception) her entire being was able to be purified by faith. Moreover, in the present argument all necessity of death and of any kind of travail or corruption is clearly excluded from that man, whereas in the other argument a question about these is seen to arise, but is settled by sufficient reasoning, as careful examination will reveal. Therefore, from both arguments it is evident that in all the things that our Lord and Redeemer suffered, He endured everything only by His gracious will.

Chapter Twenty: He who was born of the Virgin had original justice in place of original sin.

Now, regarding original sin, I think that I have adequately shown, just as I proposed to, how this sin could not in any respect be passed down from His ancestors to the man conceived from the Virgin, but how, instead, He ought to have been made just and happy, as reason requires. Therefore, since He was born from a just Father with respect to His divine nature and from a just mother with respect to His human nature — being just from the time of His very "origin," so to speak — it is not unfitting that He should be said to have original justice in place of the original injustice which all other sons of Adam have from the time of their origin.

Chapter Twenty-one: Why He could not have had personal injustice.

But since a human nature was always in Him concomitantly with the divine nature, and since His soul was never against His will burdened or at all hindered by a corruptible body, it is superfluous to argue the point that personal injustice did not touch Him. Since that soul — or, rather, since that whole man, who is Word of God and God — always existed as one person, He was never without perfect justice, wisdom, and power, all of which He always had from Himself in accordance with His person as God, even though with regard to His natures what His human nature had it received from His divine nature.

I do not deny that in addition to the argument presented here and the other one presented elsewhere there may be some other deeper rationale for how it was possible for God to assume a sinless human nature from the sinful mass, as something unleavened is taken from something leavened. If this other rationale is shown to me, I will gladly accept it; and if my accounts can be shown to be opposed to the truth — which I do not think they can be — I will abandon them.

De Conceptu Virginali

Chapter Twenty-two: The magnitude of original sin.

Furthermore, original sin can be neither more nor less than I said it is,[61] because as soon as an infant becomes rational the human nature in him lacks the justice which it received in Adam and which it ought always to possess; nor does human nature's inability excuse its not having justice, as I stated above.[62] Nevertheless, I think that original sin is not altogether as grave as I assumed earlier.[63] Since I wanted to show that original sin does not pertain to a man conceived from a virgin, I stipulated it to be so grave that nothing more could be added to it. [I made this assumption] so as not to seem, as I said, to be minimizing the gravity of original sin for the sake of the topic I was investigating.[64] I shall briefly disclose my present view on the matter.

Although because of Adam's sin it happened that no infant can be born without sin, which is followed by condemnation, I do not think that Adam's sin passes down to infants in such way that they ought so to be punished for it as if each one of them had committed it personally, as did Adam. For when the apostle says that "death reigned from Adam unto Moses, even over those who did not sin according to the likeness of Adam's transgression,"[65] he is clearly seen to signify that neither Adam's transgression nor anything equally great is imputed to them personally, even though [elsewhere] in his writings he calls all the sons of Adam (except for the Son of the Virgin) "sinners" and "sons of wrath."[66] For when he says "even over those who did not sin according to the likeness of Adam's transgression," he can be understood to mean: even over those who did not sin as much as Adam sinned when he transgressed. And when the apostle says "But the law entered-in so that the offence might abound":[67] either we shall understand that the sin in those who did not sin according to the likeness of Adam's transgression was, prior to the law, less than Adam's sin; or else, if not less, the sin which abounded in them was, subsequent to the law, more than Adam's sin — an alternative which, when I reflect upon it, I cannot understand [to be true]. In *Why God Became a Man*[68] I set forth my views on the weight of Adam's sin and on the satisfaction for this sin, as you have already read. Still, the fact remains that no one is restored to that state for which man was created and for which a reproductive nature was given to him, nor is anyone rescued from the evils into which human nature fell, unless satisfaction is made for that sin by which human nature precipitated itself into these very evils.

But someone will ask: "If individuals do not have the sin of Adam, how can you maintain that no one is saved without there being satisfaction for Adam's sin? For how can a just God demand from them satisfaction for a sin which they do not have?" But God does not demand from any sinner more than he owes; indeed, since no one can pay as much as he owes, Christ by Himself made payment for all who are saved, paying even more than they owe — as I have already said [69] in the oft-cited short work.

Moreover, in still another way we must see for what reason the sin in infants is less than the sin in Adam, even though it passes down from Adam to all infants. For "by one man," viz., by Adam, "sin entered into this world, and as a result of sin [came] death." [70]

Chapter Twenty-three: Why and how [sin] is transmitted to infants.

However, unless we understand why and how [sin] is present [in infants], we do not know why it is less [in them than in Adam]. Although I have previously discussed this point [71] to the extent required by my investigation, it will not be superfluous to repeat it briefly here. Assuredly, one cannot deny that infants existed in Adam when he sinned. Now, in him they existed causally or materially as in a seed; but in themselves they exist personally. For in him they were his very seed; but in themselves they are individual and distinct persons. In him they were not distinct from him; but in themselves they are distinguished from him. In him they were himself; but in themselves they are themselves. Therefore, they existed in him, but not as themselves, since they did not yet exist as themselves.

Perhaps someone will say: "The existence by virtue of which other men are said to have existed in Adam is something vacuous, and is as nothing, and ought not to be called existence." Then, let

De Conceptu Virginali

him claim to have been nothing or vacuous or unreal that existence by which Christ existed seminally in Abraham and David and His other forefathers. And [let him term nothing that existence] by which all things that come from seeds were in those seeds. And [let him say] that God created nothing when He created first in the seeds themselves all the things which are derived from seeds. And let him say to be nothing or to be something vacuous that which if it did not really exist then the things which we see to be existing would not exist. For were it not true that those things which nature produces from seeds were first of all something in those seeds, then they would not at all exist from them. But if it is utterly foolish to say these things, then the existence by virtue of which all other men were in Adam was not unreal or vacuous, but was real and genuine, and God did not create something vacuous when He created all other men to be in Adam. But as I said, in Adam they were not distinct from Adam; and thus they existed far differently from the way they exist in themselves.

But although it has been established that all other men were in Adam, nevertheless the Son of the Virgin alone was in Adam in a way vastly different from that of other men. Indeed, all others [except Him] were in Adam in such a way that they would exist from him by means of the reproductive nature, which was subject to his power and will. But only the Son of the Virgin did not exist in Adam in such way that He would be derived from Adam by means of Adam's nature or will. For at the time Adam sinned he had already received, with respect to these others, the power to be the one from whom they would exist and the power to cause them to exist from him. But with respect to the Son of the Virgin, Adam had received the power to be the one from whom He would exist but [had] not [received the power to cause] Him to exist from him, because it was not in Adam's power that the Son of the Virgin be propagated from him. But neither was it in Adam's power that the Son of the Virgin be derived from some other being or be made from nothing. Hence, it was not in Adam's power that the Son of the Virgin should in any way exist. For it was neither in the power of Adam's nature nor in the power of Adam's will that the Son of the Virgin should in any way exist. Nevertheless, there was in Adam the nature from which the Son of the Virgin was to be propagated — propagated, though, by the power of God, not by the power of Adam. It is true that in the lineage of ancestors down to the Virgin Mother the will motivated and the nature begat, so that partly by the natural order and partly by the voluntary order the Virgin herself derived her own existence from Adam, just like all the others. Nevertheless, in the Virgin herself neither did the will of the creature motivate the production of an offspring nor did the nature beget an offspring, but the "Holy Spirit" and "the Power of the Most High"[72] miraculously begat a man from the Virgin Woman. Therefore, with respect to the others, it was in Adam — i.e., it was in his power — that they would exist from him. But with respect to the Son of the Virgin, it was not in Adam's power that He in any way exist (just as it was not in the power of the clay from which the first man was created that the first man exist miraculously from it, and just as it was not in Adam's power that Eve exist from him in the manner she did). Nor is it the case that His existence was in the power of any of the ancestors in whom He existed from Adam to Mary. Nevertheless, He did exist in them, because that from which He was to be assumed existed in them (just as that from which the first man was created existed in the clay, and just as that from which Eve was created existed in Adam), although He was in them not by the will or power of the creature but solely by the power of God. But the more the Son of the Virgin's having been made a God-man[73] surpasses Adam and Eve's having been made mere human beings, the more the grace and miracle of His assumption [surpasses that of their creation]. Therefore, He was in Adam, when Adam sinned, in a vastly different way from that of these others who are procreated by the voluntary and the natural orders. Hence, in a certain sense Adam produces those whom the human will by motivating and human nature by begetting procreate through the power they both have received. But only God fashioned the Son of the Virgin (although He fashioned Him from Adam), because God made Him not through Adam but through Himself and, as it were, from Himself.

Therefore, what is more suitable for showing the magnitude of God's goodness and the plenitude of grace that He granted to Adam than that those whose existence was so in his power that through him they would be what by nature he was, would likewise have their existence so within the scope of his freedom

De Conceptu Virginali

of choice that he would beget them as just and happy as himself? Hence, this [prerogative] was given to him. But even though he was situated in the loftiness of such grace, he freely deserted the goods which he had received to keep for himself and his offspring. For this reason his descendants lost that which their father, although able to give them by keeping, took away from them by not keeping. This seems to me to be a sufficient reason — provided we consider the matter from the viewpoint of pure justice alone and carefully bracket off our inclinations, which frequently and extensively impede the mind from understanding what is right — for why the sin and the evils of Adam pass down to infants. However, I shall say a few words about how Adam's sin seems to me to descend to infants.

As I have said,[74] there is a sin which derives from a nature, and there is a sin which derives from a person. Thus, the sin which derives from a person can be called personal sin; and the sin which derives from a nature can be called natural sin. (It is also called original sin.) Now, just as the personal sin passes over to the nature, so the natural sin passes over to the person. For example, Adam's nature required that he eat, because his nature was created in such way as to have this need. But that he ate from the forbidden tree was the doing not of his natural will but of his personal will — i.e., of his own will. Nevertheless, that which was done by the person was not done without the nature. For the person was what was called Adam; and the nature was what was called man. Therefore, the person made the nature sinful, because when Adam sinned, the man [i.e., the nature] sinned. Indeed, it was not because he was a man that he was impelled to partake of what was forbidden; rather, he was drawn to this by his own act-of-will, which his nature did not require but which the person volunteered. A converse but similar thing happens in the case of infants. Assuredly, the fact that the justice which they should have is not in them does not result from their personal willing, as it did in Adam's case, but results from a natural deprivation which their nature has received from Adam. For in Adam, outside of whom no part of [human] nature existed, [human] nature was stripped of the justice which it possessed; and it always lacks justice unless assisted [to regain it]. Accordingly, since [human] nature exists in persons and since persons do not exist without a nature, the nature makes the persons of infants sinful. Thus, in Adam the person deprived the nature of the good of justice; and the nature, having become impoverished, causes all the persons whom it procreates from itself to be sinful and unjust because of the lack of justice. In this way, the personal sin of Adam passes over to all who are naturally propagated from him; and in them it is natural, or original, sin.

But clearly there is a great difference between Adam's sin and infants' sin. For Adam sinned of his own will, but his progeny sin by the natural necessity which his own personal will has merited. Although no one thinks that equal punishment follows unequal sins, nevertheless the condemnation of personal and of original sin is alike in that no one is admitted to the Kingdom of God (for which man was made) except by means of the death of Christ, without which the debt for Adam's sin is not paid. Yet, not all individuals deserve to be tormented in Hell in equal degree. Now, after the Day of Judgment every angel and every man will be either in the Kingdom of God or in Hell. So, then, the sin of infants is less than the sin of Adam; and yet, no one is saved without the universal satisfaction through which sin, both great and small, is forgiven. However, in the aforementioned book,[75] I have already asked and answered, as God enabled me, the question why there is no human salvation without Christ's death and how man's salvation occurs by means of His death.

Chapter Twenty-four: The sins of ancestors after Adam are not reckoned in the original sin of their descendants.

But I do not think that the sins of recent ancestors pertain to original sin. Indeed, had Adam not been able to transmit his own justice to those whom he was going to generate, then he would not at all have been able to transmit his own injustice to them. Accordingly, since no one subsequent to Adam was able to keep his own justice for his own descendants, I see no reason why the sins of recent ancestors ought to be imputed to the souls of their descendants. In fact, no one doubts that infants do not keep uprightness-of-will for the sake of uprightness itself.[76] Therefore, all infants are equally unjust in that they do not have the justice which every human being ought to have. This utter lack of justice

De Conceptu Virginali

passes down from Adam — in whom human nature despoiled itself of this justice — to all infants. Now, although in Adam human nature retained some justice, so that it kept an upright will in some respects, nonetheless it was so deprived of the gift of being able to keep justice for itself in Adam's posterity that it is not able to propagate itself with any justice in any of them. Surely, human nature was not able to remove from itself in infants more than all justice, together with all the happiness which is given to no one who in any degree lacks the required justice.

However, it does not seem possible that the injustice of [an infant's] recent ancestors could increase his deprivation of justice — a deprivation than which none greater can descend from the sin of Adam to infants. For where there is no justice, no justice can be taken away. And where no justice can be removed, no injustice can be added. Therefore, unjust ancestors are not able to add to their own infant offspring any injustice that exceeds the aforementioned deprivation of justice. But where there is no justice, nothing prevents some justice from being bestowed. Therefore, if unjust ancestors are said to add some injustice to their infant offspring, then it would seem more likely and more possible that just ancestors could give some justice to their own infant offspring. But if this were to happen, the infants of just ancestors would have some justice. And if so, then should they die without having been baptized they would be condemned less severely than the infants of unjust ancestors. Or else if they were saved, then they would be elected with regard to some antecedent merit of theirs. But this is denied by the Apostle Paul where he proves by reference to Jacob and Esau that no one is saved except by a grace which is antecedent to the merits of each individual.[77] Therefore, since just ancestors do not give justice to their own infant offspring before [their offspring's] baptism, surely unjust ancestors do not add any injustice to their own infant offspring.

But somone may say:

> Unjust ancestors do not add [numerically] any injustice to their own infant offspring, from whom they are not able to remove any justice. However, these ancestors do aggravate the original injustice which their infant offspring have from Adam. So also, then, just ancestors mitigate the original injustice in their infant offspring. Consequently, if the infant offspring of just ancestors are less unjust than those of unjust ancestors, the former ought to be condemned less than the latter.

Let him say this who dares to and who can prove it. But I do not dare to, since I see that a mixture of infants of just and unjust ancestors is elected to and reprobated from the grace of baptism. Still, even were someone to make the above claim, he could not prove it. Indeed, even as only someone who more resolutely desires or avoids what he ought to is thereby more just than someone else who is just, so only someone who more intensely loves or despises what he ought not to is more unjust than someone else who is unjust. Therefore, if it cannot be shown that once infants have souls the one in greater or lesser degree wills what he ought to or what he ought not to, then no one can prove that in the case of infants one infant is born more just or more unjust than another. It seems equally true, then, that just ancestors by means of their justice do not mitigate the original injustice in their infant offspring and that unjust ancestors by their injustice do not aggravate the original injustice in their infant offspring. Hence, if by their own sinfulness unjust ancestors are not able to increase, either in number or in magnitude, original sin in their infant prodigy, then it seems to me that the sins of ancestors since Adam are not reckoned in the original sin of their infant prodigy.

I do not deny that because of the positive merits of ancestors many and great benefits of body and of soul are imparted to their offspring. [Nor do I deny that] because of the sins of ancestors their children and grandchildren "unto the third and fourth generation,"[78] and perhaps even beyond, are scourged with various tribulations in this life and lose the goods — even goods of soul — which they might have obtained through their ancestors, had these latter been just. (It would take too long to introduce examples of such cases here.) But I do maintain that original sin is present equally in all infants who are conceived naturally — just as the sin of Adam, which is the cause of infants' being born in original sin, belongs equally to them all.

Chapter Twenty-five: How [the sins of ancestors] harm the souls of their [descendants].

But if the sins of ancestors sometimes harm the souls of their descendants, then I think that this happens in the following manner: It is not that God imputes these sins to them or that on

De Conceptu Virginali

account of their ancestors He leads them into any transgressions, but rather that even as God often rescues from sin the descendants of the just because of the merits of their ancestors, so He sometimes leaves in their sins the descendants of the unjust because of the demerits of their ancestors. For since no one is free from sin unless God sets him free, when God does not set him free from sin, He is said to lead him into it;[79] and when He does not soften, He is said to harden.[80] For it seems much more acceptable that on account of the sins of ancestors God leaves a sinful soul (to which He owes nothing except punishment) in its own sins, so that it is punished for its own sins, than that He burdens it with others' sins, so that it is tormented for their sins. Thus, then, the following statements are consistent with one another: Original sin is the same in all individuals, and "the son shall not bear the iniquity of the father,"[81] and "each one shall bear his own burden,"[82] and each one shall receive "according as he has done" in the body, "whether it be good or evil,"[83] and "unto the third and fourth generation,"[84] God visits the sins of the parents on their children (even if this occurs with respect to their souls), and whatever else we read which is seen to signify that the sins of ancestors harm the souls of their descendants. Indeed, the soul of the son dies not because of the sin of the father but because of its own sin. And when anyone is left in his own iniquity, he bears his own iniquity, not the iniquity of his father; and he bears his own burden, not another's burden. And he receives according as he has done in the body, not according as his father has done. But since on account of the sins of his ancestors he is not set free from his own iniquities, the iniquities which he bears are ascribed to the sins of his ancestors.

Chapter Twenty-six: How, nevertheless, everyone bears his own sin, not the sin of his father.

Perhaps someone may argue that all who are not saved by faith in Christ bear the iniquity and burden of Adam, but may so argue with the intent of proving thereby that either infants ought likewise to bear the iniquity of their other ancestors or else they ought not to bear Adam's iniquity. But let this objector consider carefully that infants bear their own sin, not Adam's sin. For

Adam's sin was one thing, and infants' sin is another thing, because these sins differ, as was stated.[85] For the former was a cause, whereas the latter is an effect. Adam was deprived of required justice because he himself (and not because someone else) deserted it; but infants are deprived because someone else (and not because they themselves) deserted it. Therefore, Adam's sin and infants' sin are not the same thing. Moreover, when the apostle says (as I mentioned above)[86] that "death reigned from Adam to Moses, even over those who did not sin according to the likeness of Adam's transgression,"[87] just as he signifies that the sin of infants is less than the sin of Adam, so he indicates clearly that the sin of infants is distinct from the sin of Adam.

Accordingly, when an infant is condemned on account of original sin, he is condemned not on account of Adam's sin but on account of his own. For if he did not have sin of his own, he would not be condemned. So, then, he bears his own iniquity and not Adam's, even though he is said to bear Adam's iniquity because the iniquity of Adam was the cause of his own sin. However, this cause of infants' being born in sin — a cause which was in Adam — is not in the other ancestors, because human nature in them does not have the power (as I said)[88] to propagate descendants who are just. Hence, it does not follow that sin is in infants because of the sin of their ancestors, as [it does follow that it is there] because of the sin of Adam.

Chapter Twenty-seven: What original sin is. It is equal in all [human beings].

Therefore, I understand original sin to be nothing other than that sin which is in an infant as soon as he has a rational soul — irrespective of what may have happened to his body (e.g., the corruption of its members) before it was thus animated, or irrespective of what may happen to either his body or his soul afterwards. And on the basis of the aforegiven reasons I think that in all infants who are naturally propagated original sin is equal, and that all who die with only this sin are equally condemned. Indeed, whatever sin accrues to a man over and above original sin is personal sin. And just as the person is born sinful because of the

De Conceptu Virginali

nature, so the nature is made more sinful because of the person, since when any person sins, his human nature (*homo*) sins.

I can understand this sin (which I am calling original sin) to be nothing else in these infants except the above-mentioned[89] deprivation of required justice which was caused by Adam's disobedience and through which all men are sons of wrath.[90] For the voluntary desertion of justice which the nature caused in Adam accuses the nature, and the inability to recover justice does not excuse the persons (as I have already said).[91] This inability is also accompanied by the deprivation of happiness, so that even as men are without any justice, so they are without any happiness. Because of these two deprivations men in the exile of this life are exposed to, and subject to, sins and miseries which constantly befall them everywhere, attacking them on all sides — except insofar as they are protected by divine providence.

Chapter Twenty-eight: Against those who think that infants ought not to be condemned.

There are those whose mind resists accepting [the view] that infants dying unbaptized ought to be condemned solely on account of the injustice of which I have spoken.[92] Their reasons are (1) that no man judges infants to be blameworthy as the result of another person's sin, (2) that in such a state infants are not yet just and discerning, and (3) that God (so they think) ought not to judge innocent infants more severely than men judge them. These people must be told that God ought to act toward infants in one way and man [ought to act toward them] in another way. For man ought not to demand from a nature what he has not bestowed and what is not owed to him. Nor does one man justly reproach another man for being born with a fault with which he himself is born and from which he himself is healed only by someone else. But God does rightly demand from a nature what He bestowed on it and what is rightly owed to Him.

But if we consider the matter, even this judgment by which infants are condemned is not much different from the judgment of men. For take the case of a man and his wife who not by their own merit but by favor alone (*gratia sola*) have been elevated to some great dignity and estate, and who together commit an unpardonably serious crime, and who on account of this crime are justly cast down and reduced to servitude. Who will say that the children whom they beget after their condemnation ought not to be subject to the same servitude but ought rather to be gratuitously restored to the goods which their parents rightfully lost? Such is the case with our first parents and with the descendants whom they — justly sentenced because of their own fault to [be cast down] from happiness into misery — beget into their own exile. Therefore, there ought to be like judgment for like cases; but in the case of our first parents the more reprehensible their crime can be shown to be, the more severely [it ought to be judged].

In last analysis, every man is either saved or condemned. But everyone who is saved is admitted to the Kingdom of Heaven; and everyone who is condemned is excluded therefrom. Now, assuredly, he who is admitted is elevated[93] to the likeness of those angels in whom there never was and never will be any sin — something which cannot happen as long as there is any taint of sin in him. Thus, a man with any sin at all — even a small sin — cannot be saved. Hence, if what I have termed original sin is a sin, then it is necessary that every man who is born with it and does not have it forgiven is condemned.

Chapter Twenty-nine: How the inability to have justice excuses infants after their baptism.

I have said[94] that the inability to have justice does not excuse the injustice of infants. Perhaps, then, someone will ask:

> If there is sin, i.e., injustice, in an infant before his baptism, and if (as you say) the inability to have justice is no excuse, and if in baptism only sin which was prior thereto is remitted, then since after baptism an infant, for as long as he is an infant, lacks justice and cannot even understand the justice which he should keep (if indeed justice is uprightness-of-will kept for its own sake),[95] why is he not also unjust after having been baptized? Thus, if a baptized infant dies in infancy (though not immediately after baptism) before he knows how to repent, then since he does not have the required justice, and since his inability does not excuse him, he passes from this life unjust (even as he would have done before his baptism), and he is not admitted into the Kingdom of God, into which no one who is unjust is received. But the Catholic Church does not hold to this view. Now, if in baptism a subsequent sin within infancy

De Conceptu Virginali

is remitted to infants, then why [are] not also those sins which are committed at a later stage of development [forgiven at the time of baptism]?

To this question I give the following answer. In baptism the sins which were present before baptism are completely blotted out. Accordingly, the original inability to have justice is not reckoned as sin in the case of those who have already been baptized — as [it is reckoned to them] prior [to their baptism]. Hence, just as prior to their baptism this inability could not excuse the absence of justice, since the inability was culpable, so after their baptism the inability completely excuses the absence of justice, because although the inability remains it is without any culpability. Thus it happens that the justice which before their baptism was required of infants, without any excuse on their part, is after their baptism not demanded of them as their requirement. Therefore, as long as it is only because of the original inability that they do not have justice, they are not unjust, since there is no absence in them of *required* justice. For what is both impossible and free of all culpability is not required.[96] Therefore, if infants die in such a condition, then because they are not unjust they are not condemned; rather, by the justice of Christ, who gave Himself for them, and by the justice of faith on the part of the Church, their mother, which believes on their behalf, they are saved, [being reckoned] as just.

In accordance with the capacity of my understanding I have briefly made these statements about original sin — not so much by way of asserting them as by way of provisionally inferring them — until God shall somehow reveal to me something better. But if someone has a different view, I do not reject anyone's opinion provided it can be proved to be true.

THE PROCESSION OF THE HOLY SPIRIT
(*De Processione Spiritus Sancti*)

THE PROCESSION OF THE HOLY SPIRIT[1]
(*De Processione Spiritus Sancti*)

I

That the Holy Spirit proceeds from the Son, as we Latins confess, is denied by the Greeks. They also reject our Latin teachers whom we follow with respect to this doctrine. But together with us they revere the Gospels; and in other regards they believe about the trine and one God exactly the same thing as do we, who are firmly established in this very doctrine. Therefore, if they prefer to assent to a solid truth rather than to contend for a hollow victory, I hope that on the basis of what they confess without hesitation and by the help of this same Holy Spirit they can be led rationally to what they do not yet accept. There are many men who are capable of accomplishing this task better than I. Nevertheless, since it is imposed upon me by many whose request I dare not resist — not only because of the obligation to love the truth but especially because of their love and religious desire — I call upon this same Holy Spirit to design to guide me to this end. In this hope, then, I shall undertake what these men request; and I shall use the faith of the Greeks, together with the doctrines which the Greeks both believe and confess unhesitatingly, as the most certain premises for proving what they do not believe. And on account of the lowliness of my knowledge I shall leave deeper matters to the more learned.

Indeed, the Greeks believe that God is one and unique and perfect, that He has no parts, and that He is as a whole whatever He is. They also confess that He is Father, Son, and Holy Spirit in the following way: Whether He is spoken of as Father or Son or Holy Spirit (one at a time), or spoken of (two at a time) as Father and Son or as Father and Holy Spirit or as Son and Holy

Spirit, or (three at a time) as Father and Son and Holy Spirit, the same whole and perfect God is designated — even though the name "Father" or the name "Son" does not signify the same thing as does the name "God." For it is not the same thing to be God as it is to be Father or Son. Now, the name "Holy Spirit" is construed as a relational name, because the Holy Spirit is understood to be *someone's* spirit. Although the Father is a spirit and is holy, and although the Son is a spirit and is holy, nevertheless the Father is not anyone's spirit and the Son is not anyone's spirit — as the Holy Spirit is someone's spirit. For He is the spirit of God and the spirit of the Father and the Son. For although the Greeks deny that the Holy Spirit proceeds from the Son, they do not deny that He is the spirit of the Son.

The Greeks also believe and confess that God exists from God by being begotten and that God exists from God by proceeding; for God the Son exists from God the Father by being begotten, and God the Holy Spirit exists from God the Father by proceeding. They do not think that the one who is begotten is a different God from the one from whom He is begotten, or that the one who proceeds [is a different God from the one from whom He proceeds] — even though God admits of plurality in accordance with the names signifying that there is one from whom someone is begotten and that there is one who is begotten from someone and one who proceeds from someone. In accordance with this plurality the Father, the Son, and the Holy Spirit are plural and are distinct from one another. For when God is said to be Father, He is signified to be the one from whom someone is begotten. And when God is called Son, He is understood to be the one who is begotten from someone. And when God is called Holy Spirit, then because we mean thereby not simply spirit but the spirit-of-God, God is shown to be the one who proceeds from someone.

Now, when we say that the Son is from the Father and that the Holy Spirit is from the Father, we mean that what the Son or the Holy Spirit is He has from the Father. But the Son is understood to be from the Father in one way, and the Holy Spirit [is understood to be from the Father] in another way. For the Son is from His father (i.e., is from God who is His father); but the Holy Spirit is not from God *His* father but is only from God who is Father. Therefore, the Son, with respect to the fact that He exists from God, is called the Father's son; and the one from whom the

Son exists is called the Son's father. But the Holy Spirit, with respect to the fact that He exists from God, is not the Father's son; nor is the one from whom He exists *His* father.

It is also certain that God is not the father or the son or the spirit of anyone except of God; nor is God anything except the Father, the Son, and the Holy Spirit. And just as there is one God, so there is only one Father, one Son, and one Holy Spirit. Consequently, in the Trinity there is no father except of the Son; and there is no son except of the Father; and the Holy Spirit is the spirit of no one except of the Father and the Son. Hence, the sole cause of plurality in God is that the Father and the Son and the Holy Spirit cannot be called by one another's respective name, but are distinct from one another because God is from God in the two ways mentioned above.

All of this can be expressed by the word "relation." For since the Son exists from God by being begotten and since the Holy Spirit exists from God by proceeding, by this very diversity of birth and procession they are related to one another as different and distinct from one another. Moreover, when a substance exists from a substance, two irreducible relations are produced if names are ascribed to the substance in accordance with these relations. For example, when a man exists from a man by being begotten, the man from whom the other is begotten is called father; and the other who is begotten from him is called son. Hence, it is impossible for the father to be that son of whom he is father, or for the son to be that father of whom he is son. Yet, nothing prevents a father from being a son or a son from being a father in the case where a man is both a father and a son because he is a father in relation to one man and a son in relation to another man. Assuredly, since Isaac is the father of Jacob and the son of Abraham, without inconsistency a father is a son and a son is a father. For Isaac is called father in relation to someone other than his own father, and he is called son in relation to someone other than his own son. But in the case of Isaac it is impossible for the father to be that son of whom he is father or for the son to be that father of whom he is son.

So then, with respect to God, since God is Father and Son and Holy Spirit, and since there is no father except of the Son, and no son except of the Father, and no spirit of anyone except of the Father and the Son: the Father is not the Son or the Holy Spirit;

the Son is not the Father; and the Holy Spirit is not the Father. Indeed, the Son exists from the Father, and the Holy Spirit exists from the Father; and the one from whom another exists cannot be the other who exists from him, nor can the one who exists from another be the other from whom he exists (as has been stated already). Therefore, the Father is neither the Son nor the Holy Spirit; and neither the Son nor the Holy Spirit is the Father. But the reason the Son is not the Holy Spirit, and the Holy Spirit not the Son, is that (to state for a moment a different reason, since I have not yet established that the Holy Spirit exists, and proceeds, from the Son) the Son exists from the Father by being begotten, but the Holy Spirit exists from the Father not by being begotten but by proceeding. Moreover, the Son cannot be His own spirit, nor can the Holy Spirit be that one whose spirit He Himself is.[2]

Having advanced these premises, let us inquire how, in God, the indivisible unity and the irreducible plurality are related to each other. Now, in equal measure, both we [Latins] (who say that the Holy Spirit proceeds from the Son) and the Greeks (who do not agree with us in this matter) unhesitatingly believe and confess these premises which have been stated. Therefore, without any hesitancy we both ought to accept, with mutual consent, the conclusions which follow necessarily from these premises. Now, in accordance with the property of God's unity, (which has no parts), it follows that whatever is said about the one God (who is as a whole whatever He is) is said about the whole of God the Father, God the Son, and God the Holy Spirit, because each of them considered by Himself is wholly and perfectly God. But the aforementioned opposition of relation which originates from the fact that God is from God in the aforesaid two ways prevents the Father and the Son and the Holy Spirit from being called by one another's respective name, and prevents the distinguishing properties of any one of them from being attributed to either of the others. Therefore, the consequences of this unity and of this relation are so ordered that the plurality which follows from the relation does not apply to cases in which the simplicity of the aforesaid unity is signified, nor does the unity restrict the plurality in a case where this relation is signified.[3] Thus, the unity never loses its own consequence in a case where no opposition of relation stands against it; and the relation does not lose what

De Processione Spiritus Sancti

belongs to it except in the case where the inseparable unity stands against it.

This point will become clearer if we examine it in terms of examples. Indeed, it is easy to recognize how the simplicity of unity excludes from itself the plurality which is contained in the signification of the relational names. For we confess that the Father is not the Son or the Holy Spirit, that the Son is not the Father or the Holy Spirit, and that the Holy Spirit is not the Father or the Son. Therefore, it follows that the Father and the Son and the Holy Spirit are distinct from one another and are plural. But the Father is God, the Son is God, and the Holy Spirit is God. Hence, what would follow more logically — if the above-mentioned plurality of persons retains its property — than that the Father, the Son, and the Holy Spirit are more than one God and are gods distinct from one another? But the inviolable simplicity of deity — a deity which we believe to be only one God — does not at all allow this consequence. Thus, the unity of God's being repels the consequence of the relations.

We must also consider how the plurality of relations can oppose the consequence of unity. But first let us posit some of those cases in which no opposition [of relation] opposes [the consequence of unity].[4] We say that the one God is Father and is Son and is Holy Spirit, and that they are one and the same God whether they are spoken of singly or two at a time or all three together. Therefore, if God is eternal, then because of the unity of deity it follows of necessity that the Father is eternal, the Son is eternal, and the Holy Spirit is eternal. And since whether considered one at a time or more than one at a time they are one God, there is only one eternal God. The consequence is similar if God is called creator or just or any of the other names which do not signify any of the aforementioned relations. Let us now look at how relation restricts this consequence of God's unity. We say that God is Father. Therefore, since the Father and the Son and the Holy Spirit are one God, God's unity requires that the Son be the Father and that the Holy Spirit be the Father. But the relation which prevents the Son and the Holy Spirit from being the Father opposes [this consequence]. Indeed, nature does not allow, nor can understanding comprehend, that (1) the one who exists from another is identical with this other from whom he exists, or that

(2) the one from whom another exists is identical with this other who exists from him. Now, the Son and the Holy Spirit exist from the Father. Therefore, neither the Son nor the Holy Spirit can be the Father, even though God is Father and even though the Father and the Son and the Holy Spirit are one and the same God.

This same point is recognized if God is said to be Son. For the consequence of God's unity demands that the Father and the Holy Spirit be the Son. But the Father, from whom the Son exists, cannot be this one who exists from Him. And the Holy Spirit, who exists from the Father by proceeding, is not identical with the one who exists from the Father by being begotten. Likewise, when God is said to be Holy Spirit, the aforementioned unity requires that the Father and the Son be the Holy Spirit. But the Father, from whom the Holy Spirit exists, cannot be this one who exists from Him. And the Son, who exists from the Father by being begotten, is not identical with the one (viz., the Holy Spirit) who exists from the Father by proceeding. Now, after we show that the Holy Spirit exists from the Son, it will also be clear that for this reason the Son cannot be the Holy Spirit nor can the Holy Spirit be the Son.

Let us consider still further how the above-mentioned oppositions oppose the aforementioned consequence of unity. God exists from God. Once this point has been accepted, then since the Father and the Son and the Holy Spirit are the same God, it follows in accordance with this identity that God the Father is both God from God and God from whom God exists.[5] Likewise, [God] the Son is both God from God and God from whom God exists. And the same thing holds true for [God] the Holy Spirit. Now, to ask whether each one of them is God from whom God exists is no different from asking whether each one of them is God from God. For God cannot exist from God except as the Father or the Son or the Holy Spirit [existing] from the Father or from the Son or from the Holy Spirit. Therefore, let us consider whether each one of them is God from God, and it will become evident whether each one of them is God from whom God exists.

Now, because of the previously cited opposition [of relation] the Father cannot exist from God. For God does not exist except as Father or Son or Holy Spirit, or as two or three of these together. And so God the Father cannot exist from God unless [He exists] either from the Father (i.e., from Himself) or from the

De Processione Spiritus Sancti

Son or from the Holy Spirit, or from two or three of them together. But He cannot exist from Himself, because the one existing from someone and the someone from whom he exists cannot be identical. Nor does God the Father exist from the Son; for the Son exists from Him, and thus He cannot exist from the Son. Nor does God the Father exist from the Holy Spirit; for the Holy Spirit exists from the Father, and the Father cannot be that spirit which exists from Himself. And because of this principle of opposition the Father cannot exist from two or three of them together. Now, it is necessary that God the Son exist from God the Father because the Father does not exist from the Son. But God the Son cannot exist from the Son (i.e., from Himself), because the one who exists from someone and the someone from whom he exists are not identical. However, whether God the Son exists from the Holy Spirit or whether the Holy Spirit exists from Him will be shown subsequently. But first we shall determine with regard to the Holy Spirit whether, in accordance with the previously mentioned consequence [of unity], He exists from the Father and from Himself. Indeed, it is necessary that He exist from the Father, because no opposition opposes this; for the Father does not exist from the Holy Spirit. But it is impossible that the Holy Spirit exist from Himself, since the one existing from someone and the someone from whom he exists cannot be identical. In all these cases nothing opposes the consequence of singular identity except some opposition from among the ones mentioned. And what is discerned in these cases must occur immutably in all things which are said of God.

On the basis of the above irrefutable arguments we must now ask whether the Son exists from the Holy Spirit or whether the Holy Spirit exists from the Son. I make the following claim: "either the Son exists from the Holy Spirit or the Holy Spirit exists from the Son" (just as, on the basis of the above reasoning, either the Father exists from the Son or the Son exists from the Father, and, likewise, just as either the Father exists from the Holy Spirit or the Holy Spirit exists from the Father). Anyone who denies this claim must also deny either that (1) there is only one God, or that (2) the Son is God, or that (3) the Holy Spirit is God, or that (4) God exists from God. For my claim follows from these premises. Furthermore, the Son and the Holy Spirit exist from the Father only by existing from the Father's essence, which is common to the Father and the Son and the Holy Spirit. Therefore, when it is said that the Son exists from God the Father, then if the Father and the Holy Spirit are one and the same God, it follows in accordance with the unity of deity that the Son exists also from the Holy Spirit. In the same manner, when we confess that the Holy Spirit exists from God the Father, then if the Father and the Son are the same God, it follows in accordance with the unity of deity that the Holy Spirit exists also from the Son. Therefore, from these considerations we discern clearly that "either the Son exists from the Holy Spirit or the Holy Spirit exists from the Son." For these alternates cannot both be true or cannot both be false. Accordingly, if it can be shown that the Son does not exist from the Holy Spirit, then it is necessary that the Holy Spirit exist from the Son.

Now, suppose someone says: "Even if nothing is opposed hereto, it does not follow that the Son exists from the Father and the Holy Spirit simply because the Father and the Holy Spirit are one God." Or [suppose he says]: "Even though the Son does not exist from the Holy Spirit, [it does not follow] that the Holy Spirit exists from the Father and the Son simply because the Father and the Son are one God." Let this person consider that when God exists from God, then either (1) the whole exists from the whole, or (2) a part exists from a part, or (3) the whole exists from a part, or (4) a part exists from the whole. But God has no parts. Therefore, it is impossible that God exist from God [in the following ways]: as a whole existing from a part, or as a part existing from a whole, or as a part existing from a part. Thus, it is necessary that if God exists from God, the whole exists from the whole. Hence, when the Son is said to exist from God, who is Father and Holy Spirit, [an alternative arises]: either (1) the Father will be one whole and the Holy Spirit will be another whole, so that the Son exists from the whole of the Father and not from the whole of the Holy Spirit, or else (2) if the Father and the Holy Spirit are the same whole God, then of necessity when the Son exists from the whole of God, which one whole is both Father and Holy Spirit, then the Son exists in equal measure from the Father and from the Holy Spirit — provided nothing opposes this. In the same manner, when the Holy Spirit is said to exist from the whole of God, who is both Father and Son, [an alternative arises]: either (1) the Father will be one whole and the Son

De Processione Spiritus Sancti

another whole, so that the Holy Spirit exists from the whole of the Father and not from the whole of the Son, or else (2) when the Holy Spirit exists from the Father He cannot fail to exist from the Son, if the Son does not exist from the Holy Spirit. For on no other basis can the Holy Spirit be denied to exist from the Son.

Someone will argue:

> Suppose that when the Son exists from the Father, then since the Father and the Holy Spirit are one God it follows that the Son exists from the Holy Spirit. Or [suppose that] when the Holy Spirit exists from the Father, then because the Father and the Son are the same God, the Holy Spirit also exists from the Son. [In this case], when the Father begets the Son He must also beget the Holy Spirit, because the Son and the Holy Spirit are one and the same God; and when the Holy Spirit proceeds from the Father, then because of the Son and the Holy Spirit's unity of deity the Son also proceeds from the Father just as does the Holy Spirit. On the other hand, if the unity of God in the Son and the Holy Spirit does not necessitate that each of them in like manner proceeds and is begotten, then it seems that from the fact of the Father and the Holy Spirit's being one God it does not follow that the Son exists from the Holy Spirit, or from the fact of the Father and the Son's being the same God [it does not follow] that the Holy Spirit exists from the Son — as you claim it does.

To this objection I reply: Assuredly, the Son and the Holy Spirit exist from the Father — but in different ways. For the one [exists from the Father] by being begotten, and the other [exists from the Father] by proceeding, so that for this reason they are distinct from each other — as I have said. Hence, when the one is begotten, the other who is distinct from Him by virtue of the fact that He is not likewise begotten but proceeds cannot be begotten with Him. And when the one proceeds, the other who is distinct from Him by virtue of the fact that He does not likewise proceed but is begotten cannot proceed together with Him. Hence, God's unity does not necessitate the above consequence,[6] because [that consequence] is opposed by the plurality which arises from the begottenness and the procession. For even if the Son and the Holy Spirit were not more than one for some *other* reason, they would be different for *this* reason alone. But when I say that from the fact of the Father's being one God with the Son or with the Holy Spirit it follows that either the Son exists from the Holy Spirit or the Holy Spirit exists from the Son, I do not generate here a plurality which opposes the consequence of unity. For I do not say that both alternates are true but only that one or the other is.

Therefore, by absolute and irrefutable necessity we reach the conclusion that — provided those premises are true which I said above we believe in equal measure with the Greeks — either the Son exists from the Holy Spirit or the Holy Spirit exists from the Son. But that the Son does not exist from the Holy Spirit is evident from the Catholic faith.[7] For God exists from God only by being begotten (as is the Son) or by proceeding (as does the Holy Spirit). But the Son is not begotten from the Holy Spirit. For if the Son were begotten from the Holy Spirit, He would be the son of the Holy Spirit, and the Holy Spirit would be His father. But the one is neither the father nor the son of the other. Therefore, the Son is not begotten from the Holy Spirit. And it is no less clear that the Son does not proceed from the Holy Spirit. For [in that case] He would be the spirit of the Holy Spirit — a doctrine clearly denied when the Holy Spirit is said and is believed to be the spirit of the Son.[8] For the Son cannot be the spirit of His own spirit. Therefore, the Son does not proceed from the Holy Spirit. Hence, the Son in no way exists from the Holy Spirit. And so it follows by irrefutable reasoning that the Holy Spirit exists from the Son, even as He also exists from the Father.

2

Perhaps the Greeks will deny that the Holy Spirit is God from God (as the Son is God from God) since through this doctrine we prove that the Holy Spirit exists and proceeds from the Son, and since it is not set forth in that creed[9] wherein we are blamed by the Greeks for having added the Holy Spirit's procession from the Son. But anyone who denies this, denies either (1) that the Father, from whom the Holy Spirit exists, is God, or (2) that the Holy Spirit, who exists from the Father, is God, or (3) that the essence of the Holy Spirit exists from the Father.[10] But no Christian denies that the Father or that the Holy Spirit is God. Let us see, then, whether what the Holy Spirit is essentially, He is from the Father. (I have noticed that a certain bishop in the city of Bari — a bishop who perhaps favors the Greeks — is unwilling to assent to this proposition.) Now, if it were not the case that what the Holy Spirit is essentially, He is from the Father, then since He is one and the same God as the Father there could not be found a reason for His being distinct from the Father. For the reason the Holy Spirit is distinct from the Father is not that the Father has a

De Processione Spiritus Sancti

son whereas the Holy Spirit does not have a son. Through this fact they can be *shown* to be different from each other; nevertheless, this fact is not the *reason* they are different persons. Indeed, suppose that there are two men, one of whom has a son and the other of whom does not. Although through this fact they can be shown to be different from each other, nevertheless this fact is not the reason they are different from each other. For no matter what their state is with regard to whether they have or do not have a son, they do not lose their differentiation. Thus, in the case of the Father and the Holy Spirit the fact that the one has a son whereas the other does not is not the reason they are different; rather, because they are different nothing prevents them from being unlike with respect to having and not having a son.

We can give a similar response if [the Holy Spirit] is called distinct [from the Father] because a holy spirit does not proceed from Him, as He Himself proceeds from the Father. Indeed, just as the "fact" that the Son does not have a holy spirit proceeding from Him, as does the Father (to speak after the fashion of those who deny that the Holy Spirit proceeds from the Son), is not the reason that the Son is distinct from the Father (for then it would follow that if the Holy Spirit were to proceed from the Son, the Son would not be distinct from the Father), so the fact that the Holy Spirit does not have a son or a spirit proceeding from Him, as does the Father, is not the reason the Holy Spirit is distinct from the Father. Moreover, just as the reason the Son is distinct from the Father is not that the Son has a father whereas the Father does not have a father (for if the Father were to have a father, He would still be distinct from the Son), so the reason the Holy Spirit is distinct from the Father is not that the Holy Spirit proceeds from someone whereas the Father does not proceed from anyone (for if the Father were to proceed from someone, the Holy Spirit would nonetheless be distinct from the Father, from whom He proceeds). Therefore, it is evident that the reason the Holy Spirit is distinct from the Father is not (1) that He has no son or spirit proceeding from Himself, as does the Father, and is not (2) that He proceeds from someone, whereas the Father proceeds from no one.

If the Holy Spirit does not exist from the Father, He cannot be understood to be distinct from the Father simply by virtue of being the spirit of the Father. For someone can be understood to be distinct from another before he is of that other, although he cannot be of that other unless he is distinct [from him]. For example, when one man is said to be the lord of some other man or to be the vassal[11] of another man, he is understood to be distinct from the other, of whom he is said to be, *before* he is his lord or his vassal. So then, if the Holy Spirit does not exist from the Father, nothing prevents Him from being understood to be distinct from the Father *before* He is of the Father. Hence, the fact that He is the spirit of the Father does not make Him distinct from the Father unless He is distinct from the Father for the very reason for which He is the spirit of the Father,[12] just as the Son is distinct from the Father for the very reason for which He is the Son of the Father — a reason which is no other than that the Son exists from the Father by being begotten. Thus, we see that the Holy Spirit is distinct from the Father only because He has His essence[13] from the Father — although He has it in a different way than the Son [has His essence from the Father].

But let us examine this matter more closely. Assuredly, either it was after the Holy Spirit was already what He is that He became other than the Father, or it is in the very fact that He exists that He has the reason for His being other. For it happens that someone is what he is *before* he is an "other," and it happens that someone becomes an "other" in the very fact that he exists. But it is not possible for someone to be an "other" before he is that which he is. For example, the first human being — before there was any human being from him — was himself a human being; but he was not an "other." But when first someone existed from him: this one from whom someone existed became, after he was already existing, an "other"; and that one who existed from him had, simultaneously, both his existing and his being other. Therefore, as I said, either the Holy Spirit after He was already existing became other than the Father, or else in the very fact of existing He has the reason for which He is called other. Now, if after He was already existing, it came about that He became other than the Father, then since He is *another* person only because He is other than the Father, these three persons would not always have existed; for just as the Holy Spirit would not always have been other than the Father, so the person of the Holy Spirit would not always have existed. Therefore, since these consequences are false, it is evident that in the very fact of exist-

194

De Processione Spiritus Sancti

ing the Holy Spirit has the reason for His being other [than the Father].

Now, the Holy Spirit is not able to exist except either from someone (as does the Son) or from no one (as does the Father). But if He exists from no one, as does the Father, [then an alternative arises]: either (1) each of the two so exists through Himself that neither has anything from the other, and the Father and the Holy Spirit are two gods; or (2), if each exists from no one, then since they are one God there can be found in the Christian faith no principle at all whereby they are distinct from each other, but the Father and the Holy Spirit are identical and are one person. But true faith abhors these consequences. Therefore, it is not true that the Holy Spirit exists from no one. Now, if He exists from someone He exists only from God, who is Father and Son and Holy Spirit. But the Holy Spirit cannot exist from the Holy Spirit, for no person can exist from himself. Hence, if someone denies that the Holy Spirit exists from the Son, He cannot deny that He exists from the Father.

Yet, if someone claims that although the Holy Spirit does not exist from the Father He can nevertheless be understood to be distinct [from the Father] on the basis of procession, then I think I must also reply to this claim, lest with regard to the question at hand an objection which our response does not successfully cope with can be raised against our assertion. And since that man[14] whom I perceived not to think that the Holy Spirit has His essence[15] from the Father was of no small authority among his own, and since I did not then have the opportunity to make a reply, let no one be surprised that I am dwelling so long on this topic. Accordingly, if someone wants to maintain that although the Holy Spirit does not exist from the Father He is distinct from the Father solely by virtue of procession: he understands "proceeding from the Father" to mean merely being given or sent by the Father (so that only when the Father gives or sends the Holy Spirit does the Holy Spirit proceed from the Father); or else [he understands] "proceeding [from the Father]" to mean existing from the Father.

Now, if "proceeding" meant being given or sent, then it would be as true that the Holy Spirit proceeds from the Son as that He proceeds from the Father, since He is likewise given and sent by the Son. Similarly, if for the Holy Spirit to proceed were nothing else than for Him to be given or sent, then He would be distinct from the Father and would proceed from the Father only when He is given or sent — something which no one, it seems to me, takes to be the case. For the Holy Spirit is always — even prior to creation — distinct from the Father. However, He is given or sent only to creatures. And yet, it must not be said that to be given or sent happens (*accidat*) to Him. Since the Holy Spirit is omnipresent and immutable: something indeed happens to the one who receives Him, since with respect to that one there happens something which was not previously the case and something which is able not to happen; but nothing which was not already the case happens with respect to the Holy Spirit. For example, when a blind man situated in the light does not perceive the light, nothing is added to or subtracted from the light; and if after his blindness has been removed the blind man perceives the light, there is a change in him, not in the light.[16] Clearly, then, it is not the case that the Holy Spirit is distinct from the Father by means of a procession which is construed to be such that for Him to proceed is nothing else than for Him to be given or sent. Therefore, it is evident that by means of procession He *exists* from the Father and is thereby distinct from the Father, even as the Son is distinct from the Father by virtue of no other fact than that He exists from the Father. Therefore, the Holy Spirit is God from God and proceeds from God, because He Himself is God and because the Father, from whom He exists and proceeds, is God.

But if we say that two processions of the Holy Spirit can be distinguished — one when He exists from the Father, the other when He is given or sent — I do not think that this ought to be denied, provided each is understood in its proper sense. Indeed, we rightly understand the Lord to have been speaking about that procession by which the Holy Spirit is given or sent, [when He said]: "The wind blows where it wills, and you hear the sound of it and do not know whence it comes and whither it goes."[17] For, as we see, this statement could have been made as follows: "You do not know whence the Holy Spirit proceeds or whither He recedes." For when He is given, He comes and proceeds as from concealment; and when He is withdrawn, He goes and recedes as into concealment. With regard to this procession it can be said

De Processione Spiritus Sancti

that for the Holy Spirit to proceed is the same thing as for Him to be sent.

Consequently, whether (1) the Holy Spirit proceeds only by existing from the Father, or whether (2) He proceeds only when He is given or sent to sanctify creatures, or whether (3) He proceeds in both ways: it follows that the Holy Spirit proceeds from the Son. For if (1') He exists from the Father, He is God from God; and from this fact He is proved (as I have already said) to exist and to proceed from the Son also. (For, indeed, the Holy Spirit proceeds from the one from whom He exists, and He exists from the one from whom He proceeds.) But if (2') the Holy Spirit proceeds only when He is given or sent, He proceeds from the Son, by whom He is given and sent. But if (3') He proceeds in both ways, then He is known to proceed from the Son in both ways equally.

Behold! We see that the Holy Spirit is God from God and proceeds from God — something which is not stated in the aforementioned creed.[18] Therefore, if [the Greeks] deny that He exists and proceeds from the Son because the Creed is silent about this point, let them likewise deny that He exists and proceeds from God — something which is also not stated in the Creed. On the other hand, if they cannot deny this latter view, then let them not hesitate — simply because they do not find it stated in the Creed — to confess with us that the Holy Spirit exists and proceeds from the Son.

But [the Greeks] will maintain: "When the Creed states that the Holy Spirit proceeds from the Father, then since the Father is God, the Creed sufficiently signifies that the Holy Spirit exists and proceeds from God." And in like manner we maintain: When the Creed says that the Holy Spirit proceeds from God, then since the Son is God, the Creed indicates plainly that the Holy Spirit proceeds from the Son. Now, I ask whether the reason the Holy Spirit must be understood to exist from the Father is that He exists from God or whether the reason He exists from God is that He exists from the Father. Although either fact[19] is proved from the other (for if the Holy Spirit exists from the Father He exists from God, and if He exists from God He exists from the Father — since none of the previously cited relations opposes this), it is not likewise the case that either fact is the reason for the other.

Suppose that the Holy Spirit's existing from the Father were the reason for His existing from God. Then, when He is said to exist from the Father we could not take this to mean that He exists from that in virtue of which the Father is God, i.e., from the divine essence; rather, [we would have to take it to mean that He exists] from that in virtue of which God is the Father, i.e., from that in virtue of which the Father is related to the Son. But in that case the divine essence in the Holy Spirit would exist not from the Father's deity but from the Father's relation — a thoroughly foolish statement to make. However, even if someone were to subscribe to this position, it would still follow that the Holy Spirit proceeds from the Son no less than from the Father. For, assuredly, the relation of father does not exist without the relation of son, even as the relation of son does not exist without the relation of father. So if the one relation does not exist without the other, a thing cannot exist from the relation of father without existing from the relation of son. Hence, if the Holy Spirit exists from the one relation, it will follow that He exists from both relations. Thus, if the Holy Spirit exists from the Father according to relation, He will likewise exist from the Son in this same respect.[20] But since no one is so foolish as to hold this view,[21] we must believe and confess that the reason the Holy Spirit exists from the Father is that He exists from God. But the Son is no less God than is the Father; indeed, the Father and the Son are the one and only true God. Therefore, if the Holy Spirit exists from the Father because He exists from God, who is Father, then since He exists from God, who is Son, He cannot be denied to exist also from the Son.

3

Let us also consider what the Lord says in the Gospel. For instance, He says: "But this is eternal life: that they know You, the only true God, and Jesus Christ, whom You have sent."[22] Accordingly, the phrase "the only true God" must be construed in such way that the only true God is signified only when we speak of both the Father and the Son together (i.e., in such way that the only true God is *not* signified when we name only the Father or when we name only the Son); or else the only true God is signified when we name only the Father or name only the Son.

But when we name the Father alone or the Son alone: if the only true God were not signified without the addition of the other's name, then the Father would not be perfect God and the Son would not be perfect God, but God would be a composite of Father and Son. But we believe that the Father is the perfect and only true God, and that likewise the Son is the perfect and only true God. Therefore, when we name the Father alone or the Son alone, then — if we except the relation by which they are related to each other — we signify nothing other than the same only true God, whom we discern in the uttering of each [name].

Thus, when the Lord said, "This is eternal life: that they know You, the only true God, and Jesus Christ, whom You have sent": had He added, "and the Holy Spirit proceeds from this only true God," who would dare to separate the Son from that procession, since the Father is neither more nor less this only true God than is the Son? Therefore, if the same only true God is signified when the Father or the Son alone is spoken of and when both are spoken of together, what is more clear than that when the Holy Spirit is said to proceed from the Father, He proceeds from the only true God, who is Father and Son? Accordingly, just as the Holy Spirit would be understood to proceed from the Son had the Son said that the Holy Spirit proceeds from the only true God (when the Son said that He Himself and the Father are the only true God), so when the Son says that the Holy Spirit proceeds from the Father, then without doubt He signifies that the Holy Spirit proceeds from Himself.[23]

4

The Lord also says: "The Paraclete — the Holy Spirit — whom the Father will send in my name . . ."[24] and also: "When the Paraclete comes, whom I shall send to you from the Father . . . ."[25] Therefore, when He says "whom the Father will send in my name," how is this to be interpreted? [Does it mean] that the Holy Spirit will have the Son's name, so that when the Father sends the Holy Spirit, it is the same as sending the Son? But His words "whom I shall send to you from the Father" do not admit of this construal — since the Son also sends the same spirit that the Father sends, and the Son does not send the Son. In fact, we nowhere read [in Scripture], and we wholly deny, that the Holy Spirit is the Son. So what does "whom the Father will send in my name" mean except that whom the Father will send the Son also will send? — just as when the Son says "whom I shall send from the Father," nothing else is meant except "I and the Father shall send." For "Son" is the name of Him who said "the Father will send in my name." Therefore, "the Father will send in my name" means only "the Father will send in the name of the Son." Hence, what does "the Father will send in the name of the Son" mean except that the Father will send as if the Son were sending, so that when the Father sends, the Son is understood to send.[26] But how are the Son's words "whom I shall send from the Father" to be interpreted? Assuredly, the Holy Spirit is sent from Him from whom the Son sends Him. Now, the Son sends Him from the Father. Therefore, the Holy Spirit is sent from the Father. But the one from whom the Holy Spirit is sent sends [the Holy Spirit]. Hence, when the Son says "I shall send from the Father," the Father is understood to send. So what does "I shall send from the Father" mean except "I shall send as if the Father were sending, so that my sending and the Father's sending are one and the same"?

Therefore, the Son shows very carefully that the Father's sending and His own sending are one, so that the Father does not send except when the Son sends, and the Son does not send except when the Father sends. Accordingly, what does the Son want to signify, or what does He want to be understood, except that the Holy Spirit is not related to the Father in one way and to the Son in another way, and that the Holy Spirit is not more [the spirit] of the one than of the other. Hence, it is exceedingly difficult — indeed, it is impossible — to prove that the Holy Spirit does not proceed from both. For how can the Father and the Son together give and send the Holy Spirit, and how can the Holy Spirit be [the spirit] of both, unless He exists from both? For why does the Son give the Holy Spirit rather than the Holy Spirit giving the Son, or why is the Holy Spirit [the spirit] of the Son rather than the Son being [the son] of the Holy Spirit, except for the fact that the Son does not exist from the Father and from the Holy Spirit together, as the Holy Spirit exists from the Father and from the Son together? Therefore, if the Holy Spirit does not exist from the Son, let Him not be given by the Son or be said to be of the Son — even as the Son is not given by the Holy Spirit and is not said to

De Processione Spiritus Sancti

be of the Holy Spirit, since He does not exist from the Holy Spirit. But if [the Greeks] say that the Holy Spirit does also send the Son — as the Son Himself says through the prophet:[27] "And now the Lord God and His Spirit have sent me" — this statement must be interpreted to apply to the human nature assumed by the Son, who by the common will and ordinance of the Father and the Holy Spirit appeared in the world and was going to redeem the world.

However, I ask those who deny that the Holy Spirit exists and proceeds from the Son how they interpret His so being the spirit of the Son that the Son sends Him as His own spirit. Do they think that the Father gave His own spirit to the Son, as to one not having [a spirit] from Himself? (For the Son has [a spirit] either from Himself or from another. But He cannot have it from anyone else except from the Father.) In that case, the Son would have received [this spirit] from the Father, from whom He has it, and the Father would have given the Holy Spirit to the Son as to one not having [a spirit] from Himself. At this point let [the Greeks] show (since the Father and the Son and the Holy Spirit are equal, and since each one of them is sufficient unto Himself) what reason there was — or what need the Son had — for the Father to give His own spirit to Him rather than giving His own son to the Holy Spirit. Now, we do not deny that the Son has the Holy Spirit from the Father in the following way: from whom the Son has existence, from him He has the fact that He has a spirit existing from Himself (as does the Father), since the being (*esse*) of the Father and of the Son is the same. For it is not the same thing to receive from the Father the essence (*essentia*)[28] from which the Holy Spirit proceeds and to receive from the Father the Holy Spirit. For when the Son is said to have from the Father the essence from which the Holy Spirit proceeds, no need is indicated in the Son. But when it is said that the Son receives from the Father the Holy Spirit, whom He does not have from Himself (as does the Father), we seem to signify that the Son has something less (so to speak) than does the Father and that the Holy Spirit is given to the Son as something supplemental.[29] But it is not apparent why the Son would need the Holy Spirit rather than the Holy Spirit needing the Son. Suppose that somone were to answer: "The Holy Spirit was given to the Son in order that an equal measure of gratitude would be given to the Son and to the Father, inasmuch as the Son as well as the Father would give the Holy Spirit." This belief that God assists God who is in need, as it were — similarly to a man assisting a man — is earthy and very far from an understanding of deity. For, indeed, if the Father gives the Holy Spirit to the Son, God gives God to God. For the Father is God, the Son is God, and the Holy Spirit is God; and they are one and the same God. But we do not understand God to receive God from God unless this is said when God-exists-from-God as Son and as Holy Spirit. Hence, the Holy Spirit is said to be the spirit of the Son for no other reason than that He exists from the Son.

5

We read that after the Resurrection the Lord breathed upon His disciples and said to them: "Receive the Holy Spirit."[30] What does this inbreathing signify? For we know that the breath (*flatus*) which at that time proceeded from His mouth was not the Holy Spirit; and we do not believe that the inbreathing occurred without any mystery. Hence, what can be a more accurate or more suitable interpretation here than that He did this so that we would understand that the Holy Spirit proceeds from Him? [It is] as if He had said: "Just as you see that this breath — through which I signify to you the Holy Spirit (imperceptible things being able to be signified by perceptible things) — proceeds from the depth of my body and from my person, so know that the Holy Spirit, whom I signify to you through this breath, proceeds from the hiddenness of my deity and from my person." For we believe and confess that the person of the Word and of the man[31] is one, and that in this one person are two natures, viz., a divine nature and a human nature.

But perhaps [the Greeks] will maintain: "Surely this breath was not from His *human substance*; nevertheless He breathed it out as His own breath. Therefore, we are taught by means of such a [symbolic] giving of the Holy Spirit that when the Son gives the Holy Spirit He gives and sends His own spirit but not from His *divine essence*." Let them say, then — if any hold this opinion — that just as the breath is not the human nature when it is breathed out by a man, so the Holy Spirit is not the divine substance when He is given or sent by God the Son — a view which no Christian confesses. And let them also say — if when we hear that "the heavens were established by the word of the Lord, and by the breath [*spiritus*] of His mouth all their excellence,"[32] they do not deny that here "the breath of the Lord's mouth" means the Holy Spirit — that the Holy Spirit does not exist from the essence of the Lord (of whose mouth He is called the breath), because the breath (*spiritus*) which customarily proceeds from the mouth of men is not from the substance of the one from whose mouth it proceeds. But if they do not dare to deny that the Spirit of God exists from the essence of God, and if they interpret "words for perceptible things" (i.e., "the breath of His mouth") to mean that the Holy Spirit proceeds from the hiddenness of the essence of the one of whose mouth He is said to be the breath, then let them also confess that the Holy Spirit proceeds from the essence of the one of whose lips He is said to be the breath. For in the prophet we read of Christ that "by the breath of His lips He will slay the wicked one."[33] Therefore, let [the Greeks] show the difference between "the breath of His mouth" and "the breath of His lips" (something which they cannot do); or else let them concede that the Holy Spirit proceeds equally from Him of whose mouth and from Him of whose lips He is called the breath.

But suppose they maintain that "the breath of His lips" ought not at all to be construed there as meaning the Holy Spirit but [ought to be construed as meaning] the words of Christ's preaching (which words He formed in a human manner from that breath of air), since He slays the wicked-one by His words when through His teaching He wards off wickedness from a man. Surely, audible words and perceptible breath do not do this; rather [it is done by] the Holy Spirit, of whom God says through the prophet: "I shall remove from your flesh the heart of stone and shall give you a heart of flesh. And I shall put my spirit in your midst."[34] Therefore, the Holy Spirit slays a wicked man when He converts his heart from wickedness to reverence. But if by "the wicked one" we understand the Antichrist, "whom the Lord Jesus will slay with the breath of His mouth,"[35] I do not think that anyone would attribute that power to the breath of the human voice as much as to the Divine Spirit.

Thus, if the Holy Spirit is signified by these phrases, then since He is called, equally, (1) the breath of the Lord's mouth, by whose (i.e., by the Father's) word the heavens have been established and (2) the breath of the Lord Jesus' mouth, and (3) the breath of Jesus' lips, there is no apparent reason why the Holy Spirit ought to be understood to proceed from the Father's mouth rather than from the Son's mouth. And if we take "Father's mouth" to mean the Father's essence (for His mouth is nothing other than His essence, so that just as the word of the Lord is from His essence, so the breath of His mouth is only from His essence), what is clearer than that just as the breath of the Father's mouth exists and proceeds from the Father's essence, so the breath of the Son's mouth and lips exists and proceeds from the Son's essence? For when the text says "The heavens were established by the word of the Lord, and by the breath of His mouth all their excellence,"[36] no one, I think, will take this to mean simply transitory words and the breath which is taken in from the air and emitted through the mouth of the speaker.

But in whatever way anyone tries to interpret these texts, it suffices that the breathing of the Lord upon His disciples (of which I have made mention) was done in order to signify that the spirit whom He gave proceeded from the hiddenness of this person from whose hiddenness the breath which He was breathing out was proceeding. In fact, when Divine Scripture signifies a hidden thing by means of the likenesses to perceptible things, the things which signify and the things which are signified cannot be alike in all respects; for [otherwise] this would be not a likeness but an identity. Perhaps someone might want to say that that breathing was done in the way it was simply by the wisdom of God, without any spiritual significance; but no one, I deem, is really so senseless as to think this.

6

The Son also says about the Holy Spirit: "He will not speak on His own authority, but whatsoever He will hear that will He speak."[37] What does "He will not speak on His own authority" mean except that what He will speak He will have from someone else? And what does "what He will speak He will have from someone else" mean except that He will have from someone else the knowledge of the things which He will speak? Thus, after the Son says "He will not speak on His own authority," He adds: "but whatsoever He will hear that will He speak." What is it for the Holy Spirit to hear except for Him to learn, as it were? And

De Processione Spiritus Sancti

what is it to learn except to receive knowledge? Therefore, if the Holy Spirit's knowledge is nothing other than His essence (*essentia*), then since for Him to speak is the same as for Him to teach, He exists (*habet essentiam*) from the one from whom He hears what He speaks and teaches. Now, the Holy Spirit neither hears nor exists from anyone other than either the Father or the Son. But if He exists (*habet esse*)[38] from the Father, then according to the argument previously[39] given He also exists from the Son. Accordingly, the Son also says: "He [the Holy Spirit] will glorify me because He will receive from me and will declare unto you."[40] Indeed, what else does this mean except "He will hear from me (i.e., He will know from me) that which He will declare unto you"? When the Son said "whatsoever He will hear that will He speak," He did not specify from whom the Holy Spirit would hear. But when He says "He will receive from me," He shows clearly that He Himself is the one from whom (just as from the Father) the Holy Spirit receives His knowledge and essence. [He shows this] lest anyone should attribute to the Father alone that which the Holy Spirit hears from someone. Now, when the Son says "He will not speak on His own authority, but whatsoever He will hear that will He speak" and declare unto you, the Holy Spirit is signified to exist (*esse*) and to proceed from the one from whom He hears. Similarly, when the Son says "He will receive from me and will declare unto you," He shows plainly that the Holy Spirit exists (*essentiam habere*) and proceeds from Himself (i.e., from His own essence). For what is not the divine essence is inferior to the Holy Spirit; and the Holy Spirit does not receive something from that which is inferior to Himself. Therefore, when the Son says "He will receive from me," He signifies here nothing of His own except His own essence.

7

Perhaps [the Greeks] will attempt to interpret otherwise than I have done the statement which the Son made, viz.: "He will receive from me and will declare unto you."[41] But how will they interpret the passage where [the Son] says: "No one knows the Son except the Father; and not anyone knows the Father except the Son or him to whom the Son chooses to reveal [this knowledge]"?[42] We hear that no one knows the Father or the Son except the Father or the Son and him to whom the Son reveals [this knowledge]. Now, the Son does not mean "no one" in the sense of "no human being"; rather it is as if He had said: "no one at all." Indeed, had He meant "no human being" He would not have added the words "except the Father," because the Father is not a human being. And when He says "not anyone (*quis*) knows the Father," the monosyllabic word "*quis*" signifies not only any human person but also any person whatsoever. Hence, no one whatsoever has this knowledge except the Father and the Son and him to whom the Son reveals it. Accordingly, either the Holy Spirit does not know the Father and the Son (something which it is impious to suppose), or else the Son reveals to the Holy Spirit the knowledge of Himself and the Father (which knowledge is nothing except the essence of the Holy Spirit).

But what if [the Greeks] make the following claim?: "As far as regards the wording of the text the Son admits no one to this knowledge except Himself, the Father, and him to whom the Son reveals it. Nevertheless, the Holy Spirit must not be said either to be excluded from this knowledge or to receive it from the Son; for the Father and the Son know each other only insofar as they are one with the Holy Spirit. And so when [the text] says that the Father and the Son know each other, the Holy Spirit must be meant at the same time. And when the Son reveals, He reveals not to the Holy Spirit but to creatures." If, I repeat, [the Greeks] make this claim then we immediately and firmly draw the following inference. In a case where Truth clearly denies (according to what the words of His mouth declare) that the Holy Spirit knows the Father and the Son unless the Son reveals this knowledge, [the Greeks] say that we ought not so much to pay attention to the words as to the unity of essence which is one and inseparable for the three. If so, then we ought all the more to preserve the consequence of this unity (a consequence about which I spoke earlier)[43] in the case where no authority (either in writing or in thought) denies this consequence, and where no authority sets forth anything which is contrary to it or in any respect opposed to it.

If the Greeks are unwilling openly to resist the truth, then let them choose one of the two alternatives: either (1) the Holy Spirit does not know the Father and the Son unless the Son reveals [this

De Processione Spiritus Sancti

knowledge to Him], or (2) because of the fact that insofar as the Father and the Son know each other they are one with the Holy Spirit, then when they are said to know each other it follows necessarily that the Holy Spirit is included in this knowledge. Surely, there is no middle course — provided [the Greeks] do not want altogether to take away this knowledge from the Holy Spirit or altogether to take away truth from the words of Truth, both of which things true confession curses. For Truth speaks as follows: "No one knows the Son except the Father; and not anyone knows the Father except the Son and him to whom the Son chooses to reveal [this knowledge]."[44] Now indeed, if they opt for the Holy Spirit's knowing the Father and the Son because of the Son's revelation, then the Holy Spirit has this knowledge from the Son, and this knowledge is, for the Holy Spirit, nothing else than His being. Hence, He exists and proceeds from the Son, since He proceeds from the one from whom He exists. On the other hand, suppose they [opt for] maintaining: when the Father and the Son are said to know each other, then because the essence through which they know each other is the same for the Holy Spirit, it follows that the Holy Spirit shares this knowledge. [In that case], when they read that the Holy Spirit proceeds from the Father, about whom the Son says "I and the Father are one":[45] let them confess with us, because of the essential identity of the Father and the Son, that the Holy Spirit without doubt proceeds also from the Son.

8

Now, when we state that the Son is begotten from the Father and that the Holy Spirit proceeds from the Father and the Son, someone may make the following objection: that (1) we are establishing grades and intervals (as if the Holy Spirit could not exist unless the Son were first begotten from the Father, so that the Holy Spirit is later than the Son), and thus that (2) it is more correctly said that they both exist equally from the Father — the Son by being begotten and the Holy Spirit by proceeding — so that the Son does not exist from the Holy Spirit nor does the Holy Spirit exist from the Son (even as brightness and heat exist equally from the one sun — the brightness not existing from the heat, and the heat not existing from the brightness). If someone makes this objection to our assertion, then we reply [as follows].

We do not posit grades of dignity in God, who is one; nor do we establish intervals in eternity (which is outside of all time) [when we affirm] that the Son exists from the Father or that the Holy Spirit exists from the Father and the Son. For just as all of us who hold the Christian faith confess that the Son is neither lesser nor later than the Father (even though the Son exists only from the Father), so also we who say that the Holy Spirit exists and proceeds from the Son confess that He is neither lesser nor later than the Son. To be sure, although brightness and heat proceed from the sun and are not able to exist unless the sun from which they come exists, nevertheless we discern nothing earlier or later in these three — viz., in the sun, the brightness, and the heat. Thus, since this holds true in the case of temporal things, how much less in the case of eternity (which is not confined by time) can the previously mentioned three persons be understood, in existing, to be susceptible to an interval.

Now, as for its being said that the Son and the Holy Spirit can so exist from the Father alone that the Son does not exist from the Holy Spirit nor the Holy Spirit from the Son (even as brightness and heat proceed together from the one sun, so that neither exists from the other): it is wrong to raise this objection against us. For when we say that the Son exists from the Father and that the Holy Spirit exists from the Father, we maintain that God the Son and God the Holy Spirit exist from God the Father, and that these three persons are only one God, and that this very being exists from this very same being itself. But in the case of the sun we do not say, when brightness or when heat exists from the sun, that the sun exists from the sun, or that the sun and what exists from the sun are the same thing, or that the three things are one sun. For if the sun and the brightness were one sun, or if (similarly) the sun and the heat were one sun: it would be necessary for either the brightness to exist from the heat (since it would exist from the whole of the sun, which would be identical with the heat) or the heat to exist from the brightness (since it would exist from [the whole of] the sun, which would not be different from the essence of the brightness). Nevertheless, let us suppose that the Son and the Holy Spirit exist equally from the Father alone, in the way that heat and brightness exist from the one sun. Now, if this were the case, what basis would those who say this have for affirming that the Holy Spirit is [the spirit] of the Son and denying that the

De Processione Spiritus Sancti

Son is [the son] of the Holy Spirit? For just as there is no reason to admit that the heat is the brightness' [heat] or that the brightness is the heat's [brightness], so truth would not allow that the Holy Spirit is the Son's [spirit] rather than that the Son is the Holy Spirit's [son]. Therefore, if [the Greeks] do not dare to deny that the Holy Spirit is [the spirit] of the Son, let them deny that the Son and the Holy Spirit exist equally from the Father alone in the way that brightness and heat exist from the sun alone. Hence, if they raise against us this objection which I have mentioned regarding the brightness and heat of the sun, it counts neither for them nor against us.

9

In order not to separate the Son altogether from participating with the Father in the procession of the Holy Spirit, [the Greeks] maintain (as we are told) that the Holy Spirit proceeds from the Father *through* the Son (*per filium*). But it is not clear how this can be understood to be the case — especially since they nowhere read any text from which they can prove it clearly. Suppose they think that the following text which we read about God supports them: viz., that "all things are from Him and through Him and in Him,"[46] so that (1) the Father is the one from whom all things exist, and the Son is the one through whom all things exist, and the Holy Spirit is the one in whom all things exist, and so that (2) the Holy Spirit is included among all the things which exist through the Son. Now, indeed, we accept without scruple the view that all things exist from the Father and through the Son and in the Holy Spirit. But it is exceedingly difficult to maintain that the Holy Spirit is included among all the things which the apostle states to exist though the Son. For it is impossible to include any one of the three persons among all these things and to exclude the other two. But if it were the case that the Father and the Son and the Holy Spirit are among all the things which exist from the Father and through the Son and in the Holy Spirit, let a rational mind behold how much confusion would follow. Therefore, when the apostle says "All things are from Him and through Him and in Him," surely we ought to understand ["all things" to mean] all divinely created things — which exist from God and through Him and in Him as one thing exists from another thing and through another and in another. For whatever has been created is not identical with God but is different from Him. However, the Holy Spirit is not different from God but is the same being as the Father and the Son.

Assuredly, no other way can be discerned by means of which they can show that the Holy Spirit proceeds from the Father through the Son, as they say. Now, the Father and the Son do not differ in unity of deity; and the Holy Spirit proceeds only from the *deity* of the Father. Therefore, if the Son has the same deity [as the Father], then it is impossible to understand how the Holy Spirit could proceed from the deity of the Father *through* the deity of the Son but not *from* the deity of the Son. [This view is impossible to understand, that is,] unless perhaps someone were to claim that the Holy Spirit proceeds not from the Father's deity but from His paternity, and proceeds not through the Son's deity but through His filiation. But this view is stifled by its own obvious foolishness.

But suppose someone argues that when I say that the Holy Spirit proceeds from the deity of the Father and the Son, I am unable to separate the deity of the Holy Spirit from the deity of the Father and the Son, since the three have one and the same deity. [And suppose he alleges] it to follow that if the Holy Spirit proceeds from the deity of the Father and the Son, then He proceeds as well from His own deity and therefore proceeds from Himself. Now, to this objection I recall having above already[47] adequately given the answer that no person can exist from Himself. Now, when the Son exists from the essence of the Father: then although the essence of the Son is the same essence as (and not a different one from) the essence of the Father, nevertheless the Son does not exist from Himself but exists only from the Father. Similarly, although the Holy Spirit exists from the essence of the Father and the Son, which is identical with His essence, He does not exist from Himself but exists only from the Father and the Son.

[The Greeks] will ask: "Why can we not also say that the Holy Spirit proceeds from the Father *through* the Son, just as we say that all things were created by the Father *through* the Word, which is the Son? For when the Father creates through His word, He creates through no other than through what He Himself is —

De Processione Spiritus Sancti

viz., through the essential power which is the same as the Word's — and yet He is said to create through the Word. Why can we not say likewise that the Holy Spirit proceeds from the Father through the Word, since He proceeds from the Father only from and through what is common to the Father and the Son (even though the Holy Spirit proceeds not as does creation but as that which proceeds from itself)?"

Let us see what follows if we say this; and let there be peace between us. Assuredly, what has been created by the Father through the Word has been created by the Word. For, indeed, the Word says: "Whatever the Father does, this the Son does also."[48] Therefore, since the Holy Spirit proceeds from the Father through the Son, let us say likewise that He proceeds also from the Son, even as what has been created by the Father through the Word has also been created by the Word. Or do [the Greeks] perhaps judge that the Holy Spirit proceeds from the Father through the Son in the way that a lake is said to exist from a spring through a river, when a spring flows into a river and the river accumulates into a lake?[49] Now, in this example the river is not in the spring but is outside the spring, whereas the Son is in the Father and not outside the Father. Therefore, it is not the case that the Holy Spirit exists from the Father through the Son in the way that a lake exists from a spring through a river. Nevertheless, even if it were the case, then even though the Holy Spirit existed from the Father through the Son, He could not be denied to exist from the Son — just as even though the lake exists from the spring through the river, it must be said to exist from the river. For if anyone denies that the lake exists from the river simply because the river first exists from the spring, then let him say that he exists from Adam and not from his own father, since through his own father he exists from Adam. Let him also deny — on the ground that they first existed from Adam — that the Son of the Virgin exists from Mary and from David and from Abraham. And let him claim to be false what was said to Abraham, viz., "In your seed all nations will be blessed," and what was said to David, viz., "From the fruit of your loins I will place one upon your throne," and what was said to Mary, viz., "Blessed is the fruit of your womb."[50] And let him say that Christ is the seed or the fruit of Adam and not of them, since they descend from

Adam. But according to this line of reasoning the Son of the Virgin is not even from Adam but is from the clay from which Adam was created.

But [the Greeks] will reason as follows: "Although the Holy Spirit exists from the Father and the Son (just as you say that the lake exists from the spring and from the river), we are correct in saying that the Holy Spirit proceeds not from the Son but from the Father through the Son. For, indeed, the dispute between us is over the word 'procession': you affirm and we deny that the [Holy Spirit's] procession is from the Son. For, lo, you see that the river proceeds from the spring as from its source of origin. But even though the lake exists from the river, it does not proceed from the river; rather it accumulates from the river. So, then, even if the Holy Spirit exists from the Son, He is not properly said to proceed from the Son but is properly said to proceed from the Father, as from His source."

Perhaps this reasoning would be correct if in being begotten from the Father the Son proceeded outside the Father, and if there were then a small spatial interval, and if the Holy Spirit were understood to exist from the Father before existing from the Son. For the river flowing from the spring proceeds outside the spring and after an interval accumulates into a lake; and the lake exists from the spring before existing from the river, and thus the lake exists from the spring through the river, not from the river through the spring. But in being begotten from the Father, the Son does not pass outside the Father but remains within Him and does not differ from the Father spatially or temporally or essentially; moreover, that from which the Holy Spirit proceeds is one and the same for the Father and the Son. Therefore, it cannot be comprehended, and it ought not to be said, that the Holy Spirit proceeds from the Father but not from the Son. Hence, there is no apparent reason to say that the Holy Spirit does not proceed from the Son but proceeds from the Father *through* the Son. For even if He [proceeds] *through* the Son, He cannot avoid [proceeding] *from* the Son.

Nevertheless, what if someone — in order not to concede that the Holy Spirit proceeds from the Son, from whom He exists (as a lake exists from a river) — wants to say that the Son proceeds more properly from the Father than the Holy Spirit proceeds from the Son, even though the Holy Spirit exists from the Son? (For

De Processione Spiritus Sancti

the river seems to him to proceed more properly from the spring than the lake proceeds from the river.) Well, we do not deny that the one who is begotten does proceed in a certain respect from the one from whom he is begotten. And we affirm that the Holy Spirit in His unique way proceeds not as from two springs but truly from one spring. He proceeds in such way, however, that the Son's procession does not lose, and the Holy Spirit's procession does not acquire, the name "begottenness." Therefore, there is no reason why the Son ought to be said to proceed from the Father rather than the Holy Spirit's being said to proceed from the Son.

Let us consider more carefully how the lake exists equally from the spring and the river, so that we may recognize by means of this example — inasmuch as what is eternal can be understood by means of something spatial and temporal — that the Holy Spirit exists from the Father and the Son. For as I wrote[51] to Pope Urban (of venerable memory) in my letter on *The Incarnation of the Word*, we find in the examination of these three many things which apply, by virtue of a certain likeness, to the one God and the three persons. It is evident that what is called the spring and the river and the lake is one and the same water, not three waters, even though the spring, the river, and the lake are three. So let us distinguish between the spring and the river and the lake, and let us see why these separate things, although they are three, are understood to be one water. Indeed, in the spring the water bubbles up from the depths; in the river it flows down from the spring; in the lake it accumulates and remains. Therefore, "spring" signifies water bubbling forth from the depths; "river" signifies that the water flows from the spring; and "lake" signifies that the water accumulates there. However, we see that the river does not exist from that with respect to which the water is called a spring; instead it exists from that which the spring is, viz., from water. And the lake does not exist from that with respect to which the water is called a spring or a river; instead, it exists from the water itself, which is one and the same water in the spring and the river. Therefore, the lake does not exist from that in virtue of which the spring and the river are different but exists from that in virtue of which they are one. Thus, if the spring is no more that from which the lake exists than is the river, the lake cannot be understood to exist from the spring rather than from the river. Similarly, then, when God is called Father or Son or Holy Spirit, one essence and one God is understood to be present in these three; and the name "God" signifies this essence. But "Father" signifies the one who begets, "Son" the one who is begotten, and "Holy Spirit" the one who proceeds in a unique and ineffable manner. Therefore, just as the lake does not exist from that in virtue of which the spring and the river differ from each other but exists from the water, in virtue of which they are one, so the Holy Spirit does not exist from that in virtue of which the Father and the Son differ from each other but exists from the divine essence, in virtue of which they are one. Therefore, if the Father is no more that from which the Holy Spirit exists than is the Son, we cannot understand why the Holy Spirit would exist from the Father rather than from the Son.

10

But if [the Greeks] argue that the Holy Spirit cannot exist from two causes or two sources, then we make the following reply. Just as we believe that the Holy Spirit exists not from that in virtue of which the Father and the Son are two but from that in virtue of which they are one, so we say not that He has two sources but that He has one source. Indeed, when we call God the source of creation, we understand the Father and the Son and the Holy Spirit to be one source, not three sources; similarly, although the Father and the Son and the Holy Spirit are three, [we understand them to be] one creator and not three creators. For the Father or the Son or the Holy Spirit is the source or the creator through that in virtue of which they are one, not through that in virtue of which they are three. Therefore, although the Father is the source and the Son is the source and the Holy Spirit is the source, there are not three sources but is one source. Similarly, when the Holy Spirit is said to exist from the Father and the Son, He exists not from two sources but from one source, which is Father and Son — even as He exists from one God, who is Father and Son (if God can properly be said to have a cause or a source).

Indeed, a source is seen to be [the source] only of a thing's beginning, and a cause is seen to be [the cause] only of an effect. But the Holy Spirit never began to exist; nor is He the effect of anything. What begins to exist advances from not-being to be-

De Processione Spiritus Sancti

ing; and the word "effect" is seen to be properly applied to something which is brought about. However, since it is true that the Son exists from the Father and that the Holy Spirit exists from the Father and the Son: then — provided it is taken in a certain unique and ineffable sense, because otherwise it cannot be asserted — the Father can acceptably be called the source (in some sense) of the Son, and the Father and the Son can be called the source of the Holy Spirit. Nevertheless, we do not acknowledge two sources — the one source being the Father in relation to the Son and the other source being the Father and the Son in relation to the Holy Spirit — just as we do not believe that the Father, from whom the Son exists, is one God and that the Father and Son, from whom the Holy Spirit exists, is another God. Yet, each of them[52] exists in His own way from the same God and from the same source. The one exists by being begotten; the other exists by proceeding — provided this procession is construed in a certain unique and ineffable manner. For procession is spoken of in many ways; of these ways this one is understood to be unique, even as the Son's begottenness is recognized to be unique. This same thing is understood to be the case if we say that the Father is the cause of the Son, and that the Father and the Son are the cause of the Holy Spirit. For we cannot say that there are two different causes — the cause of the Son, and the cause of the Holy Spirit — but [can only speak of] one cause, just as there are not two gods but is one God, from whom the Son and the Holy Spirit exist.

11

Someone may ask: "At the time the Lord used the words[53] 'When the Paraclete — the Spirit of Truth — comes, who proceeds from the Father . . .' why did He not add 'and from the Son' or 'and from me' if He meant for it to be interpreted in this way?" But in His sayings it is not unusual that when He attributes something as if to the Father alone or to Himself alone or to the Holy Spirit alone, He intends for what is said in the case of the one to be understood to hold true in the case of the other two as well. For instance, when He says "Blessed are you, Simon bar Jona, because flesh and blood has not revealed it to you but my father who is in Heaven,"[54] must not the Son and the Holy Spirit be understood to have revealed together with the Father? For since the Father does not reveal with respect to the fact that He is Father but with respect to the fact that He is God, and since the Son and the Holy Spirit are this same God, it follows that what the Father reveals the Son and the Holy Spirit also reveal. Likewise, the Son says[55] "No one knows the Son except the Father; and not anyone knows the Father except the Son and him to whom the Son chooses to reveal [this knowledge]" — as if only the Son knew and revealed the Father and Himself, and as if only the Father knew the Son. [When he says this] we must take it to mean that revealing and knowing are common to the three persons; for the Father and the Son and the Holy Spirit know and reveal with respect to the fact that they are one, not with respect to the fact that they are distinct from one another. Moreover, when the Son says that the Father knows the Son and that the Son knows the Father and reveals Himself and the Father, clearly He intends for it to be understood that the Father knows the Holy Spirit and that the Son knows and reveals the Holy Spirit. For the Holy Spirit too is the very same thing that the Father and the Son are. Likewise, when the Son says "He who sees me sees the Father also,"[56] the Holy Spirit must not be excluded; for he who sees *that* with respect to which the Father and the Son and the Holy Spirit are one cannot see one of these three without seeing the other two. Furthermore, the Son says[57] to the Apostles regarding the Holy Spirit: "When He, the Spirit of Truth, comes He will teach you all truth" — as if only the Holy Spirit would teach all truth, although in fact He does not teach all truth independently of the Father and independently of the Son. For it is not with respect to the fact that He is someone's spirit (viz., the Father and the Son's spirit) but with respect to the fact that He is one with the Father and the Son (i.e., with respect to the fact that He is God) that He teaches all truth.

So do you see how, in the examples I have presented, what the Son attributes as if to one person alone cannot be excluded from the other two persons? In Sacred Scripture we read many texts of this kind, so that what is said of one person singularly is understood to apply to all three indifferently. For whatever is said of one person should be understood to hold true of the other two as well — except when that in virtue of which they are different from one another (as I said)[58] is known to oppose it. Consequently, when we believe that the Holy Spirit proceeds from

De Processione Spiritus Sancti

the Father: since God exists from God (i.e., since the Holy Spirit's essence exists from the Father's essence, which is understood to be common to the three), we must also confess that the Holy Spirit exists from the Son if the Son does not exist from the Holy Spirit. For the Holy Spirit exists from that which the Son is and which the Father is.

But someone will say: "Because what we read in one place about one of them alone is elsewhere clearly indicated to hold true of the other two, we know (1) that the Son and the Holy Spirit reveal what the Father alone is said to reveal, (2) that the Father and the Holy Spirit reveal and know what the Son alone is said to do, and (3) that the Father and the Son teach what the Holy Spirit alone is promised to be going to teach. But when [the Lord] says that the Holy Spirit proceeds from the Father, we do not read elsewhere that He proceeds from the Son. Hereby we are cautioned against asserting by our own discretion that which has nowhere [in Scripture] been stated."

To this argument we reply: It is rather the case that by means of those things which have thus been said, we are taught to understand similarly, in similar sayings, those things which have been left unsaid. This is especially the case where we see very clearly that the things which are not said follow by rational necessity (and without any other rational considerations contradicting them) from the things which are said. For when the Lord says to the Father: "This is eternal life: that they know You, the only true God, and Jesus Christ, whom You have sent,"[59] ought we to exclude the Holy Spirit from this health-giving and life-giving knowledge simply because we nowhere read: "This is eternal life: that they know the Father, the only true God, and also the Holy Spirit," or "This is eternal life: that they know the Son, the only true God, and also the Holy Spirit"? Or when we read "Just as the Father has life in Himself, so He has granted to the Son to have life in Himself":[60] shall we deny that the Holy Spirit has from the Father, from whom He exists, the fact of having life in Himself (as the Father and the Son have) simply because the Son nowhere says this about the Holy Spirit (as He does say it about Himself)? Moreover, when He says "The Father is in me and I in the Father"[61] and "He who sees me sees the Father also":[62] shall we deny (1) that the Holy Spirit is in the Father and the Son, and that the Father and the Son are in the Holy Spirit, or (2) that

He who sees the Son sees the Holy Spirit as well as seeing the Father — if these statements are not read in the same passage in which they are made about the Father and the Son?

Rather, since the Father and the Son and the Holy Spirit are one and the same God, then when eternal life is said to consist in knowing the Father and the Son — the only true God — the Holy Spirit must be taken to be inseparably included in this knowledge. And when we read that "as the Father has life in Himself, so He has granted to the Son to have life in Himself," we ought not to think that this life is alien to the Holy Spirit or that the Holy Spirit does not have it in Himself. And when we hear "The Father is in me and I in the Father" and "He who sees me sees the Father also": we ought to know, by means of what is thus said, that the Holy Spirit is not outside the Father and the Son, that the Father and the Son are not outside the Holy Spirit, and that in seeing the Son one sees the Holy Spirit as well as the Father. For as the Father is not one God, the Son another God, and the Holy Spirit still another God, so God does not have within Himself anything other than God, and God does not exist outside of God, and God is not unlike God. In fact, where in the Prophets or the Gospels or the Apostles do we read in these very words that the one God is three persons, or that the one God is a trinity, or that God exists from God? Not even in that creed[63] in which the [doctrine of] the procession of the Holy Spirit from the Son is not set forth do we find the word "person" or "trinity." Nevertheless, since these statements follow very clearly from the statements we do read, we steadfastly believe them in our hearts and confess them with our mouths. Therefore, we ought to accept with certainty not only those things which we read in Sacred Scripture but also the statements which follow from them by rational necessity and which no other rational considerations contradict.

12

Although what has already been said above can suffice, I will add still another consideration on the basis of which the Holy Spirit is known to exist from the Son. The Greeks confess with us that the Holy Spirit is the spirit of God and the spirit of the Father and the spirit of the Son. Therefore, I ask whether they understand Him to be the spirit of God and the spirit of the Father and

De Processione Spiritus Sancti

the spirit of the Son in the same way or in different ways. Now, it is certain that He is not called God's spirit in the sense of [God's] possession — as, for example, when a horse is called someone's [horse], or a house is called someone's [house]. For the one who possesses is greater than what is possessed. But God is not greater than the Holy Spirit — because the Holy Spirit is God, and God is not greater than God. Nor is the Holy Spirit called God's spirit in the sense of being God's member — as a man's hand or foot [is a man's member]. For God does not have a member or any part. In what sense, then, is the Holy Spirit to be understood to be the spirit of God except in the sense that what He is He is from God? Now, the name "Father" signifies nothing other than either God who is the Father or else the Father's relation to the Son, from which relation He has the name "Father." A similar thing must be said about the Son. For, indeed, what is understood by the name "Son" except either God who is the Son or else the relation by which the Son is related to the Father and because of which He is called the Son? But anyone with sense comprehends that the Holy Spirit is the spirit of the Father or of the Son not with respect to the fact that the one is the Father and the other is the Son but with respect to the fact that both are one and the same God.[64] Therefore, when the Holy Spirit is called the spirit of God and the spirit of the Father and the spirit of the Son, the signification is the same.

Now, the Holy Spirit is called the spirit of God and the spirit of the Father because He exists and proceeds from God and from the Father. Thus, He exists and proceeds also from the Son, because He is called the spirit of the Son in this same sense. Now, when the Holy Spirit is called the spirit of God and the spirit of the Lord: if we do not understand that He is the spirit of the Son in the same sense that He is the spirit of the Father, then either we will be excluding the Son from being called God and Lord, or else "the spirit of God" or "the spirit of the Lord" will be understood to have a twofold sense. But from where do [the Greeks] get this latter view? Or — when we read "the spirit of God" or "the spirit of the Lord" — where in Sacred Scripture do we read something which is not understood in the same sense regarding the Father and regarding the Son? Or what do we find from which this conclusion follows? Suppose [the Greeks] say: "When the Holy Spirit is called the spirit of the Father, this is understood in two ways, for He is the spirit of the Father both because He exists from the Father and because He is given by the Father; but He is the spirit of the Son only because He is given by the Son." This is the view about which I am asking: where do they get it? Suppose they answer: "This view is not stated in any authentic passage [of Scripture], and it does not follow from what is written in Scripture." Well, then, when we say that the Holy Spirit proceeds from the Son: since we recognize that this doctrine follows of necessity from that which they read and believe, why do they find fault with us on the ground that they do not read these words in Scripture?

Therefore, let [the Greeks] themselves judge which one of the following views ought to be adopted, even though the Sacred Page does not say anything about either: (1) our view that the Holy Spirit proceeds from the Son (a view which we prove to follow from those things which we rightly believe); or (2) their view that the Holy Spirit is the spirit of the Father in one way and the spirit of the Son in another (a view which they cannot prove either by authority or by reason or from things which are certain). If indeed they say (as I hear) that the Holy Spirit is the spirit of the Son in a way different from His being the spirit of the Father: assuredly, either they ought to cease holding this view since they nowhere read it itself or anything else from which to prove it; or at least they ought not to reproach us, who say (even though we do not read this in these very words) that the Holy Spirit proceeds from the Son, for we demonstrate that this view follows from those things which we believe equally [with them]. Now, if they cease making this assertion, let them believe equally with us that the Holy Spirit is the spirit of the Father and — in the same sense — of the Son, and let them recognize that He proceeds from the Son as well as from the Father. And if they cease to reproach us, let them acknowledge with us the basis upon which they know that we ought not to be reproached.

13

[The Greeks] reproach us for having added, in that creed[65] which both we and they equally accept and affirm, that the Holy Spirit proceeds from the Son. And they ask why this addition was made, and why it was not first shown to their church, so that what

De Processione Spiritus Sancti

needed to be added could be considered jointly and could be added by mutual consent. To this reproach, however, we have a sufficient reply. For if we are asked why it was done, we say: It needed [to be done] on account of certain men who, lacking understanding, did not recognize that implicit in the truths which the universal church believes, and following from these truths, is [the doctrine] that the Holy Spirit proceeds from the Son. [It needed to be done] in order that these men would not hesitate to believe this doctrine. Just how necessary this addition was is recognized by reference to those who deny this doctrine simply because it was not placed in the Creed. Therefore, since need urged this addition and since no rational consideration prevented it and since true faith allowed it, the Latin Church faithfully asserted what it knew ought to be believed and confessed. For we know that not all the things that we ought to believe and confess have been recorded there. Nor did those who composed this Creed intend for the Christian faith to be content to believe and confess only those things which they set down in it. For to mention only one instance: in the Creed the Lord is not said to have descended into Hell — a doctrine which, nonetheless, both we and the Greeks believe in equal measure. But if they say that a creed fixed by such great authority ought not at all to have been corrupted, we do not judge to be a corruption a case where we add nothing contrary to what has already been stated therein. And although we can defend this addition as not being a corruption, still if someone wants to insist contentiously that it is a corruption, we reply that we have not corrupted the Creed but have added something new. For with the Greeks we keep and venerate intact the version translated in accordance with the nature of the Greek text. But the version which we regularly use in the hearing of the people, we publish with the above addition as prescribed by the Latin tradition.

Now, as for the question why this addition was not made with the consent of the Greek Church, we answer: (1) it was especially difficult for the Latins to gather the Greek bishops for consultation on this matter, and (2) it was not necessary for the Latins to call into question that about which they had no doubt. For what church is there which, extended throughout a single kingdom, is not permitted to establish in accordance with right faith something which is usefully read and sung in the assembly of the people? How much more, then, the Latins were permitted to proclaim steadfastly that doctrine agreed upon by all the nations and kingdoms using the Latin language!

14

Let us briefly summarize what we have accomplished above on the basis of many considerations. By incontestable reasoning we have established that the Holy Spirit exists from the Son as well as from the Father and that, nevertheless, the Holy Spirit exists not as from two [sources] but as from one [source].[66] For the Holy Spirit exists from the Father and the Son's oneness — i.e., from their deity — and not from that in virtue of which they are distinct from each other. But God, from whom the Holy Spirit exists, is Father and Son; therefore, the Holy Spirit is truly said to exist from the Father and from the Son, who are two. Now, the Father is not earlier or later than the Son, nor greater or lesser; and the one is God neither more nor less than is the other. Consequently, the Holy Spirit does not exist from the Father before existing from the Son, nor from the Son before existing from the Father; nor is He greater or lesser as He exists from the Father than as He exists from the Son; nor does He exist more or less from the one than from the other. For suppose He existed earlier or later from, were greater or lesser [as He exists from], or existed more or less from, the one than from the other. Then, of necessity, it would follow that either (1) the Holy Spirit would not exist from that in virtue of which the Father and the Son are one, or else that (2) this oneness would not be perfectly and absolutely one but would contain some diversity from which would occur the difference which I said the Holy Spirit [would have] in existing from this oneness. But it cannot be denied that the Holy Spirit exists from that in virtue of which the Father and the Son are one, for otherwise He would not exist from God. And it ought not to be believed that in this oneness there is anything with respect to which there is any diversity. Therefore, it is not the case that the Holy Spirit exists earlier or later from, is greater or lesser [as He exists from], or exists more or less from, the Father than from the Son or from the Son than from the Father. For it is not possible for one and the same Holy Spirit, who exists once and as a whole from God as a whole, to exist in greater or lesser degree from the one and supremely simple God.

But if it is said that the Holy Spirit exists principally[67] from the Father — as if He existed from the Father more than from the Son — then it must not be said in such way that any one of the aforesaid differences is understood to be present. But since that which the Son is He has from the Father, it is not unacceptable to assert that the Son has from the Father, from whom He exists, the fact that the Holy Spirit exists from Him.[68] Nevertheless, the Son so exists from the Father that He is in every respect the same thing as the Father and is one and the same God as the Father. Thus, just as the sole and simple God cannot be greater or lesser than Himself, nor earlier or later than Himself, and just as He has no diversity within Himself, so the Son is neither earlier nor later, neither greater nor lesser, than is the Father. Nor does the Son have in Himself anything different from the Father; rather, just as the Son has it from the Father to exist perfectly, so He has it from the Father to be equal and similar to the Father in every respect — indeed, to be the very same thing [as is the Father]. Hence, just as although the Son exists from the Father, the Son is no less God than is the Father, so although the Son has from the Father the fact that the Holy Spirit exists from Him, the Holy Spirit exists no less from the Son than from the Father. For insofar as the Son is one and the same God as the Father — i.e., insofar as the Son is God — He is not different from the Father and does not have any dissimilarity. For the Father is not one God and the Son another God, nor are they dissimilarly that which they are; rather, the one is different from the other insofar as the one is the Father and the other is the Son. And just as the Son is not a different God from the Father, so with respect to the fact that the Son is God He does not have anything from any other than from Himself.

Now, when we say that God exists from God and that the Son exists from the Father, we construe this to mean not that one God exists from another God but that the same God exists from the same God — even though we say "The one exists from the other," i.e., that the Son exists from the Father. For (as was said earlier)[69] just as in accordance with the name signifying unity God receives no diversity, so in accordance with the names signifying that God exists from God, necessarily He admits of plurality. Therefore, if it is said that the Holy Spirit exists principally from the Father, nothing else is signified than that the Son, from whom the Holy Spirit exists, has from the Father the fact that the Holy Spirit exists from Him — since that which the Son is He has from the Father. There is no parallel here with the case of created things, where when we assert that something exists principally, we intend to signify that what is said to exist principally is greater than that other to which it is compared. For example, when a steward of some lord feeds, by the lord's command, the members of the household, the lord principally and more than the steward is rightly said to feed the household. For it is not the case that all the things which are the lord's are equally the steward's, as it is the case that whatever is the Father's is equally the Son's.

Perhaps someone will marvel and ask: "How can it be comprehended that one thing exists from another without the other from which it exists somehow existing more principally and more valuably, and without the thing which exists from this other somehow existing inferiorly and as something secondary? [Is this not] especially the case when that which exists from something else is seen to need, in order to exist, the other from which it exists, though that other from which it exists does not at all need this thing which exists from it?" To this query we must reply: Just as the existence of God is vastly different and diverse from created existence, so when we say that God exists from God by being begotten and by proceeding, this begottenness and this procession must be understood in a far different way from when, in other cases, we say that something proceeds or is begotten.[70] For in the case of God neither naturally nor temporally nor in any respect is anything earlier or later, more or less, or at all in need of anything. Rather, the whole of what God is is not so much equal to and similar to and coeternal with itself as it is identical with itself and altogether sufficient unto itself through itself; in the case of God nothing proceeds or is begotten in the sense of passing from not-being to being. Therefore, just as our intellect cannot pass beyond eternity in order to pass judgment on God's source, so to speak, so it cannot and ought not to conceive of or to judge God's begottenness and procession after the likeness of creation.[71] Now, [in God] that which is begotten or that which proceeds is no other than that from which it proceeds or is begotten, viz., the one and only God. Consequently, just as God

De Processione Spiritus Sancti

is not greater or lesser than Himself: so in the case of the three (viz., the Father and the Son and the Holy Spirit) there is not anything greater or lesser; and no one of them is what He is any more or less than is another of them, even though it is true that God exists from God by proceeding and by being begotten.

Behold! We have seen from how much truth and by how great a necessity it follows that the Holy Spirit proceeds from the Son. Now, if [this doctrine] is false, then either one or more of the premises from which we said that it follows is false (a consequence which goes against the Christian faith which we affirm with the Greeks), or else we have not argued consistently. But it cannot be shown [that we have argued inconsistently]. Thus, if [this doctrine] is false, the Christian faith is destroyed. Moreover, to someone with understanding, it is obvious that if [this doctrine] is assumed to be false, no truth follows from it. Now, let us also consider what happens when [this doctrine] is propounded as true. Surely, if it is true that the Holy Spirit proceeds from the Son as well as from the Father, it follows that the Holy Spirit is the spirit of the Son as well as of the Father, and that He is sent and given by the Son as well as by the Father (both of which things Divine Authority teaches); and no falsity at all follows. So, on the one hand, to deny [the doctrine of] the procession of the Holy Spirit leads to such great falsehood that (contrary to the Christian faith) it destroys the premises from which we have shown this [doctrine of] procession to follow, and it begets no truth. And, on the other hand, to affirm [this doctrine] establishes very much truth (as we have shown) and does not entail any falsehood at all. Accordingly, let a rational mind ask itself on what rational basis it could exclude from the Christian faith this [doctrine of] procession.

In fact, if it is an error to believe in the procession of the Holy Spirit from the Son, then Divine Authority itself leads us into this error when it teaches us both the premises from which the [doctrine of] procession follows and those conclusions which follow from it. And Divine Authority nowhere either denies it or in any way states anything which contradicts it. Therefore, if the objection is raised that because Divine Authority nowhere affirms the [doctrine of] procession, it ought not to be affirmed, then likewise let the claim be made that because Divine Authority nowhere denies the [doctrine of] procession or says anything contradictory to it, it ought not to be denied. Furthermore, we claim that Divine Authority does sufficiently affirm [this doctrine] when (1) it makes those assertions from which [this doctrine] is demonstrated and when (2) it in no way expresses anything on the basis of which this doctrine can be denied.

15

As I promised, then, it has become clear that (1) the Son and the Holy Spirit cannot be called by each other's name because of the fact that the Holy Spirit exists from the Son (as well as because of the fact that the Son exists by being begotten, whereas the Holy Spirit exists by proceeding) and that (2) by reason of this fact alone the Son cannot exist from the Holy Spirit. For since (as was said)[72] either the Son exists from the Holy Spirit or the Holy Spirit exists from the Son: if the Holy Spirit did not exist from the Son, then it would follow that the Son existed from the Holy Spirit.

Hence, on the basis of the aforementioned rational considerations it is evident that: (1) the Father is God from whom God exists, but is not God from God; (2) the Son is God from God and also God from whom God exists; (3) the Holy Spirit is God from God, but is not God from whom God exists. And although two — viz., the Son and the Holy Spirit — exist from the Father, nevertheless they are not two gods existing from the Father; rather, they are one God, who is Son and Holy Spirit. And although the one from whom the Son exists and the one who exists from the Son — viz., the Father and the Holy Spirit — are two, they are not two gods; rather, they are one God, who is Father and Holy Spirit. And although the Holy Spirit exists from two — viz., from the Father and from the Son — He does not exist from two gods; rather, He exists from one God, who is Father and Son.

However, if the Father and the Son and the Holy Spirit are considered in pairs: then from those things which have been said it is evident that, necessarily, either the one exists from the other (because the other does not exist from Him) or else He does not exist from the other (because the other exists from Him). For if we compare the Father and the Son, we see that the Son exists from the Father because the Father does not exist from the Son;

and the Father does not exist from the Son because the Son exists from the Father. And likewise if we consider the Father and the Holy Spirit, we find that the Holy Spirit exists from the Father because the Father does not exist from the Holy Spirit; and the Father does not exist from the Holy Spirit because the Holy Spirit exists from the Father. So too, if we examine how the Son and the Holy Spirit are related to each other, we will recognize that the Holy Spirit exists from the Son because the Son does not exist from the Holy Spirit; and the Son does not exist from the Holy Spirit because the Holy Spirit exists from the Son. Therefore, it is evident (as I said earlier)[73] that although the previously mentioned relations are present in one being, they cannot introduce their plurality into the unity, nor [can] the unity [introduce] its singularity into the relations.

16

Moreover, among the Father and the Son and the Holy Spirit there are six differences which arise in accordance with their names: viz., (1) having a father, (2) not having a father, (3) having a son, (4) not having a son, (5) having a spirit proceeding from oneself, and (6) not having a spirit proceeding from oneself. Each [of the persons], considered by Himself, has one of these differences which is proper and by which He differs from the other two [persons]; and He has two differences which are both common and proper in such way that by the difference which He shares with the one [person] He differs from the other [person]. For (A) only the Father has a son; and in this respect He differs from the other two. The Father has a holy spirit proceeding from Him; and this characteristic is common to Him with the Son but is that by which He differs from the Holy Spirit. But, like the Holy Spirit, the Father does not have a father; and in this respect He differs from the Son. (B) Only the Son has a father; and in this respect He differs from the Father and the Holy Spirit. And, as has been said, the Son has it in common with the Father that a holy spirit proceeds from Him; and in this respect the Son differs from the Holy Spirit. But, like the Holy Spirit, the Son lacks a son; and in this respect the Son differs from the Father. (C) It is only the Holy Spirit from whom someone else does not proceed. The Holy Spirit has it in common with the Father (as I said)[74] that

He does not have a father; and in this respect He is unlike the Son. Moreover, the Holy Spirit has it in common with the Son (as has already been shown) that He does not have a son; and in this respect He is unlike the Father.

Accordingly, it is the Father alone who exists from no one else and from whom two others exist. And, inversely, it is the Holy Spirit who exists from two others and from whom no one exists. And it is the Son alone who exists from one other and from whom one other exists. But it is common to the three that [each one] stands in relation to both of the others. For the Father is related to the Son and the Holy Spirit in that they exist from Him. And the Son [is related] to the Father and the Holy Spirit because the Son exists from the Father and because the Holy Spirit exists from the Son. And the Holy Spirit [is related] to the Father and the Son because He exists from them both.

Thus, each [of the three persons] possesses His distinguishing properties; and, after the fashion of different human persons, the collection of distinguishing properties[75] is not the same in the other [two persons]. Indeed, human persons are different from one another by virtue of the fact that the collection of distinguishing properties which each person has is not the same in the case of another person. Nevertheless, there is a difference [between the persons of God and human persons]. For in the case of human persons, if there is one person there is one man; and if there is one man there is one person. Likewise, if there are several persons there are also several men; and if there are several men the persons also do not escape plurality. But in the case of God, even though there are three persons there is one God; and even though there is one God the persons do not at all lose their plurality. Thus, insofar as God is spoken of in relation to God He admits of a difference of persons, just as do several men. But in that which God is in Himself — i.e., in His deity — He retains an inseparable oneness, after the likeness of a single man. For there is a plurality of human persons only in case there are several men; one man does not have a plurality of persons. But the one God is three persons; and the three persons are one God. In this way, then, God does not wholly retain the characteristic feature of one or more other persons.

Although in the previously mentioned epistle on *The Incarnation of the Word* I have said[76] a little about why this last point is

De Processione Spiritus Sancti

true, I will repeat it briefly here. It often happens that several things harmonize into one thing which has the same name and the same quantity as each of them had before they became one. Suppose we add a point to a point without any space in-between; or suppose we place one line on another line which is equal to it in length, or place one surface on another surface which is equal to it in length and breadth. Surely, what results is only one point or one line or one surface. If someone cares to make an investigation, he will find similar results in many other examples. In this way, then, if — although there is not a plurality of eternities — eternity is said to be within eternity, there is only one eternity. And light within light is only one light. Similarly, whatever is ascribed to God's essence does not increase His quantity or admit of plurality should it be repeated within itself. But since God is eternity: just as nothing at all is external to eternity, so nothing at all is external to God; [77] and just as eternity within eternity is only one eternity, so God within God is only one God.

However, we learn from true faith that God exists from God by being begotten, and that God exists from God by proceeding. But since there is not anything external to God: when God is begotten from God or when God proceeds from God, the one who proceeds or is begotten does not pass outside of God but remains within God.[78] So since God within God is only one God: when God is begotten from God, the one who begets and the one who is begotten are only one God; and when God proceeds from God, the one who proceeds and the one from whom He proceeds are only one God. Hence, since God has no parts but is wholly whatever He is, it follows inescapably that the Father is God as a whole, the Son is God as a whole, and the Holy Spirit is God as a whole — and they are one and the same God, not different gods. When God exists from God, God is within God and there is only one God. So because of this fact, the Father and the Son and the Holy Spirit retain in their deity a singularity after the fashion of a single human being. But when God exists from God either by being begotten or by proceeding, He who exists from another cannot be one and the same as the other from whom He exists. Because of this fact [the Father and the Son and the Holy Spirit], in accordance with the names signifying these relations, retain a plurality, which is like the plurality of different human persons.

However, we must note that (1) the deity does not exist apart from the person, nor the person apart from the deity. And [we must also note] that sometimes we ascribe to each of the persons their respective distinguishing properties, whereas sometimes [we ascribe] to one of the persons, as if it were His distinguishing property, a property which He shares with the other two. For example, when we say "Among the three persons it is only the Father who exists from no other; it is only the Son who exists from one other and from whom one other exists; and it is only the Holy Spirit from whom no other exists," we name each of the persons and attribute to each His respective distinguishing property. But when we read that "No one knows the Son except the Father; and not anyone knows the Father except the Son,"[79] and read that "No one knows the things of God except the Spirit of God,"[80] then although what Scripture says of the one person it seems to deny of the others, nevertheless the respective property which Scripture ascribes to each of them (as if it were His distinguishing property) is common to all three. For neither the Father nor the Son lacks knowledge of Himself and of the things which are God's; nor does the Holy Spirit [lack knowledge of] the Father or of the Son. But we have already adequately discussed both why and when what is said about the one, as if of Him alone, is taken to be true of the other two as well.

At the urging of others, and on behalf of the Latins against the Greeks, I have presumed to write these things about the procession of the Holy Spirit, relying not on myself but on the Holy Spirit. And on this occasion I have presumed to add something about the unity of deity and about the trinity of persons, even though among those using the Latin language there are countless others who could do this better than I. Therefore, let whatever I have said that is worthy of acceptance be attributed not to me but to the Spirit of Truth.[81] But if I have set forth anything which must be corrected in certain respects, let [these errors] be imputed to me and not to the judgment of the Latin Church.

THREE LETTERS ON THE SACRAMENTS

THE SACRIFICE OF UNLEAVENED AND LEAVENED BREAD
(*Epistola de Sacrificio Azimi et Fermentati*)

BISHOP WALRAM TO ANSELM
(*Epistola Waleramni Episcopi ad Anselmum*)

THE SACRAMENTS OF THE CHURCH
(*Epistola de Sacramentis Ecclesiae*)

THE SACRIFICE OF UNLEAVENED AND LEAVENED BREAD.[1]
(*Epistola de Sacrificio Azimi et Fermentati*)

Anselm, servant of the Church of Canterbury, to Walram, bishop of Naumburg.[2]

To a knowledgeable man I speak briefly. If I were sure that Your Wisdom did not favor[3] the successor[4] of Julius Caesar and of Nero and of Julian the Apostate over the successor and Vicar of the Apostle Peter, most willingly would I greet you as "reverend and most beloved Bishop." But since insofar as possible we ought not to fail anyone in the defense of the truth which you are seeking against the Greeks who have come to you, I have sent you the treatise which I published against them on *The Procession of the Holy Spirit*.

I

Now, about the sacrifice concerning which the Greeks do not hold the same opinion as do we: to many judicious Catholics, it seems that what the Greeks do is not contrary to the Christian faith. For [the Christian faith] consecrates bread — consecrating both unleavened and leavened bread. And when we read of the Lord (when He produced His body from bread) that "He took bread and blessed it," the word "unleavened" or the word "leavened" is not added.[5] (Nevertheless, that He blessed unleavened bread is certain — not perhaps because what He was doing required this, but because the meal at which it was done had this custom.) And when elsewhere He called Himself and His flesh bread — [doing so] because just as a man lives temporally by means of common bread, so he lives eternally by means of this other bread — He did not specify leavened or unleavened, because both kinds are equally bread. For just as both the new man prior to sin and the man grown old in the leaven of sin do not differ [from each other] in substance, so unleavened bread and leavened bread do not differ in substance (as some people suppose they do). Hence, the Lord is seen to have called Himself and His flesh bread and to have produced His Body from bread only for the following reason: [to indicate] that just as common bread, whether unleavened or leavened, gives transitory life, so His Body gives eternal life, irrespective of whether [the bread of His Body] is leavened or unleavened. Nevertheless, in the Law, where nearly every action bore a symbolic meaning, the eating of unleavened bread at Passover was commanded in order to indicate that the Messiah whom [the Jews] were expecting was going to be pure and sinless, and in order to admonish us who were to eat of His Body to be likewise free from all "leaven of malice and wickedness."[6] However, now that we have passed from ancient foreshadowing to a new reality, now that we eat the unleavened flesh of Christ, we have no need of this former symbolism in the bread from which we produce this flesh.

2

Nevertheless, it is perfectly clear that it is better to consecrate unleavened bread than to consecrate leavened bread — not only because to do so is much more suitable, pure, and exact, but also because the Lord did this. Hence, it is not to be passed over in silence that when the Greeks anathematize the "azimites" — for this is what they call us — they are anathematizing Christ. However, if they say that we judaize, let them likewise say that Christ judaized. And if they dare to claim that Christ produced His [eucharistic] Body from unleavened bread in order, because of Judaism, to observe the precept given regarding unleavened bread, then they err most egregiously, since they think that He infected such a pure newness with the leaven of obsolescence. Accordingly, it is evident that when He used unleavened bread for that consecration, He did not do so in order to observe the precept regarding unleavened bread. Rather, [He did so] either in order to approve the "azimites" while reproving the "fermentarians," whose existence He foresaw, or else assuredly so that if indeed the fermentarians were approved He would approve the azimites as well.

3

As for their saying that we judaize: it is not true. For we consecrate unleavened bread not in order to observe the Old Law but in order to perform the rite more exactly and to imitate the Lord who performed it without judaizing. For when we do something which the Jews did to observe Judaism, then provided we do this not for the sake of Judaism but for some other reason, we do not judaize. For suppose that during the days of Passover someone eats unleavened bread — either because he has no other kind or because he prefers it to leavened bread. Or suppose that some man as a result of an ailment is required to circumcise his foreskin, or that someone in order that his ox not go hungry does not muzzle it while it is threshing. No one except a fool would judge that someone doing these things is judaizing. Therefore, when we consecrate unleavened bread — not in order to signify through the symbol of unleavened bread that the Lord Jesus would be unleavened, but in order to consecrate this bread into His Body by the working of divine power, even as He Himself did — we in no way thereby observe the oldness of the Law but we render honor to the truth of the Gospel.

In fact, when the Lord Jesus performed this rite and said to His disciples "Do this in remembrance of me":[7] if He had not wanted us (to whom He gave this commandment in [giving it to] the Apostles) to do this with unleavened bread, He would have forewarned us in [forewarning] the Apostles, and would have said, "Do not do this with unleavened bread." Therefore, since in saying "Do this" He did not rule out unleavened bread, who is there whose intellect dares to rule out what the Lord Himself has done and to prohibit that which the Lord not only did not prohibit by any word but even prescribed by His action? And who, I say, but one who is "wiser than it behooves to be wise"[8] trusts so greatly in his own wisdom that he presumes even to make the following claim?: When the Lord said "Do this," then just as we rightly understand it to mean "[Do] what I am doing," so we must doubtlessly take it to mean "but not with that with which I [am doing it]."

Likewise, if we ought to perform the things of God by means of things which we deem to be the more suitable: since it is evident that the consecration we are discussing ought to be celebrated with respect to the substance of the bread, whether unleavened or leavened, what bread do we deem to be more suitable for producing the reality of the Lord's Body than that bread which the Old Law chooses for signifying, and which the Gospel chooses for exhibiting, this reality? Therefore, if we reply to the Greeks that we perform this rite with unleavened bread not because of any symbolism but for the aforementioned reasons, no basis can be discerned here upon which the Greeks [can] rightly judge us worthy of anathematization, or at least of reproach.

4

But if [the Greeks] say that we cannot consecrate unleavened bread without a symbolic meaning and that hereby we are proven to judaize, then it follows that they also are not able to use leavened bread for this rite without a symbolic sense. For by the word "leaven" both the Old Testament (*vetus scriptura*) and the New signify sin: the Old when it curses the eating of leavened bread during its Passover, and the New when it instructs us to feast during our Passover "not on the old leaven, nor on the leaven of malice and wickedness."[9] Moreover, we say that we do not judaize even if we subscribe to a symbolic significance in [the use of] unleavened bread. For we do not signify that the Messiah is going to come without the leaven of sin, as do the Jews; rather, as do Christians, we indicate that He has already come without sin. Hereby we are reminded to be unleavened, as is the Passover[10] of which we Christians partake. However, [the Greeks] profess themselves to be neither Jews nor Christians, in that they signify in the symbolism of leavened bread neither that God is going to come without sin (as do the Jews) nor that He has already come without sin (as do the Christians). Rather, they seem to favor the pagans, who think that Jesus was leavened by sin, as are other men.

But if [the Greeks] say that Christians ought not to use symbols because the old things (wherein symbols were necessary) have passed away,[11] then let them deny (to mention only one point) that baptism is a symbol of someone's death and burial — thus contradicting the apostle who says: "All of us who are baptized in Christ Jesus are baptized into His death. For we are buried together with Him by baptism into death."[12] Or if they concede to us the use of symbols except in the case of those things which the Old Law used symbolically (and thus [claim] that unleavened bread must not at all be used symbolically because it is used symbolically in the Old Law): let them not baptize in water (1) since "in Moses all our fathers were baptized in the cloud and in the sea"[13] (an event which we cannot deny to have occurred foreshadowingly) and (2) lest they appear to baptize with the baptism of John, who baptized in water. Therefore, if — even though that old baptism (which was a foreshadowing of this new baptism) was done in water — we are blameless for baptizing in water, which has a symbolic use: what is this "wisdom" of the Greeks? Because of the fact that the old Passover (through which our Passover was foreshadowed) was celebrated with unleavened bread, the "wisdom" of the Greeks abominates our sacrificing the Body of Christ (who is our Passover)[14] with the symbol of unleavened bread — whether [we do so] in order to commemorate the fact that He whose Body we sacrifice was unleavened (i.e., free from the stain of sin), or whether [we do so] in order to be reminded that we who partake of His Body ought to be unleavened, in accordance with the words of the apostle. For the apostle says: "Purge out the old leaven so that you may be new dough, even as you are unleavened. For Christ our Passover is sacrificed. Therefore, let us feast not with the old leaven nor with the leaven of malice and of wickedness, but with the unleavened bread of purity and truth."[15]

5

Therefore, whether our consecration of unleavened bread has a symbolic significance or whether it has no symbolic significance, the Greeks cannot at all show us to be blameworthy. Instead, either we alone act rightly and they act wrongly, or else if they act rightly we act more rightly and more correctly. Assuredly, when they set forth against us that which is recognized to count in no way against us or for them, they sufficiently manifest that they have no rational basis to support their position and to defeat ours. For as I have read in your letter, they raise in objection against us the fact that the apostle says, "The letter kills but the Spirit makes alive,"[16] and that the Prophet Amos says "Offer a sacrifice of praise with leaven."[17] Thus, not rightly interpreting the words of the apostle, they try to show that the letter which the old Passover commands to be celebrated with unleavened bread kills us when we observe the letter by consecrating unleavened bread. For the apostle means that the letter kills in the case where it reveals sin by giving the command to turn aside from sin, because unless grace renders assistance in doing what is commanded, the letter causes a man to be disobedient and sinful. In his epistle to the Romans the same apostle exhibits this clearly when he says: "I did not know sin except because of the Law. For I would not have known lust unless the Law had said 'You shall not covet.' But sin, having been occasioned by the commandment, worked in me all forms of lust. For without the Law sin would have been dead. I was once alive without the Law; but when the commandment came sin revived, and I became dead. And the commandment that was meant to give life was found to be unto my death. For having been occasioned by the commandment, sin seduced me and by the commandment killed me."[18] Thus, without the assistance of grace, the letter kills. But the Spirit makes alive, just as the same apostle said to Titus: "When the goodness and kindness of God our Savior appeared: God saved us — not by the works of justice which we have done but according to His mercy, by the laver of regeneration and of renewal by the Holy Spirit, whom He poured forth upon us abundantly through Jesus Christ our Savior, so that having been justified by grace we would be his heirs in accordance with our hope for everlasting life."[19]

And so after [the apostle] said "Our sufficiency is from God, who has made us fit ministers of the new testament, not in the letter but in the Spirit,"[20] he added: "For the letter kills but the Spirit makes alive." [It is] as if he were to say: "God has made us ministers of the new testament, which is not in a letter that kills, as was the old testament, but in a life-giving Spirit." But his further statement applies to both the letter that kills and the Spirit that gives life:

> If the ministration of death, engraven with letters upon stones, was glorious — so that the children of Israel could not steadfastly behold the face of Moses because of the glory of his countenance, a glory which was done away with — how shall not the ministration of the Spirit be more glorious? For if the ministration of condemnation is glory, much more the ministration of justice abounds in glory. For because of the more excellent glory, that which was

glorious was not in this respect glorified. For if that which passes away is glorious, much more that which does not pass away is glorious. Having, then, such hope we experience great confidence, and are not like Moses, who placed a veil over his face so that the children of Israel could not look steadfastly upon the appearance of that which passes away. But the senses of the Israelites have grown dull. For until the present day, whenever the Old Testament is read this same veil remains and is not taken away (for in Christ it is taken away). And until the present day, when Moses is read a veil is placed over their hearts. But when [Israel] shall turn to the Lord, the veil will be removed. Now, the Lord is a spirit; and where the Spirit of the Lord is, there is liberty. But all of us who behold with unveiled faces the glory of the Lord, are transformed into the same image, from glory to glory, as by the Spirit of the Lord. Therefore, since we have this ministration in accordance with which we have obtained mercy, we faint not.[21]

To these statements I think it superfluous to add anything about the letter that kills and the Spirit that gives life. Accordingly, it is quite evident that the objection which the Greeks raise regarding the letter that kills neither profits them nor injures us.

6

Now, as to what [the Greeks] quote[22] from the prophet — "Come to Gilgal and do wickedly" and "Offer a sacrifice of praise with leaven" — we must construe these words as having been spoken either by way of approving such a sacrifice or by way of reproving it. Now, if the prophet prescribes this sacrifice, then (to speak in accordance with the Greeks) the letter kills them, for they observe the letter in sacrificing with leavened bread. On the other hand, if these words were spoken in reproof, then how impudent it is of them to sacrifice what the prophet curses as a sacrifice! And how unreasonably they quote this text as an authority in their favor! But since the prophet associated this sacrifice with a wicked action, there is no doubt that he spoke these words not by way of commandment but by way of reproof. For he said: "Come to Bethel and do wickedly." And shortly thereafter, continuing his rebuke, he said: "And offer a sacrifice of praise with leaven." Therefore, let the fermentarians defend their position with rational considerations as strong as those with which the azimites corroborate theirs; or else let them cast away their own leaven and become azimites. Or if they cannot do the former and are unwilling to do the latter, let them at least not reproach the azimites.

7

On the third point of contention — as I understand it — you have written that the Greeks denounce our marriages in which blood relatives [from one clan] are joined in marriage with blood relatives from another clan. I see no authority or reason for their doing so. For if they forbid this from being done in their marriages, either they do not extend relationships unto the seventh generation as do we, or else what they prescribe is seen to be impossible to be observed. For in one clan there are often more than one hundred men and women seeking marriage. Accordingly, it would be necessary to find this many other clans from each of which one man or one woman would be selected, with each of whom would be conjoined one man or one woman from that one clan. Therefore, if the Greeks' marriages are entered into within seven generations, they are unquestionably abominable, and the Greeks ought not to reproach our marriages in which blood relatives are conjoined with blood relatives from a different clan (something which no authority and no rational consideration forbids). Or else, it is impossible (as I said) to observe what the Greeks prescribe: viz., to seek out, for marriages with the members of one clan, as many other clans as in this one clan there are men and women requesting marriages. Now, that which is done without any authority or any rational basis, and is even done against reason, is undoubtedly reasonably deemed worthy of rejection.

BISHOP WALRAM TO ANSELM[1]
(*Epistola Waleramni Episcopi ad Anselmum*)

To the most serene Lord Anselm, most reverend archbishop of the holy church of Canterbury: Walram, bishop of Naumburg by the grace of God [offers] a servant's homage, constant prayers, and himself, completely devoted in all respects. [When one is dealing] with Minerva, it is most foolish to suppose oneself to be versed in learned matters. Moreover, among distinguished men of learning it is not within my power to reason convincingly by the force of my arguments. But sighing with the prophet "Open my eyes and I will behold the wonderous things of Your law,"[2] with supreme devotion I lift up my eyes to the mountain of Your Highness,[3] so that from thence help may come to me. Your help is "help from the Lord, who made heaven and earth."[4] "He who is joined to the Lord is one spirit,"[5] so that it is thereby evident that from His fullness you search out the deep things of God;[6] but I in my smallness hear His voice but am utterly ignorant of "whence He comes or whither He goes."[7]

I

God is undivided trinity, and all who are in God are one in Him. Diversity in the Church is directly opposed to unity. And what proceeds against itself by dissension among its parts cannot remain standing for long. Now, Palestine believes one thing about the sacraments of the Church, Armenia another, and our Rome and three-part Gaul still another. Moreover, the Roman Church performs the mystery of the Lord's Body in one way, the Gallic Church in another way, and our Germany much more differently still. We have received from the ancient Fathers the rite of sacrifice, and I wonder greatly as to whence this novelty has crept into the house of the Lord. "Jesus Christ yesterday and today, He is forever," always one, always the same, undergoing no change.[8] He who tends toward diversity dissents from Christ. Christ is the bread of angels[9] who came down from Heaven and was made the bread of men, the food of the poor, and the fullness of those who reign with Him — so that those who worthily partake of Him live forever and ever. All of us who partake of one bread are, though we be many, one bread and one body in Christ.[10] Christ is the way on which we should walk, the one whom we should imitate. He who wanders away from Christ walks in peril. While sacrificing, let us do even what Christ did; for He has said: "Do this as often as you partake."[11]

2

Indeed, the Armenians believe that with *leavened* bread they are offering a sacrifice of praise. But they are not walking with Christ in "newness of life."[12] True imitators of Christ ought to feast not on "the old leaven" but on the "unleavened bread of purity and truth."[13] "Even a little leaven corrupts the whole lump."[14] Insofar as possible let not the incorruptible Body of Christ be infected with any corruption. Let all such corruption be absent from the sacrifice of purity. Let those who long to put on the incorruption of Christ's Body strip themselves of the old man by means of the purity of the new sacrifice. In the production of the Body of Christ any substance except the substance that Christ sacrificed is unacceptable. And if I dare to say so, the rule for sacrificing — the rule He gave — must be kept.

3

We bless the bread separately and the chalice separately. The canons and the ancient Roman Ordo prescribe this — namely, that from the beginning, in the canon, we trace a particular cross over each. We hold this as a public and time-honored custom everywhere, "from generation unto generation,"[15] and we are amazed at your diversity. Christ did this, and He commanded us to do it. "Do this," He said, "as often as you partake."[16] Taking bread, He blessed it separately, and in like manner the chalice. He made a separate sign of the cross over each, as our Ordo — indeed, as the Roman Ordo — prescribes. And so our custom grew up from Him who is the same "yesterday and today and forever."[17] On the matter of individual signs of the cross the authority of Christ gives approval to us. Now, I greatly wonder how the difference in sacrificing came about. There is "one faith, one baptism,"[18] one friend, spouse, and dove of Christ. It is greatly harmful to the unity of the Church to be at variance in the sacraments and to allow whatever one pleases.

4

Furthermore, several while consecrating cover the chalice from the beginning: some do so with a corporal, others with a folded cloth, according to the likeness of the shroud which, we read, was found in the sepulcher "not lying with the linen clothes, but apart, wrapped up in one place."[19] Christ is "the way, the truth, and the life."[20] He is the way on which we ought to walk so that we may come to Him. "He who says that he abides in Christ ought to walk just as Christ walked."[21] None but true imitators of the Life come to the Life. The pascal Victim was immolated uncovered in body on the altar of the cross. He willed to be offered uncovered in body, who unveiled to His own all that He heard from the Father. In His immolation He revealed Himself "as He is";[22] and "with unveiled faces" we shall behold His glory, so as to be conformed to Him in all respects, "having been made like the body of His glory," so that He may be all things to us in eternal bliss."[23] And to use His own words: "It is finished."[24] He said this so that we would not doubt that "old things have passed away and that all things are new."[25] The veil of the temple was rent from top to bottom.[26] And until this present day a veil is upon the hearts of the Jews,[27] so that though having eyes they do not see and having ears they do not understand.[28] We, however, to whom God has revealed [these things] by His Spirit,[29] ought not to confound the mysteries of sacrificing but, following the example of the Lord Jesus, to make them clear. Let us not with Moses impose a veil as do the Jews; but offering with the Lord Jesus, let us strive to be conveyed from glory unto glory.[30] Let Jesus, who was naked on the altar of the cross, appear naked on the altar of our immolation. What we proclaim in words, let us carry out by deeds. That bread is truly the Body of Christ, and it ought to be sacrificed as being the sacrifice of Christ's body. Uncovered on the altar of the cross, Christ's body was wrapped in linens in the sepulcher. Naked in His suffering, He was wrapped up at His burial, through the devotion of His disciples. Burying [Him] as it was the custom of the Jews to bury, they evidenced their zealous devotion to their Master; but they were still ignorant of the truth of the sacrament. They buried Him as a Jew who resembled the Jews, because they had not yet carefully pondered the mystery of the cross. "The Spirit searches all things, even the deep things of God."[31] But the Spirit had not yet been given to them because Jesus, crucified in His weakness, had not yet been glorified. But once glorified, Jesus put away the clothes of corruption; He took off corruptible things, having put on incorruption; He left the sepulcher and manifested His glory to those who loved Him. Why, then, by wrapping with a corruptible shroud do we proclaim, so to speak, Christ's weakness and His concealment in such darkness — when most truly we proclaim Him as the power of God and the light of the world? Let not that light from light[32] which enlightens every man be put in any way under the bushel of a shroud.[33] Rather, just as He Himself — both priest and victim — offered Himself, so let our sacrifice too be offered to Him. Placed uncovered, let it shine forth in the house of Christ unto life for all. Our sacrifice will be most acceptable when it is similar to Christ's sacrifice.

Nevertheless, even we wrap the life-giving sacrifice — not at the beginning, as is your custom, but at the end, with Joseph and Nicodemus. That which is offered both with the appearance and with the reality of the original ought not to be at variance in regard to its immolation. He who differs in sacrificing does not walk as Christ Himself walked.[34] But if in this part of the sacrifice the purity [of the sacrifice] is pled, it is very easy to safeguard, with us, the cleanliness by means of a protective cover — without at the beginning of the sacrifice deviating from a most ancient rite of the Church.

5

Let your eyes see my imperfection.[35] And just as you are filled, as by the hands of the virtues, with the whole fullness of prudential knowledge, so may you have compassion on my extreme imperfection. The Catholic Church glorifies God in me because the grace of divine goodness is apparent in my transformation. "By the grace of God I am what I am."[36] From Saul [I have been transformed to] Paul; from being an enemy of the Roman Church [I have been transformed to] its intimate friend, in highest favor with Pope Paschal, sharing the secrets of the cardinals. In this regard I am hopeful of prosperous success in all matters. Joseph was in the house of Pharoah; I was in the palace of Emperor Henry.[37] It was not iniquity nor any sin of mine[38] if — banish the thought — I was like Nero the Incestuous or Julian the Apostate.[39] Thanks be to God because under the rule of Your Holiness the wolf and the lamb pasture together, the lion and the calf lie down together, and a little child leads them.[40] And because the scepter of your kingdom is a scepter of justice,[41] we praise the strength of God for the fact that the wild beasts have become tame out of fear of the Church and because they harm no one on the mount of the Lord's powers. "The lion will roar; who will not be afraid?"[42] But because the just man is bold as a lion:[43] your heart, like the heart of strong-handed David himself, does not fear in such things but triumphs in all things by the power of God. May the Lord, who has anointed you with "the oil of gladness above your fellows,"[44] crown you with "mercy and compassion"[45] in the kingdom of blessedness.

THE SACRAMENTS OF THE CHURCH[1]
(*Epistola de Sacramentis Ecclesiae*)

To my lord and friend Walram,[2] venerable bishop of Naumburg by the grace of God: Anselm, servant of the Church of Canterbury [sends] greeting, reverence, prayers, and the affection of love.

I rejoice and thank God because, as you have written, the Catholic Church glorifies Him in you. For in your transformation the grace of divine goodness is apparent; and you enjoy friendship and close acquaintance with Lord Pope Paschal,[3] so that now I am permitted to greet Your Holiness as a friend. As for the fact that Your sublime Humility compares me to Minerva and calls me "Mountain": I do not apply [these epithets] to myself, because I discern in myself no reason why they ought to be ascribed to me. However, I am obliged not to be ungrateful to Your Benevolence, since the abundance of your good will toward me produces these ascriptions. For those whom we love we are wont to regard more highly than they deserve. So my heart does not take pride in your praise, which does not apply to me; instead, it gratefully delights in your love, which ought always to be cherished.

I

Your Reverence asks about the sacraments of the Church, because they are not everywhere performed in the same way but are dealt with differently in different places. Assuredly, if they were celebrated in one way and with one mind throughout the whole Church, it would be a good and praiseworthy thing. However, there are many differences which do not conflict with the fundamental importance of the sacrament or with its efficacy or with faith in it; and these cannot all be brought together into one practice. Accordingly, I think that these differences ought to be harmoniously and peaceably tolerated rather than being disharmoniously and scandalously condemned. For we are taught by the holy Fathers that, provided the unity of love is preserved within the Catholic faith, a different practice does no harm. But if one asks whence these different customs arise, I deem [the source to be] nothing other than the differences of human dispositions. Even though men do not disagree about the truth and the validity of the sacrament, nevertheless they do not agree on the aptness and suitability of the manner of administration. For what one person deems to be more suitable, another often deems to be less suitable. Now, I do not believe that to disagree concerning such differences is to wander from the truth of the matter.

2

To be sure, in sacrificing the Body and the Blood of the Lord some make one sign of the cross over each during the canon from the beginning, whereas others make one sign over each only when the bread or body is named individually and when the chalice or blood is named individually. But these latter make one sign of the cross over both when the offering or victim is named — because just as Christ, who sacrificed Himself for us, is one, so there is one offering or victim in the bread and wine which we offer. I do not see that in doing this these latter dissent more from Christ, who blessed each individually, than all those dissent who do not consecrate the chalice after a supper, as Christ did, and who do not always do it in the evening, as Christ did, and who call both together by one name — "offering" or "victim" — which Christ did not do. From this we may conclude that in such an action, provided we mutually preserve the truth of the thing, we may differ from one another without blame, since we differ from the very author of the sacrifice itself without offense.

Now, when we say "these gifts, these offerings, these holy sacrifices" — whether separate signs of the cross are made individually over the bread and over the wine, or whether both are consecrated together by one sign of the cross — I do not see in this diversity any reprehensible dissension, except that perhaps it is more fitting to sign both with one cross, as both are sanctified with one word of blessing. For when we bless several men or bless distinct things collectively, we do not impart to each a particular sign of the cross, but we believe that a single sign of the cross suffices for all.

3

Some cover the chalice from the beginning — some with a corporal, others with a folded cloth — to keep it clean. They do not leave the chalice uncovered, as Christ was crucified uncovered in order (as you indicate) to show Himself revealed to the world. I do not see that they should be reproved on account of the nudity of Christ, which they do not signify while sacrificing, any more than because they do not show in the same sacrifice that He was crucified outside the city, outside a house, and under the open sky. Yet these things are not devoid of great significance. For "Christ, who suffered for us, leaving us an example so that we would follow in His footsteps,"[4] also gave us in these things an example of enduring incomparable contempt and poverty for the sake of justice. For He was held in such contempt and was judged so execrable that He was not deemed worthy to die inside any dwelling of men, or among any men except the execrable, or under any roof except the sky, from beneath which He could not be driven away. Thus, according to the prophet, He was regarded as "the scorn of men and the rejected of the people."[5] Moreover, He was so poor that when He came into the world He was born not in His own house but in another's. And once born He was placed, for lack of a room, in the manger of brute animals. And living in the world, He had no place to rest His head. And dying, He had nothing with which to cover His nakedness. And dead, He had nothing with which to be enshrouded; and He had neither a sepulcher nor a place where His dead body could be reposited.

One should imitate all these things in one's life by deeds, as reason demands, rather than signifying the nakedness of Christ by the nudity of the sacrifice. Nor can I imagine why one should see to it that the sacrifice not be covered with a cloth because Christ suffered naked, any more than that it not be performed under a roof or within a city because Christ suffered under the open sky outside the city. But if it is not the custom to offer it out from under a roof on account of the disturbances of the weather, there seems to be a similar reason for not leaving the chalice uncovered during the sacrifice because of certain inconveniences which can occur.

Therefore, I consider it safer and more careful to cover the chalice — lest a fly or something undesirable fall into it, which to our knowledge often happens — than to expose it, uncovered, to possible impurities.

These things I answer to Your Wisdom according to my way of thinking, rejecting no one's better reasoning. About those who sacrifice with leavened bread I have erstwhile sent you a letter.

ABBREVIATIONS

M	*Monologion*
P	*Proslogion*
DV	*De Veritate*
DL	*De Libertate Arbitrii*
DIV	*Epistola de Incarnatione Verbi*
CDH	*Cur Deus Homo*
DCV	*De Conceptu Virginali et de Originali Peccato*
DP	*De Processione Spiritus Sancti*
DC	*De Concordia Praescientiae et Praedestinationis et Gratiae Dei cum Libero Arbitrio*
PF	*Ein neues unvollendetes Werk des hl. Anselm von Canterbury* (Philosophical Fragments)
DT	*De Trinitate* (Augustine)
PL	*Patrologia Latina* (ed. J. P. Migne)
S	*Sancti Anselmi Opera Omnia* (ed. F. S. Schmitt). E.g., S I, 237:7 indicates Volume I, page 237, line 7.

VOLUME III: NOTES

TO JOHN THE MONK

1. This letter (#129) and the Letter to Fulco (#136) were written between 1090–1092.
2. Roscelin. Note the mention of Roscelin by name in the letter which follows.
3. Fulco, bishop of Beauvais.

TO FULCO, BISHOP OF BEAUVAIS

1. See n. 1 of the preceding letter to John the Monk.
2. Lanfranc died in May, 1089.
3. The Council of Soissons, which condemned Roscelin's view in 1092.
4. Anselm alludes to the Apostles' Creed, the Nicene Creed (381), and the Quicumque, respectively.

THE INCARNATION OF THE WORD

1. The final recension of this letter was published about the beginning of 1094.
The mss. of the letter contain divisional marks. At these places in his edition of the Latin text F. S. Schmitt has placed Roman numerals, which he intended to inclose in brackets. See S II, 3n.
2. Urban II, pope from 1088–1099.
3. Anselm was abbot from 1078–1093.
4. In this treatise Anselm nowhere refers to Roscelin by name. It is clear, however, whom he has in mind. See the letters to Fulco, bishop of Beauvais, (#136) and to John the Monk (# 129). Anselm does not seem actually to have had firsthand contact with Roscelin's views, but to have been relying upon written and verbal reports. At the end of section 11 of the present treatise he explicitly acknowledges the limitation of his acquaintance.
5. The Council of Soissons, which condemned Roscelin's view in 1092.
6. Rainaldus was archbishop of Rheims from 1083 to 1096.
7. I.e., after March of 1093.
8. Dan. 2:34–35.
9. Eph. 5:8.
10. Cf. S II, 21:3.
11. Isa. 7:9. Note the end of P 1 and the end of P 4.
12. Acts 15:9.
13. Ps. 18:9 (19:8).
14. Ps. 18:8 (19:7).
15. Matt. 11:25.

Notes

16. I Cor. 2:14.
17. Rom. 8:13.
18. I Cor. 2:15.
19. Ps. 118:99 (119:99).
20. Ps. 118:100 (119:100)
21. Literally: ". . . surpasses knowledge from hearing."
22. Rom. 1:21.
23. I Tim. 1:18–19.
24. Literally: ". . . who think that universal substances are only a *breath* of voice." Playing on this expression, Anselm speaks of blowing the heretics of dialectic right out of the discussion.
25. In this treatise Anselm never refers to Roscelin by name. (See n. 4 above.) At S II, 23:9 he calls him *"ille disputator"* and at S II, 19:16 *"ille . . . contra quem ista dixi."* But elsewhere he refers to him simply as "he" or "that one." For purposes of readability we have inserted the words "my opponent."
26. In the previous paragraph.
27. Viz., that the Father was incarnate with the Son.
28. Viz., that there are not three persons in God, that there are no relations in God, that the heresy of Sabellius is true.
29. Cf. the end of Ch. 3.
30. In Chs. 7, 8, and 9 respectively.
31. Literally: ". . . that even if there were three gods they would not help him to keep the Father and the Holy Spirit from incarnation — something which he thinks cannot occur without a plurality of gods."
32. Note M 22–24.
33. Note CDH II, 16 (S II, 121:9–12).
34. Cf. CDH II, 7.
35. Cf. CDH II, 9.
36. I.e., the same unbefittingness as in the hypothetical case where the Holy Spirit was incarnate.
37. Cf. Phil. 2:6; DCD 28.
38. Note DCD 4 (S I, 242:3–10); CDH II, 9 (S II, 105:22–24); DC I, 6 (S II, 256:24); DC III, 14 (S II, 288:9–10). Cf. Augustine's statement at PL 42:687.
39. Phil. 2:7.
40. Phil. 2:6.
41. John 10:30; 14:9.
42. See Col. 1:15 and Heb. 1:3.
43. *"Homo"* can be used to signify "human being" in the sense of "a human being" (i.e., "a man") and in the sense of "a humanity" (i.e., "a human nature"). Anselm will argue that the Son of God assumed a humanity, rather than assuming an individual man. He is contending against the nominalists of his day, who denied that the Son of God could have assumed a human nature, since (according to them) a human nature is not something real.
44. John 1:14.
45. Alternative translation: "Now, when the word 'humanity' is used. . . ."
46. Cf. DG 20 (S I, 166:5).

Notes

47. Anselm means that the nature is generically (rather than numerically) common to all men.
48. John 1:14.
49. Or: the word "humanity."
50. Or: ". . . that the Word and human nature. . . ." N.B. The Word assumed human nature only in the restricted sense that He assumed *a* human nature. He became a man, rather than becoming Man. See CDH, Bk. I, n. 1.
51. Section 1 (S II, 4:6–9).
52. Cf. M 79.
53. This example is repeated in DP 9.
54. The text plays upon the words *"infistulatus"* and *"incarnatus."*
55. Note the second half of DP 16; also see DC I, 5.
56. Note M 59 (S I, 70).
57. Note M 79 (S I, 86:5–8).
58. I John 3:2.
59. I Cor. 13:12.
60. In section 6.
61. M 42 and 56.

WHY GOD BECAME A MAN

Commendation to Pope Urban II

1. F. S. Schmitt has supplied the heading (*"Commendatio operis ad Urbanum Papam II"*).
2. Job 14:5.
3. Isa. 7:9. Note DIV 1 (S II, 7:11–12) and P 1 (S I, 100:18–19).

Preface

1. Anselm was caught up in the struggle over investiture.
2. Here and at S II, 102:7 (Bk. II, Ch. 7), 132:11 (Bk. II, Ch. 21), and 164:18 (DCV 23) Anselm writes *"homo-deus"* instead of his usual *"deus-homo."* Since he regards these expressions as substitutes, the translators have preferred to render both as "God-man."
3. For those of his treatises to which Anselm gave chapter titles, his custom was to place all of these titles before the text itself. Note his allusion in the preface to M (S I, 8:21–23).

BOOK I

1. This work was begun between 1094 and 1097; it was completed during the summer of 1098.

How to translate the title *"Cur Deus Homo"* has long been the subject of controversy. English and American translators have settled upon "Why God Became Man"; and French and German translators have fixed upon the corresponding equivalences: *"Pourquoi Dieu S'Est Fait Homme"* and *"Warum Gott Mensch Geworden [Ist]."* A more correct translation, however, will include the indefinite article: "Why God Became a Man" (*"Pourquoi Dieu S'Est Fait un*

Notes

Homme"; "Warum Gott ein Mensch Geworden [*Ist*]"). This fact is evident from the following considerations.

a. The title is drawn from three fuller expressions in the text: (1) "*deus homo factus est,*" (2) "*deus se facit hominem,*" (3) "*deum fieri hominem.*" (Note 48:2–3; 60:3–5; 118:1–2; 121:3; 121:9; 124:7; 125:25; 126:25; 130:29–30; 133:6.)

b. These fuller expressions are substitutes for the expression "*Deus incarnatus est*" (or "*Deus incarnatus factus est*"). In fact, in DCV 17 (S II, 158:10–11, 14) Anselm poses the question "*Cur necesse fuit deum incarnari?*", and answers it with the words "*Ideo deus factus est homo, quia non sufficeret ad redimendos alios . . . homo non-deus.*" (Also cf. (in CDH II, 9) S II, 105:3–4 with 105:12–14.)

c. Both the expression employing "*incarnari*" and the expression employing "*factus est homo*" parallel the Scripture verse John 1:14: "*Verbum caro factum est.*" (Note DIV 11. S II, 29:3–4, 19.)

d. Anselm's theory of incarnation teaches that the Son of God became the man Jesus by assuming a human nature. Therefore, God became a man, viz., the God-man; He did not become Man, viz., the God-Man. This difference is important. But it is lost sight of in the customary translation of "*Cur Deus Homo*" as "Why God Became Man." For too often in the past the reader unfamiliar with Anselm has gained the false impression that, on Anselm's view, God assumed unindividuated human nature and thus became Man as such, or the universal Man. But DIV 11 (S II, 29:26–30:6) shows clearly that Anselm rejects this view. And CDH I, 8 (S II, 60:3–5) speaks with equal clarity of *illum hominem . . . quem filius se ipsum fecit* ("that man whom the Son caused Himself to become" [viz., Jesus]). The appearance of the phrase "*illum hominem*" is meant to preclude the phrase "*quemlibet hominem.*" (Note DIV 11. S II, 29:6–12.) Since Anselm's use of "*filius se fecit illum hominem*" is but a consistent expansion and specification of what he meant by "*Deus se fecit hominem,*" and since "*Cur deus se fecit hominem*" is but a consistent expansion of what he meant by the title "*Cur Deus Homo,*" this title is more accurately (i.e., less misleadingly) rendered with the indefinite article than without it.

At any rate, the interpretation (as contrasted with the translation) of Anselm's topic is clear: He is discussing why the Son of God became incarnate (as a human being), or why He became (incarnate as) the man Jesus, or why He assumed a human nature, or why there had to be a God-man, etc. — all of which statements are unobjectionable ways of expressing the interpretation.

Note Augustine's expressions in *On the Trinity:* (1) "*Verbum Dei dico carnem factum, id est, hominem factum . . .*" (4:21.31. PL 42:910); (2) "*Christus . . . factus est homo*" (7.3.4. PL 42:937). Also note 8.5.7 (PL 42:952).

2. I Pet. 3:15.
3. Ecclesiasticus 3:22.
4. Anselm never completes this other work. See PF.
5. Ps. 44:3 (45:2).
6. Or more literally: "But [I will do so] subject to the following condition, under which I want everything I say to be accepted: viz., that. . . ."
7. Cf. DC III, 6 (S II, 271:28–272:7).

Notes

8. See Rom. 5:19.
9. See Luke 20:36.
10. In *A Meditation on Human Redemption* (S III, 85:46ff.) Anselm also deals with this claim.
11. Cf. DV 8 (S I, 187:2–17).
12. Col. 2:14.
13. Ps. 77:39 (78:39).
14. John 8:34.
15. Matt. 3:17.
16. Ch. 6 (S II, 54:1–5).
17. Phil. 2:8–9.
18. Heb. 5:8.
19. Rom. 8:32.
20. John 6:38.
21. John 14:31.
22. John 18:11.
23. Matt. 26:39.
24. Matt. 26:42.
25. Viz., Jesus.
26. John 14:31.
27. John 18:11.
28. Phil. 2:8.
29. Heb. 5:8.
30. Phil. 2:8.
31. Phil. 2:9.
32. Ps. 109:7 (110:7).
33. Luke 10:22.
34. John 16:15.
35. Luke 2:52.
36. John 6:38.
37. John 7:16.
38. Rom. 8:32.
39. Cf. DCD 1 (S I, 234:15–17).
40. Matt. 26:39.
41. Matt. 26:42.
42. James 1:17.
43. John 6:44.
44. Note PF 38:6–13.
45. Cf. PF 38:19–23.
46. Isa. 53:7.
47. John 10:17–18.
48. Note the beginning of CDH I, 3.
49. Note DIV 10 (S II, 26:3–4).
50. Viz., Jesus. N.B. DIV 11.
51. Cf. DV 12 (S I, 194:30–34) and DC III, 2 (S II, 264:26–265:5). Also note Ps. 35:11 (36:10).
52. One who commits a sin is required (1) to recommence paying to God the honor of being subordinate to His will and (2) to make compensation, or satis-

Notes

faction, for the honor he has stolen by committing the sin. Only by meeting both of these requirements would the sinner fully restore God's honor. The first requirement — viz., to be subordinate to God's will — was binding upon human nature even before Adam sinned. The second could not acceptably have been exacted from human nature had Adam not stolen what belonged to another (viz., what belonged to God). Note CDH I, 20 (S II, 87:26–28) and DCV 2 (S II, 141:17–19).

53. Cf. Matt. 6:12.
54. Cf. Rom. 12:19.
55. Cf. Rom. 13:1, 4.
56. Cf. DL 1 (S I, 208:18–21).
57. I.e., He would be powerless to exact the repayment and powerless to punish.
58. Literally: "What kind of honor for God the punishment of a sinner is."
59. Cf. PF 25:9; 37:1.
60. Cf. CDH I, 11 (S II, 68:11–15).
61. Cf. CDH I, 10 (S II, 67:1–6).
62. Cf. DCD 5 and 23.
63. See CDH I, 10 (S II, 67:9–10).
64. II Cor. 9:7.
65. See CDH II, 21.
66. Cf. DCD 24.
67. DCD 2 and 3.
68. Literally: "From this reasoning it is evident that elect men will not be less in number than are reprobate angels."
69. Ecclesiasticus 18:1. Note Augustine's doctrine of *rationes seminales*.
70. Acts 10:35.
71. Cf. the discussion in DCD 25.
72. II Pet. 3:12–13.
73. I.e., the day the saint enters Heaven, viz., the day of his death.
74. Deut. 32:8.
75. See CDH I, 2 (S II, 50:7–10).
76. Deut. 32:8.
77. Gal. 3:7.
78. John 6:71.
79. CDH I, 16.
80. Cf. P 4 and *On Behalf of the Fool* 4 regarding the distinction between *cogitare secundum rem* and *cogitare secundum vocem*.
81. Matt. 6:12.
82. Cf. the similar expression at the end of P 4 (S I, 104:6–7).
83. Here we do not follow the chapter division in Bodley 271.
84. I, 10 (S II, 67:1–6).
85. Cf. M 68 (S I, 78:23–79:1).
86. Matt. 7:12.
87. CDH I, 12 (S II, 70:2–3).
88. Cf. I Cor. 6:19–20.
89. Gal. 5:6.
90. Ezk. 18:27.

Notes

91. See the Preface to CDH (S II, 42:11–13).
92. In the preceding chapter.
93. Anselm often speaks of what God *can* or *cannot* do in the sense of what it is acceptable for Him to do. For example, see also *A Meditation on Human Redemption* (S III, 88:111) and P 11 (S I, 109:22).
94. Ps. 50:7 (51:5).
95. Here we do not follow the chapter division in Bodley 271.
96. See CDH I, 16 (S II, 74:12–13).
97. Cf. DCV 2 (S II, 141:15–16).
98. Literally: "Perhaps if in him there is no cause of inability, he can to some extent be excused. But if there is blameworthiness in this inability, then. . . ."
99. CDH I, 14 (S II, 72:16–18).
100. Ps. 35:7–8 (36:7).
101. CDH I, 21 (S II, 89:27–28).

BOOK II

1. See CDH I, 9 (S II, 61:29–30).
2. Cf. M 68 (S I, 78:21–23).
3. CDH I, 9 (S II, 61:25–62:6).
4. Cf. CDH I, 18 (S II, 80:10–13).
5. Note M 70–72.
6. CDH I, 19.
7. Cf. CDH II, 17.
8. CDH I, 21.
9. CDH I, 16, 19.
10. Ps. 65:20 (66:20) and elsewhere.
11. *Homo-deus*. See n. 2 of CDH Preface.
12. Cf. CDH I, 4.
13. Cf. the end of CDH I, 3 (S II, 51:7–9).
14. See DIV 11.
15. See DIV 10.
16. Cf. DIV 10.
17. Note DCD 28 and DIV 10 (S II, 27:1–3).
18. II Cor. 4:4. Col. 1:15.
19. John 8:55.
20. Note DV 8 (S I, 188:18–22); DL 5 (S I, 217:1–6); DCD 12 (S I, 253:22–27); CDH II, 17 (S II, 123:15–22); CDH II, 18 (S II, 128:27–30).
21. Cf. DCD 18.
22. Note the beginning of DCD 18 and the second mode of causing cited at PF 29:34ff. See also DCD 1 (S I, 234:6–9).
23. At the end of CDH II, 5.
24. I.e., neither mortality nor immortality.
25. Literally: ". . . since neither makes or destroys human nature. . . ."
26. Cf. CDH II, 3 (S II, 98:23–25).
27. John 10:17–18.
28. CDH I, 21; CDH II, 6.
29. This view is stated in the previous chapter.

Notes

30. Cf. Baruch 3:38.
31. Cf. II, 16 (S II, 119:14).
32. CDH I, 21.
33. CDH I, 21 (S II, 89:9–11).
34. I Cor. 2:8.
35. I.e., to kill the God-man.
36. See Ps. 50:7 (51:5) and Rom. 5:12.
37. CDH I, 8–10; II, 10–11.
38. Literally: "If you had carefully considered the things said above, you would have recognized, I think, that this problem was solved in them."
39. CDH II, 10.
40. CDH II 5 and 10.
41. CDH II, 7. Cf. DIV 11.
42. I.e., it could not have cleansed the Virgin and the others of their sins.
43. That is, you are finding problems where none exist.
44. CDH I, 1 (S II, 49:25–26).
45. CDH II, 5 and 10.
46. Cf. PF 24:16.
47. Note DV 8 (S I, 188:18–22); DL 5 (S I, 217:1–6); DCD 12 (S I, 253:22–27); CDH II, 10 (S II, 107:5–6); CDH II, 18 (S II, 128:27–30).
48. Note PF 23:13–24.
49. Note PF 24:16–25 and the beginning of DC I, 2.
50. CDH II, 7 and 9.
51. CDH II, 5.
52. Cf. CDH II, 7.
53. Isa. 53:7.
54. Note DC I, 2.
55. That is, the notion of subsequent necessity applies to the example of the heavens but the notion of antecedent necessity does not apply to the case of speaking.
56. John 10:18.
57. Anselm presents this other rationale in DCV.
58. See CDH I, 1 (S II, 48:2–5).
59. E.g., CDH I, 9.
60. See *A Meditation on Human Redemption* (S III, 87:96).
61. That is: if He had turned aside from the death that was inflicted upon Him because He obediently kept justice.
62. In this section "*debere*" is translated as "to be obliged to," "to owe," "ought to."
63. Note DCD 1.
64. Note PF 36:21–37:5.
65. See n. 61 above.
66. Note DV 8 (S I, 188:18–22); DL 5 (S I, 217:1–6); DCD 12 (S I, 253:22–27); CDH II, 10 (S II, 107:5–6); CDH II, 17 (S II, 123:15–22).
67. Note PF 36:26–29 and DV 8 (S I, 188:15–18).
68. CDH II, 11 (S II, 111:22–25).
69. Note *A Meditation on Human Redemption* (S III, 87:93–95).

Notes

70. Literally: "With what great reason human salvation follows from His death."
71. See CDH II, 14.
72. Cf. John 16:15.
73. CDH II, 18 (S II, 127:17-22).
74. See Luke 6:47-48.
75. See CDH I, 6, 7 and *A Meditation on Human Redemption* (S III, 86:1-2).
76. Cf. *A Meditation on Human Redemption* (S III, 88:126-128).
77. CDH I, 17.
78. *Homo-deus*. See n. 2 of CDH Preface.
79. *Angelus-deus*.
80. That is: "For unless they rise without anyone else's assistance. . . ."
81. CDH II, 9.
82. CDH II, 16 (S II, 119:18-19).
83. Cf. CDH II, 15 (S II, 116:3-7).

THE VIRGIN CONCEPTION AND ORIGINAL SIN

1. This treatise was written between the summer of 1099 and the summer of 1100.
2. See CDH II, 16-17. Note Ch. 19 of the present work, where Anselm summarizes the differences between these two arguments.
3. I.e., in CDH.
4. Note DIV 11 (S II, 29:4-9).
5. Cf. CDH I, 23 (S II, 91:21).
6. See n. 52 of CDH, Bk. I.
7. Cf. CDH I, 20.
8. Wisd. of Sol. 9:15.
9. Ex. 20:5.
10. I.e., so as not to appear tendentious in treating this topic, I shall stipulate for the sake of the argument that the sins of one's recent ancestors are included in the notion of original sin. Thus, by referring to these sins no one can propose that original sin is more grave than I am already supposing it to be. Cf. the beginnings of Chs. 8 and 22. See Ch. 24, where Anselm argues that the sins of ancestors are not reckoned in original sin.
11. I.e., consists of the sins of one's recent ancestors in addition to the condition of obligation and inability.
12. Cf. DCD 16.
13. N.B. DV 12.
14. This elaboration comes in DC III, 11.
15. Gal. 5:17; Rom. 7:25.
16. Rom. 7:22.
17. Rom. 7:23.
18. I Esdras 7:21.
19. Josue (Joshua) 8:31.
20. Num. 25:7-11.
21. Note Eph. 5:3.

Notes

22. Cf. CDH II, 12.
23. Note DCD 1 (S I, 235:6-7).
24. Cf. DCD 26 (S I, 274:19-24).
25. Literally: ". . . and is driven into various dangers to his soul — this is what evil deeds are — we say that injustice causes these deeds."
26. Note DCD 26 (S I, 274:8-15). See also DC I, 7.
27. E.g., DCD 9, 16, and 1.
28. See DV 12.
29. CDH I, 14 (S II, 72:16-21).
30. CDH I, 15 (S II, 73:22-25).
31. Job 14:4.
32. Ps. 50:7 (51:5).
33. Gen. 2:17.
34. Rom. 8:10.
35. Rom. 5:12.
36. Rom. 5:19.
37. Ch. 7.
38. Ch. 2.
39. At the end of Ch. 2.
40. Wisd. of Sol. 9:15. See DCV 2 (S II, 141:20-21).
41. "*in aetate perfecta.*" Cf. DC I, 6 (S II, 256:10): "*ad intelligibilem pervenit aetatem.*"
42. Rom 5:14.
43. Gen. 5:2.
44. Note CDH I, 16.
45. Ch. 2.
46. CDH II, 1.
47. Literally: "Therefore, since all the things which occur — if they are carefully considered — are done either by. . . ."
48. I.e., freedom from sin, its debt, and its penalty.
49. Note DCD 18.
50. I.e., a rational nature which is subjected to evil.
51. See the beginning of Ch. 3.
52. Job 14:4; Ps. 50:7 (51:5).
53. See Ch. 3.
54. Note Ch. 10 (S II, 152:1-3).
55. CDH II, 6.
56. Ch. 8.
57. Wisd. of Sol. 9:15.
58. Literally: "Thus, I began to ask how this could be understood regarding the necessity of sin and of Adam's debt."
59. CDH II, 16.
60. *Loc. cit.*
61. Ch. 2.
62. Ch. 2.
63. At the end of Ch. 2.
64. I.e., so as not to appear to minimize its gravity for tendentious reasons.
65. Rom 5:14.

Notes

66. Rom 5:8; Eph. 2:3.
67. Rom 5:20.
68. CDH I, 21–25.
69. See CDH I, 25; II, 14.
70. Rom. 5:12.
71. I.e., the point about how sin is present in infants. See Chs. 7, 10.
72. Luke 1:35.
73. *Homo-deus.* See n. 2 of CDH Preface.
74. Ch. 1.
75. Viz., CDH.
76. Note the definition of "justice" in DV 12.
77. Rom. 9:10–13.
78. Ex. 20:5.
79. Note Matt. 6:13.
80. Note Job 23:16; Rom. 9:18. Cf. PF 39:18–20.
81. Ezk. 18:20.
82. Gal. 6:5.
83. II Cor. 5:10.
84. Ex. 20:5.
85. Ch. 23.
86. Ch. 22.
87. Rom. 5:14.
88. Ch. 10.
89. Ch. 23.
90. Eph. 2:3.
91. Ch. 2.
92. Ch. 23.
93. See CDH I, 16–18.
94. Ch. 2.
95. N.B. DV 12.
96. That is: one is not liable for an inability for which he bears no culpability.

THE PROCESSION OF THE HOLY SPIRIT

1. This treatise was completed in the summer of 1102.
In his edition of the Latin texts F. S. Schmitt has placed Roman numerals where the mss. indicate divisions.
2. The Holy Spirit is the spirit of the Son as well as of the Father.
3. Note M 43.
4. Literally: "We must also consider how the plurality of relations opposes the consequence of unity if we first posit some of those cases in which no opposition opposes."
5. Anselm goes on to reject this inference, which is contradicted by the considerations of relation. Throughout this treatise, though, Anselm's argument distinguishes two notions: *(A)* God from whom God exists and *(B)* God from God. God the Father is *A* because the Son is begotten from Him and because the Holy Spirit proceeds from Him; He is not *B*, since He neither proceeds nor is begotten. God the Son is *B* since He is begotten; and He is *A* since the Holy Spirit

Notes

proceeds also from Him. God the Holy Spirit is *B* since He proceeds from the Father and the Son; but He is not *A*, since neither the Father nor the Son proceeds from Him or is begotten from Him. In Ch. 15 Anselm summarizes these distinctions.

6. Literally: "And so this unity does not have that force of consequence. . . ." What Anselm means is that because of considerations arising from the plural relations God's unity does not require the conclusion that both the Son and the Holy Spirit are begotten and that both the Son and the Holy Spirit proceed.

7. In some contexts, as in the present one, Anselm uses "*catholica fides*" to refer — whether primarily or secondarily — to the Quicumque, or Athanasian Creed (Cf. CDH I, 25. S II, 96:11–12). In other contexts he does not use it in this way (Cf. *The Sacraments of the Church* 1. S II, 240:9).

8. The Greeks concede that the Holy Spirit is the spirit of the Son (S II, 178:11–12).

9. The Nicene Creed (i.e., the Nicene-Constantinople Creed of 381) is under discussion throughout this treatise.

10. Literally: "denies that the very thing which the Holy Spirit is exists from the Father."

11. *Homo*.

12. Viz., the following reason: that He exists from the Father by proceeding.

13. Literally: "only because He has from the Father His being-what-He-is." Or alternatively: "only because He has it from the Father to be what He is."

14. The Bishop of Bari.

15. Literally: "that which He is."

16. Cf. M 25.

17. John 3:8. In Latin "*spiritus*" may mean either wind or spirit, depending upon the context.

18. See n. 9 above.

19. Viz., the fact that the Holy Spirit exists from the Father and the fact that the Holy Spirit exists from God.

20. I.e., according to relation.

21. I.e., the view that the Holy Spirit exists from the Father qua father.

22. John 17:3.

23. I.e., from the Son Himself.

24. John 14:26.

25. John 15:26.

26. Literally: "so that in the Father's sending the Son's sending is understood."

27. Isa. 48:16.

28. Although Anselm is not here making a distinction between *esse* and *essentia*, the English word "essence" seems the best translation of "*essentia*" in the present context. See M, n. 12.

29. Literally: ". . . the Son seems to be signified to have something less (so to speak) than the Father has, and [it seems to be signified that] the Holy Spirit is given to Him as something supplemental."

30. John 20:22.

31. Viz., Jesus. See DIV 11 and CDH II, 9.

Notes

32. Ps. 32:6 (33:6).
33. Isa. 11:4.
34. Ezk. 36:26–27.
35. II Thess. 2:8.
36. Ps. 32:6 (33:6).
37. John 16:13.
38. Anselm interchanges *"habet essentiam"* and *"habet esse."* The reader is here reminded that Anselm uses *"essentia"* in various senses: being, existence, a being. From the viewpoint of Anselm's terminology, it makes no difference (in English) whether we say that the Holy Spirit has His existence from the Father or that He has His essence from the Father. Similarly, we may say either that the Holy Spirit's knowledge is identical with His essence or identical with His being. Cf. S II, 197:8–9 with 199:16–17. See M, n. 12.
39. See the end of DP 2 (S II, 190:8–19).
40. John 16:14.
41. John 16:44.
42. Matt. 11:27.
43. See DP 1.
44. Matt. 11:27.
45. John 10:30.
46. Rom. 11:36.
47. DP 1 (S II, 182:2–3).
48. John 5:19.
49. This example also occurs in DIV 13.
50. Gen. 22:18; Ps. 131:11 (132:11); Lk. 1:42.
51. DIV 13.
52. Viz., the Son and the Holy Spirit.
53. John 15:26.
54. Matt. 16:17.
55. Matt. 11:27.
56. John 14:9.
57. John 16:13.
58. DP 1 (e.g., S II, 181:2–4).
59. John 17:3.
60. John 5:26.
61. John 14:10–11.
62. John 14:9.
63. See n. 9 above.
64. Cf. the concluding paragraphs of DP 2 (e.g., S II, 190:2–7).
65. See n. 9.
66. See DP 10.
67. Cf. Augustine's Sermon 71 (PL 38:459).
68. I.e., from the Son.
69. DP 1 (e.g., S II, 180:30–181:2).
70. Note M 65.
71. Cf. P 3 (S I, 103:3–6).
72. DP 1 (S II, 183:18–19).
73. See n. 69.

Notes

74. A few lines earlier.
75. Note DG 20 (S I, 166:5) and DIV 11 (S II, 29:6–9).
76. See DIV 15.
77. Note M 22–24 and P 19–20, where Anselm has already explained this statement, which must not be construed pantheistically.
78. Cf. M 59.
79. Matt. 11:27.
80. I Cor. 2:11.
81. See John 16:13.

THE SACRIFICE OF LEAVENED AND UNLEAVENED BREAD

1. This letter was written between 1106–1107. In its ms. form it contains no divisions. F. S. Schmitt's edition of the text retains — but in bracketed Roman numerals — the divisions of the Gerberon edition. See S II, 223 n.
The same dating and absence of division is found in the two letters which follow this one.
2. Walram was bishop from 1091 to 1111.
3. Anselm is here alluding to the investiture controversy which was raging in Germany. In this dispute Walram had at first sided against the papacy.
4. Viz., Henry IV, emperor from 1056 to 1106.
5. Matt. 26:26.
6. I Cor. 5:8.
7. Luke 22:19.
8. See Rom. 12:3.
9. I Cor. 5:8.
10. Christ is our Passover. I Cor. 5:7.
11. II Cor. 5:17.
12. Rom. 6:3–4.
13. I Cor. 10:1–2.
14. I Cor. 5:7.
15. I Cor. 5:7–8.
16. II Cor. 3:6.
17. Amos 4:5.
18. Rom. 7:7–11.
19. Titus 3:4–7.
20. II Cor. 3:5–6.
21. II Cor. 3:7–4:1.
22. Amos 4:4–5.

BISHOP WALRAM TO ANSELM

1. See n. 1 of the previous letter.
2. Ps. 118:18 (119:18).
3. See Ps. 120:1 (121:1).
4. Ps. 120:2 (121:2).
5. I Cor. 6:17.
6. I Cor. 2:10.
7. John 3:8.

Notes

8. Heb. 13:8.
9. Note Ps. 77:25 (78:25).
10. I Cor. 10:17.
11. I Cor. 11:25.
12. Rom. 6:4.
13. I Cor. 5:8.
14. I Cor. 5:6.
15. Luke 1:50.
16. I Cor. 11:25.
17. Heb. 13:8.
18. Eph. 4:5.
19. John 20:7.
20. John 14:6.
21. I John 2:6.
22. I John 3:2.
23. II Cor. 3:18; Phil. 3:21; I Cor. 15:28.
24. John 19:30.
25. II Cor. 5:17.
26. Matt. 25:51.
27. II Cor. 3:15.
28. Cf. Rom. 11:8.
29. I Cor. 2:10.
30. II Cor. 3:18.
31. I Cor. 2:10.
32. "Light from light" is a phrase belonging to the Nicene Creed (381).
33. John 8:12.
34. I John 2:6.
35. Ps. 138:16 (139:16).
36. I Cor. 15:10.
37. Henry IV reigned from 1056 to 1106.
38. Ps. 58:5 (59:3).
39. Note the opening lines of the previous letter.
40. Isa. 11:6.
41. Heb. 1:8.
42. Amos 3:8.
43. Prov. 28:1.
44. Heb. 1:9.
45. Ps. 102:4 (103:4).

THE SACRAMENTS OF THE CHURCH

1. See *The Sacrifice of Unleavened and Leavened Bread*, n. 1.
2. See *The Sacrifice of Unleavened and Leavened Bread*, n. 2.
3. Paschal II was pope from 1099 to 1118.
4. I Pet. 2:21.
5. Ps. 21:7 (22:6).